Creativity in Load–Balance Schemes for Multi/Many–Core Heterogeneous Graph Computing:

Emerging Research and Opportunities

Alberto Garcia–Robledo
Center for Research and Advanced Studies of the National Polytechnic Institute (Cinvestav–Tamaulipas), Mexico

Arturo Diaz–Perez
Center for Research and Advanced Studies of the National Polytechnic Institute (Cinvestav–Tamaulipas), Mexico

Guillermo Morales–Luna
Center for Research and Advanced Studies of the National Polytechnic Institute (Cinvestav–IPN), Mexico

A volume in the Advances
in Computer and Electrical
Engineering (ACEE) Book Series

Published in the United States of America by
> IGI Global
> Engineering Science Reference (an imprint of IGI Global)
> 701 E. Chocolate Avenue
> Hershey PA, USA 17033
> Tel: 717-533-8845
> Fax: 717-533-8661
> E-mail: cust@igi-global.com
> Web site: http://www.igi-global.com

Library of Congress Cataloging-in-Publication Data

Names: Garcia-Robledo, Alberto, 1985- author. | Diaz-Perez, A. (Arturo),
    author. | Morales-Luna, Guillermo, author.
Title: Creativity in load-balance schemes for multi/many-core heterogeneous
    graph computing : emerging research and opportunities / by Alberto
    Garcia-Robledo, Arturo Diaz-Perez, and Guillermo Morales-Luna.
Description: Hershey, PA : Engineering Science Reference, [2018] | Includes
    bibliographical references.
Identifiers: LCCN 2017022369| ISBN 9781522537991 (hardcover) | ISBN
    9781522538004 (ebook)
Subjects: LCSH: Parallel processing (Electronic computers) | Graph
    algorithms. | Multiprocessors.
Classification: LCC QA76.58 .G345 2018 | DDC 004/.35--dc23 LC record available at https://lccn.
loc.gov/2017022369

This book is published in the IGI Global book series Advances in Computer and Electrical Engineering (ACEE) (ISSN: 2327-039X; eISSN: 2327-0403)

British Cataloguing in Publication Data
A Cataloguing in Publication record for this book is available from the British Library.

All work contributed to this book is new, previously-unpublished material.
The views expressed in this book are those of the authors, but not necessarily of the publisher.

For electronic access to this publication, please contact: eresources@igi-global.com.

Advances in Computer and Electrical Engineering (ACEE) Book Series

ISSN:2327-039X
EISSN:2327-0403

Editor-in-Chief: Srikanta Patnaik, SOA University, India

MISSION

The fields of computer engineering and electrical engineering encompass a broad range of interdisciplinary topics allowing for expansive research developments across multiple fields. Research in these areas continues to develop and become increasingly important as computer and electrical systems have become an integral part of everyday life.

The **Advances in Computer and Electrical Engineering (ACEE) Book Series** aims to publish research on diverse topics pertaining to computer engineering and electrical engineering. **ACEE** encourages scholarly discourse on the latest applications, tools, and methodologies being implemented in the field for the design and development of computer and electrical systems.

COVERAGE

- Digital Electronics
- VLSI Fabrication
- Microprocessor Design
- Sensor Technologies
- Algorithms
- Computer science
- VLSI Design
- Electrical Power Conversion
- Circuit Analysis
- Programming

IGI Global is currently accepting manuscripts for publication within this series. To submit a proposal for a volume in this series, please contact our Acquisition Editors at Acquisitions@igi-global.com or visit: http://www.igi-global.com/publish/.

Titles in this Series

For a list of additional titles in this series, please visit:
https://www.igi-global.com/book-series/advances-computer-electrical-engineering/73675

Design and Use of Virtualization Technology in Cloud Cmputing
Prashanta Kumar Das (Government Industrial Training Institute Dhansiri, India) and Ganesh Chandra Deka (Government of India, India)
Engineering Science Reference •©2018 • 315pp • H/C (ISBN: 9781522527855) • US $235.00

Smart Grid Test Bed Using OPNET and Power Line Communication
Jun-Ho Huh (Catholic University of Pusan, South Korea)
Engineering Science Reference •©2018 • 425pp • H/C (ISBN: 9781522527763) • US $225.00

Transport of Information-Carriers in Semiconductors and Nanodevices
Muhammad El-Saba (Ain-Shams University, Egypt)
Engineering Science Reference •©2017 • 677pp • H/C (ISBN: 9781522523123) • US $225.00

Accelerating the Discovery of New Dielectric Properties in Polymer Insulation
Boxue Du (Tianjin University, China)
Engineering Science Reference •©2017 • 388pp • H/C (ISBN: 9781522523093) • US $210.00

Handbook of Research on Nanoelectronic Sensor Modeling and Applications
Mohammad Taghi Ahmadi (Urmia University, Iran) Razali Ismail (Universiti Teknologi Malaysia, Malaysia) and Sohail Anwar (Penn State University, USA)
Engineering Science Reference •©2017 • 579pp • H/C (ISBN: 9781522507369) • US $245.00

Field-Programmable Gate Array (FPGA) Technologies for High Performance Instrumentation
Julio Daniel Dondo Gazzano (University of Castilla-La Mancha, Spain) Maria Liz Crespo (International Centre for Theoretical Physics, Italy) Andres Cicuttin (International Centre for Theoretical Physics, Italy) and Fernando Rincon Calle (University of Castilla-La Mancha, Spain)
Engineering Science Reference •©2016 • 306pp • H/C (ISBN: 9781522502999) • US $185.00

For an enitre list of titles in this series, please visit:
https://www.igi-global.com/book-series/advances-computer-electrical-engineering/73675

701 East Chocolate Avenue, Hershey, PA 17033, USA
Tel: 717-533-8845 x100 • Fax: 717-533-8661
E-Mail: cust@igi-global.com • www.igi-global.com

Table of Contents

Preface

THE CONVERGENCE OF NETWORK SCIENCE AND HPC

Recent years have witnessed the rise of Network Science, defined as "the study of network representations of physical, biological, and social phenomena leading to predictive models of these phenomena." Such representations are known as complex networks. Big Data and Network Science share interesting properties: both deal with data that are large (volume), complex (variety), and dynamic (velocity). Complex network applications, such as Social Network Analysis, biological network analysis and link analysis for fraud/cybercrime detection, have renewed the interest in graph algorithms like Breadth-First Search (BFS), centrality calculation, force-based visualization, and multi-level partitioning.

The efficient computation of large graphs has direct implications in different of scientific and data analysis fields, including computational biology, bioinformatics, computer networking, web search, and knowledge discovery. Graph theoretic problems constitute fundamental kernels in emerging scientific computing areas following a holistic approach, such as systems biology and social network analysis; and have applications in medicine and even national security. Real-world massive and complex phenomena such as the Internet, protein-protein interactions, the world-wide web, neural networks, social interactions and transportation networks are being modeled and analyzed as graphs.

To efficiently solve large-scale graph problems, it is necessary to exploit High Performance Computing (HPC) systems together with novel parallel algorithms, as well as to overcome the existing breach between irregular problems, like large sparse graph processing, and modern parallel hardware architectures. High Performance Computing (HPC) accelerates the innovation process for discovery and invention of new products. HPC has become the third leg of science, along with theory and experimentation, and currently represents a key component in the path to competitiveness of nations such as the U.S.

HPC is a dynamic field that is continuous progress: super-computers are increasing its capacity by exploiting accelerators such as Graphic Processing Units (GPUs); the number of cores in commercially available multi-core CPUs continues to increase and will represent the standard in the years to come; and the languages used to program parallel computers are evolving to provide more friendly programming environments.

However, HPC graph computing is an infant field, in sharp contrast with numerical scientific computing and other disciplines that benefit from HPC. There is a list of factors that difficult the design of efficient parallel traversal algorithms for graphs, including unstructured problems, data-driven computations, irregular memory access and poor locality, revealing the existing gap between complex network algorithms and modern parallel architectures; as well as the need for works that present new parallel strategies that combine special features of modern hardware architectures in order to accelerate the characterization of large and evolving networks.

The High-Performance Computing and U.S. Manufacturing Roundtable has pointed out that the U.S. is failing to educate new scientist and engineers in the designing and developing of effective algorithms and code for the available HPC computers. Network Science is a young field and has been mostly addressed from a theoretical physics-statistics perspective. Works that approach the new array of problems in Network Science from the Computer Science and Data Analytics perspectives are still scarce, and books on the parallel processing of large-scale graphs are almost non-existent.

On the other hand, there is clear divergence of the programming models and tools exploited in the HPC and Big Data ecosystems, slowing down the development and the progress of these fields. As stated by Reed and Dongarra (2015): "The tools and cultures of HPC computing and Big Data Analytics have diverged, to the detriment of both; unification is essential to address a spectrum of major research domains."

TOPOLOGY-AWARE HETEROGENEOUS COMPUTING PARTITIONING

To overcome the limitations of modern parallel architectures for graph processing, CPUs can be combined with GPUs, in an approach known as heterogeneous computing. A fundamental problem in heterogeneous computing is to decide how to partition the graph to distribute it between the CPU and the GPU. On the one hand, the performance of new Bulk Synchronous Parallel (BSP) heterogeneous platforms depends on minimizing the computation time of partitions. On the other hand, the characterization of the topology of complex networks through metrics like the k-core decomposition provides insights that can be exploited for a variety of purposes.

In the context of the above-mentioned challenges, the objective of our publication is to bring together the Network Science, the Big Data and the HPC communities, by providing accessible methods for methodologically processing complex networks through known and novel methods on complex network analysis and high-performance processing. Specifically, we seek to contribute to the progress of Network Science, HPC and Big Data by providing experimental evidence on the suitability of networks and state-of-the-art parallel architectures, as well as efficient load-balancing algorithms that are suitable for large-scale graph processing, all in all while following a Computer Science approach based on computational experiments and our first-hand experience with processing real-world complex network datasets.

We feature novel algorithms that exploit the topology of large graphs for efficient graph processing, partitioning, and mapping in order to unleash the combined power of multi-cores and GPU's. The performance of an existing BSP heterogeneous computing platform is studied by exploiting the proposed algorithms when traversing large real-world and synthetic graphs.

BOOK ORGANIZATION

This book is organized in 2 sections. In Section 1, comprised of Chapters 1 through 3, we introduce the need for high-performance computing for the analysis of massive complex networks (Chapter 1). Next, we go on to describe widely used complex network concepts, metrics as well as algorithmic kernels (Chapter 2). Finally, we study in an experimental manner the performance parallel algorithms for one of these kernels on graphs with varying structure (Chapter 3).

In Section 2, comprised of Chapter 4 through 7, we explore the state-of-the-art and current challenges related to the problem of partitioning in both homogeneous and heterogeneous parallel platforms with a focus on graph HPC computing (Chapter 4). This review lays the groundwork and prepares the context for the material of the next chapter: novel topology-aware heuristics for unbalanced graph partitioning with heterogeneous computing in mind (Chapter 5). We close Section 2 of the book with a review of trends in large-scale complex network analysis: from processing to storage (Chapter 6); and a case study on the analysis of a citation network by exploiting some Network Science techniques covered throughout the book (Chapter 7). The following subsections summarize the content of each of the 7 main chapters.

Chapter 1: The Need for HPC Computing in Network Science

The size of complex networks introduces large amounts of traversal times that can be tackled by exploiting pervasive multi-core and many-core parallel hardware architectures. However, there is a list of factors that difficult the design of efficient parallel traversal algorithms for graphs: unstructured problems, data-driven computation, irregular memory access, poor locality, and low computing load. In Chapter 1 we introduce the synergy between Network Science and High Performance Computing, and motivate the combined use of multi/many-core heterogeneous computing and Network Science techniques to tackle the above-mentioned challenges and to efficiently traverse the structure of massive real-world graphs.

Chapter 2: Core Kernels for Complex Network Analysis

The emergence of Network Science has motivated a renewed interest in classical graph problems for the analysis of the topology of complex networks. For example, important centrality metrics, such as the betweenness, the stress, the eccentricity, and the closeness centralities, are all based on BFS. On the other hand, the k-core decomposition of graphs defines a hierarchy of internal cores and decomposes large networks layer by layer. The k-core decomposition has been successfully applied in a variety of domains, including: large graph visualization and fingerprinting, analysis of large software systems and fraud detection.

Complex networks encode intriguing properties in their topology that reveal important details of their functional organization and the underlying real-world phenomena. In Chapter 2, well-known metrics and techniques used to characterize the structure of complex networks are introduced. In addition, the recurrent algorithms in complex network applications, BFS and k-core decomposition, are described. In Chapter 2 it is also described a coarsening approach based on the contraction of edges and the k-core decomposition to obtain coarse and reduced version of large complex networks that preserve well-known graph and complex network topological properties.

Chapter 3: Accelerated Network Traversal Using Multi/Many-Cores

Current works report that it is possible to use GPU's to accelerate BFS traversals on real-world data, such as social, infrastructure, citation, circuit, and road networks. The performance of platforms under new paradigms depends on minimizing the computation time of partitions by increasing the suitability of partitions to processors. However, there is a lack of studies on the suitability of parallel architectures for processing different families of graphs, including small-world and scale-free networks.

Moreover, no works methodologically study how the structural properties of the experimented networks, such as the density and the degree distribution, influence the performance of the exposed parallel implementations. In this chapter, we conduct an experimental characterization of the performance multi/many-cores when traversing synthetic networks of varying topology in order to reveal the suitability of multi-cores and GPU's for processing different families of graphs. More specifically, in this chapter an experimental characterization of the performance of BFS on multi/many-cores is developed, by methodologically comparing two BFS algorithmic approaches on synthetic networks of varying topology, in order to reveal the influence of the network topology on the performance of multi-core CPUs and GPUs.

Chapter 4: Partitioning of Complex Networks for Heterogeneous Computing

The most fundamental problem in BSP parallel graph computing is to decide how to partition and then distribute the graph among the available processors. In this regard, partitioning techniques for BSP heterogeneous computing should produce computing loads with different sizes (unbalanced partitions) in order to exploit processors with different computing capabilities.

In Chapter 4 three major graph partitioning paradigms that are relevant to parallel graph processing are reviewed: balanced graph partitioning, unbalanced graph partitioning, and community detection. Then, it is discussed how any of these paradigms fits the needs of graph heterogeneous computing where the suitability of partitions to hardware architectures (rather than the minimization of communications) plays a vital role. Finally, it is shown how the decomposition of networks in layers through the k-core decomposition provides the means for developing methods the produce unbalanced graph partitions that match multi-core and GPU's processing capabilities.

Chapter 5: Topology-Aware Load-Balance Schemes for Heterogeneous Graph Processing

Inspired on the insights presented in Chapters 2, 3, and 4, in Chapter 5 it is shown how the coreness of complex networks can be exploited for graph partitioning to accelerate BFS on large real-world and synthetic graphs in the context of a heterogeneous BSP multi/many-core platform. We present two complex network heuristics: the KCMAX (K-Core MAX) and the KCML (K-Core Multi-Level): novel k-core-based graph partitioning approaches that produce unbalanced partitions of complex networks that are suitable for heterogeneous parallel processing based on the degree, the k-core coarsening and the k-core of graphs.

We then use KCMAX and KCML to explore the configuration space for accelerating BFSs on large complex networks in the context of TOTEM, a BSP heterogeneous GPU + CPU HPC platform. We study the feasibility of the heterogeneous computing approach by systematically studying different graph partitioning strategies, including the KCMAX and KCML algorithms, while processing synthetic and real-world complex networks.

Chapter 6: Trends and Challenges in Large-Scale HPC Network Analysis

The storage and analysis capabilities needed for large-scale graph analytics have motivated the development of a new wave of HPC technologies, including: MapReduce-like BSP distributed analytics, No-SQL data storage and querying; and homogeneous and hybrid multi-core/GPU graph supercomputing. In Chapter 6 we review these trends and current challenges for HPC large-scale graph analysis, including the processing and storage of large-scale graphs that cannot fit the main memory, as well as opportunities for research.

Chapter 7: A Case Study on Citation Network Analysis

Throughout this book, we study algorithms that represent the building blocks of a variety of complex network metrics. Examples are: the AS-BFS algorithm, which represents the algorithmic kernel to implement metrics like the betweenness and the stress centrality; and the k-core decomposition, that allow us to create a visual fingerprint of a large network to visually asses its complexity patterns, as well as its similarities to other complex networks. Network centrality analysis is a prominent example where metrics like the betweenness and the k-core decomposition find a practical application. In Chapter 7, we present a case study of centrality network analysis in the field of bibliometrics, where we conduct a topology analysis of an arXiv scientific citation network from the field of high-energy physics theory, in order to methodologically obtain groups of central arXiv papers according to different topological perspectives of the studied graph. Later in Chapter 7, we also discuss the potential benefits that the parallel kernels and the topology-aware partitioning algorithms covered in this book can offer in the context of the presented case study.

CONCLUSION

We believe that our publication can be a valuable help to a broad readership, including data analysts and computer scientists alike, especially those interested in HPC, Big Data and Network Science. We also expect this book to be a valuable tool for a wide variety of applications and domains that benefit from Network Science, such as bioinformatics, networking, data mining, physics, and social science, to name a few. Our ultimate goal is to contribute to the unification of Big Data and HPC by presenting Network Science as a common ground.

Acknowledgment

This work is the product of years of work at the IT Lab of the Research Center for Research and Advanced Studies, in Tamaulipas, Mexico. The Authors acknowledge all the people that directly or indirectly made possible the development and completion of this project.

The authors would like to acknowledge Jedidiah Yanez-Martinez and Gilberto Estrada-Bernon for their important contributions to the study case presented in the last chapter of this book.

The authors also acknowledge the General Coordination of Information and Communications Technologies (CGSTIC) at Cinvestav for providing HPC resources on the Hybrid Cluster Supercomputer "Xiuhcoatl", that have contributed to the research results reported within this document.

Alberto Garcia-Robledo would like to express his gratitude to Arturo Diaz-Perez and Guillermo Benito-Morales Luna, for their continuous support and inestimable guidance during the development of this research work

Last but not least, Alberto Garcia-Robledo would like to give thanks to his family, for all their care and love; and to express his sincere gratitude to Mahboobeh Zangiabady for all her invaluable help and support during the writing of this book.

Section 1

Chapter 1
The Need for HPC Computing in Network Science

ABSTRACT

The size of complex networks introduces large amounts of traversal times that can be tackled by exploiting pervasive multi-core and many-core parallel hardware architectures. However, there is a list of factors that make the design of efficient parallel traversal algorithms for graphs difficult: unstructured problems, data-driven computation, irregular memory access, poor locality, and low computing load. In this chapter, the authors introduce the synergy between Network Science and High Performance Computing and motivate the combined use of multi/many-core heterogeneous computing and Network Science techniques to tackle the above-mentioned challenges and to efficiently traverse the structure of massive real-world graphs.

INTRODUCTION

We are in the Big Data era, where data are linked and form large complex networks. Networks Science is an emerging and interdisciplinary research field with the goal of developing the necessary theory and tools that increment our understanding of natural and technological phenomena modeled by complex networks. Big Data and Network Science share interesting properties: both deal with large scale (volume), complex (variety), and dynamic (velocity) phenomena. The combination of Big Data and Network Science offers a number of potential applications for the data-driven analysis of massive systems with a holistic approach.

DOI: 10.4018/978-1-5225-3799-1.ch001

The efficient computation of large-scale graphs occurring in Network Science has direct implications in different scientific and data analysis fields, including computational biology, bioinformatics, computer networking, Web search, and knowledge discovery. Real-world massive and complex phenomena such as the Internet, the Wide World Web, global social interactions and transportation networks are being modeled and analyzed as graphs.

To efficiently solve large-scale graph problems it is necessary to exploit High Performance Computing (HPC) systems together with novel parallel algorithms, as well as to overcome the existing breach between irregular problems (like large sparse graph processing) and modern parallel hardware architectures. HPC is a dynamic field that is in continuous progress: super-computers are increasing their capacity by exploiting multi-cores and accelerators such as Graphic Processing Units (GPUs); and the number of cores in novel many-core CPUs such as the Intel Phi continues to increase and will represent the standard in the years to come.

Moreover, the HPC industry is utilizing existing general-purpose CPUs combined with GPUs or tightly-coupled accelerators at different scales to improve the performance of data analytics on large volumes of data. This is known as *heterogeneous computing*.

Heterogeneous computing is based on the idea of breaking down a task in such a way that different architectures do part of the work at the same time or in a synchronized manner. Thus, given a platform that includes, say, a CPU and a GPU, a fundamental problem is to decide how to partition and then distribute the graph between the CPU and the GPU to maximize performance. Widely used scientific graph partitioners like Chaco and METIS produce equivalent partitions and focus on reducing communication costs by minimizing the edge cut. However, in heterogeneous computing the power of different processors varies, so the size of the partitions should not be the same.

To efficiently solve a variety of problems in complex networks of the present and the future, it is necessary to design novel algorithms that: (1) exploit the structure of the graph by means of topological metrics; and (2) adopt a heterogeneous multi/many-core approach that combines the computing power of different parallel architectures, such as multi-core CPUs and GPUs. However, how to methodologically produce partitions that fit the capabilities of different parallel architectures and reduce the computation time of partitions?

In this chapter we introduce the synergy between Network Science and High Performance Computing, and motivate the combined use of multi/many-core heterogeneous computing and Network Science techniques to tackle the above mentioned question and to efficiently process the structure of massive real-world graphs.

COMPLEX NETWORKS AND NETWORK SCIENCE

Network Science has been defined by the Committee on Network Science for Future Army Applications (2005) as "*the study of network representations of physical, biological, and social phenomena leading to predictive models of these phenomena.*" The main study objects in Network Science are *complex networks*.

A complex network is a graph $G = (V, E)$, i.e. a discrete mathematical object integrated of a non-empty set V of $n = |V|$ vertices or nodes and a set $E \subset V^{(2)}$ of $m = |E|$ edges or links connecting pairs of vertices.

Unlike random graphs[1] and graphs arising in scientific applications, like 3D meshes[2], complex networks show properties that emerge only when modeling massive phenomena. Complex networks are integrated of thousands to billions of nodes and links.

The emerging "science of networks" is motivating a renewed interest in classical graph problems, such as the efficient computing of shortest paths, vertex connectivity and graph traversals. Algorithms for these problems represent building blocks for a new set of applications related to the analysis of the structure of massive real-world graphs.

An example of such an algorithm is Breadth-First Search (BFS). BFS discovers the vertices of a graph by levels: starting from a given vertex, BFS visits all the vertices at distance one from that vertex, then all the vertices at distance two, and so on. A full BFS graph traversal takes only $O(n + m)$ time. Due to their efficiency on sparse graphs, BFS and other classical algorithms represent the main building block of a new set of applications related to the analysis of the global structure and centrality of nodes of massive real-world phenomena:

1. *Statistics analysis*. It is the computation of metrics and statistics that summarize important aspects of the structure of complex graphs, such as the average path length, the average clustering coefficient, and the degree distribution. The measurement of these properties is the first step for the analysis of the structure of a national airport (Guida and Maria, 2007), the analysis of a subway train system (Angeloudis and

Fisk, 2006), and the evaluation of the redundancy and connectivity of a water distribution system (Yazdani and Jeffrey, 2011).

2. *Community detection.* It is the partitioning of a network in communities of densely connected vertices in order to find functional groups in protein complexes (Pereira-Leal et al., 2004), find groups of Web pages of related topics (Flake et al., 2002), and identify groups of scientists with common research interests in a massive citation network (Girvan and Newman, 2002).

3. *Centrality measurements.* It is the quantification of the importance of vertices and edges by using centrality indexes, in order to identify key protein in a PPI network or in a gen regulation network (Koschutzki and Schreiber, 2008), to calculate the ranking of a Web page (Page et al., 1999), to identify key agents in a network of terrorists (Memon et al., 2008), and to measure the reputation of a single person in a social network (Freeman, 1979). Additionally, centrality measurements can be used to evaluate the capacity of a network to resist attacks (resilience) (Holme et al., 2002).

4. *Motif enumeration.* It is the identification and counting of small subnetworks or motifs that appear with a greater frequency in a complex network than in a random network. Motifs represent interconnection patterns that allow us to understand the design principles of a network (Milo et al., 2002). In biology, the searching of motifs has been used to find topological units of potentially preserved functions.

5. *Specific domain problems*, such as the alignment of biological networks (Singh et al., 2008) (searching of the best matching between two networks in order to discover orthologous genes) and the searching of similar subnetworks in protein complexes (Shlomi et al., 2006).

Complex graphs model real-world phenomena made up of thousands or millions of entities. For example, in 2008 Google reported the indexation of a billion of Web URLs (Alpert and Hajaj, 2008); in 2010, Facebook registered more than 500 millions of users (Sweney, 2010); and in April 2017, GenBank reported 200 millions of protein sequences stored in its biological database (National Center for Biotechnology Information, 2017).

Unfortunately, the calculation of metrics like the diameter and the centrality of massive graphs involves as many BFS traversals as the total number of vertices. This results in $O(n^2 + nm)$ time, which on real-world complex networks can be tackled only by means of *parallel computing*.

HIGH-PERFORMANCE COMPUTING ARCHITECTURES

Parallel computing is a kind of computation in which multiple tasks are processed concurrently in order to solve a problem in less time (Mattson, 2009). Multiple processing elements (cores, processors, computer nodes, etc.) are required in order to exploit parallelism and truly execute processes and threads concurrently.

We can think of a parallel computer as a "collection of processing elements that cooperate and communicate to solve large problems fast" (Almasi and Gottlieb, 1989). Nowadays parallel computers are ubiquitous: multi-core laptops, multi-core desktop computers, graphics hardware, modern video game consoles, smartphones, supercomputers, etc.

According to The IEEE Standard Dictionary of Electrical and Electronics Terms (Radatz, 1997) a parallel architecture is "a multi-processor architecture in which parallel processing can be performed", where the term "parallel" is defined as the "simultaneous transfer, occurrence, or processing of the individual parts of a whole, such as the bits of a character and the characters of a word using separate facilities for the various parts."

Parallel computing has been successfully used to boost science, engineering and industry for decades under the name of *High Performance Computing (HPC)*. HPC accelerates the innovation process for discovery and invention of new products. Along with theory and experimentation HPC is considered the third leg of science, and now represents a key component in the path to competitiveness of nations such as the U.S. (The Council on Competitiveness, 2009)

Parallel Architectures

During the past forty years, the HPC field has seen four major eras (Keyes et al., 1997):

1. **Stone Age:** "Solve my problem faster". The first motivation of developing parallel computers was speed up. However, a seminal work of Gene Amdahl, widely known as the Amdahl's law, exposed that it does not matter how many processors a parallel machine may have, the maximum speed up that a parallel program can achieve is severely limited by the fraction of the program that cannot be parallelized (Amdahl, 1967).

5

Many used the Amdahl's law to predict the doom of parallel computers (Reinders, 2007).

2. **Bronze Age:** "Solve my problem bigger, in constant time". More than two decades after, Gustafson and Barsis reevaluated the Amdahl's law at Sandia National Labs. They demonstrated that parallelism is useful when the power of a parallel machine grows with the problem size (Gustafson, 1988), turning the attention to scalability and setting a new goal: to keep the time constant as the problem size grows. This triggered the development of machines with increasing number of processors, and vector computers became dominant in this era. However, most parallel machines were special purpose and expensive from both, the hardware and software perspectives (Trobec et al., 2009).

3. **Iron Age:** "Solve my problem cheaper". In order to find a workaround for the costs of developing special purpose parallel hardware and software for that hardware, the attention was turned to the crafting of parallel computers with cheap desktop systems configured as *clusters computers* interconnected via special or commodity networks (e.g. Ethernet, FDDI). The super-computing era was about to arise.

4. **Modern Age:** "Solve my problem smarter". Massively parallel super-computers, multi-core commodity hardware, Grid computing, and the Cloud draw the big picture of the modern era of parallel computing. Use of thousands of processors is now an usual practice in national laboratories and super-computer centers (Committee On Modeling Simulation And Games, 2010). Development of methods and algorithms for modern parallel systems are now a necessity in order to leverage the full potential of available super-computers and commodity multi-core computers.

Today, HPC is not restrained to special-purpose high-end expensive machines anymore. Parallel mechanisms are found in every kind of computers: from smartphones and commodity desktop computers to powerful supercomputers. Parallel architectures are implemented using both hardware and software techniques at different levels (Gebali, 2010, Rauber and Runger, 2010):

1. *Bit-level parallelism*, where we apply a logical operation to multiple bits, simultaneously exploiting the parallelism inherent to the hardware. Examples of this are bit-parallel addition, multiplication, and division of binary numbers.

2. *Data-level parallelism*, where we operate on multiple data at the same time. Examples of this are vector processors and systolic arrays, which apply the same operations to different portions of the data in parallel.
3. *Instruction-level parallelism (ILP)*, where the processor simultaneously executes more than one instruction at the same clock cycle. This is a common technique in modern superscalar processors known as instruction pipelining.
4. *Thread-level parallelism (TLP)*, where multiple threads are executed simultaneously on several processing elements, sharing the same memory space. The most common example is a multithreaded application that exploits multiple cores of a multicore processor.
5. *Process-level parallelism*, where multiple processes are running simultaneously on several machines, and each machine has its own memory space. A common example of this is a cluster supercomputer.

Semiconductor industry has taken three different paths for microprocessor design: the multicore, the manycore and the hybrid approaches (Wen-mei et al., 2008; Vajda, 2011).

Multi-Core Processors

Chip Multi Processors (CMPs) or multicore processors have few but complex cores with a on-chip hierarchy of large caches for general-purpose and high-performance computing. They can be found in desktop, laptop and server processors. Recently, multicores began to gain importance in mobile devices such as smartphones and tablets, which have to process a wide variety of Internet and multimedia applications.

Multicore chips do not necessarily run as fast as the fastest single-core processors, but they offer better overall performance when a program exploits the cores in parallel. Moore's law still applies in the current multicore scenario, in fact "multicores are a way to extend Moore' s law so that the user gets more performance out of a piece of silicon" (Geer, 2005).

The dominant approach to mitigate the gap between the CPU speed and the memory access time is to exploit available chip space to provide more on-chip cache memory. The trend in processors with heavy data reuse (e.g. Intel Core i7) is to make cache sizes as big as the die area and power budget will allow. Caches are specially important in multicore systems due to the increasing number of cores that are trying to access the slow off-chip memory (Blake et al., 2009).

Graphic Processing Units

The manycore trajectory is based on the premise that a larger number of simpler but specialized cores can achieve better throughput and improved raw performance for a certain domain of applications with abundant parallelism, such as 3D graphics processing and networking (Vajda, 2011, Kirk and Wenmei, 2010). Unlike multicore processors, manycore architectures are designed to allow the efficient execution of a massive number of threads.

A GPU is a special-purpose high-performance processor composed of many multi-thread cores. GPUs were initially designed as graphics accelerators for the PC and video game industry. However, GPUs are being used to accelerate a wide variety of scientific algorithms. Its popularity has increased since GPUs offer massive parallelism, huge memory bandwidth, and a general-purpose instruction set. Parallel architectures such as CUDA (Compute Unified Device Architecture) and programming interfaces such as C for CUDA and OpenCL facilitate co-processing between CPUs and GPUs.

Modern GPUs are more general than earlier GPUs that were specifically designed to efficiently render 2D images, 3D triangles and other geometric objects. Theoretical peak performance of GPUs is now close to three teraflops. This make GPUs attractive to accelerate many compute-intensive algorithms that are likely to be benefited from this kind of architecture (Brodtkorb et al., 2010).

Multi-core CPUs and GPUs are pervasive and inexpensive in commodity hardware, such as desktop computers, workstations, laptops, and low-cost hybrid servers; placing another brick on the wall of the nascent *personal supercomputing*.

Supercomputer Clusters

A supercomputer is a "*computer that leads the world in terms of processing capacity, particularly speed of calculation, at the time of its introduction* (ScienceDaily, 2017)." The first registered successful supercomputer was the CDC-6600, a mainframe computer built by Control Data Corporation in 1965 that achieved a performance of 9 millions of floating-point computations per second (megaflops).

Today supercomputers, such as the Titan Cray XK7 at the DOE/SC/Oak Ridge National Laboratory, are able to perform quadrillions of floating-point computations per second (petaflops). Since the emergence of CDC-6600 the performance of supercomputers has improved about 10^{10} times. The performance of supercomputers has improved faster than the Moore's law, at a stable rate of 10-fold per four years (Xie et al., 2010).

The predominant architecture in the TOP500 is the cluster computer. Modern cluster supercomputers consist of thousands of compute nodes. Each node is powered by general-purpose high-performance multicores, such as the Intel Xeon or the Power BQC, or manycore processors such as the Xeon Phi and the Sunway SW26010. Hybrid cluster architectures have attached co-processors such as GPUs. Nodes are highly-interconnected following a network topology, such as a fat-tree, a 3D torus, a 3D mesh. The topology is implemented by high-speed interconnection networks like Gigabit Ethernet or Infiniband (a discussion about HPC interconnection topologies and networks can be found in (Abts and Kim, 2011).

Supercomputing has contributed to many critical computing areas which involves national security, economic and social developments, and scientific discovery and innovation; and it is considered as an indicator of the national scientific and technological strength.

Petascale super-computers allow us to look for similarities and relationships between entire populations of chronic and acute patients in order to design more effective vaccines (ScienceDaily, 2009). On the other hand, physicians are looking at the space, through galaxies, dark holes and stars, in an effort to understand the origin and the physics that rule the dark matter. Peta-scale supercomputers have allowed modeling the universe in order to navigate beyond quantities seen in state-of-the-art sky surveys in a reasonable amount of time (PhysOrg.com, 2009).

COMPLEX NETWORKS VS. HPC

Parallel applications show a good performance when they present an appropriate coupling among the problem to be addressed, the algorithm used to solve it, the software used to express the algorithm, and the hardware used to execute the software.

However, there is a list of factors that difficult the design of efficient parallel traversal algorithms for graphs (Lumsdaine, 2007, Madduri, 2008, Stark, 2011, Dehne and Yogaratnam, 2010, Hendrickson and Berry, 2008) (Figure 1):

Figure 1. Parallel computing vs. graph processing

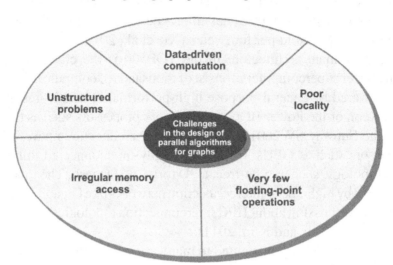

1. **Unstructured Problems:** Usually, complex network problems are highly irregular. This makes it hard to obtain balanced partitions of the graph and prevents a balanced distribution of the graph to the processing units, causing poor scalability.
2. **Data-Driven Computations:** The traversal of complex networks is determined by the graph structure and cannot be directly expressed in code. Since the structure of the graph is not known *a priori*, load distribution is again hard to achieve.
3. **Irregular Memory Access:** Unstructured graph instances cause irregular memory accesses to graph-related data structures. Execution time of affected algorithms are memory-bounded rather than CPU-bounded.
4. **Poor Locality:** Unstructured graph instances also cause poor data locality. The performance of graph algorithms on complex networks can be severely affected by memory contention, even in cache-based architectures.
5. **Low Computing Load:** Most of graph algorithms are based on the exploration and visitation of vertices (e.g. BFS) and do neither perform arithmetic nor logic operations on the data. Moreover, a wide variety of graph algorithms does not require floating point operations at all.

The memory wall arises when it is not possible to find enough concurrency to keep the hardware busy and hide memory latency times. Lack of concurrency and locality needed to scale performance and hide synchronization events between threads cause a growth of idle times that prevent graph algorithms to fully exploit the parallelism provided by parallel architectures. The gap between the concurrency that we expect to extract from graph algorithms and the concurrency that current hardware supports is growing. In consequence, algorithms behind graph applications like those based on path search seem to have hard limits in both concurrency and locality.

These factors reveal the existing gap between complex network algorithms and modern parallel architectures; as well as the need for the design of new parallel strategies that combine special features of modern hardware architectures to accelerate the exploration of large and evolving networks.

HETEROGENEOUS HIGH-PERFORMANCE COMPUTING

The emerging hybrid strategy, commonly found in specialized DSPs, represents a new tendency in the CPU market. A hybrid multicore integrates a full-featured multicore with other processors with different Instruction Set Architectures (ISAs) or very different capabilities.

The heterogeneous computing approach provides the following advantages:

- **Multi-Granularity Parallelism:** Accelerators such as GPUs offer a substantial amount of parallelism, enabling fine and medium-grained parallel strategies.
- **Multiple Computing Resources:** With multiple hardware accelerators, it is possible to distribute computing intensive kernels to the most appropriate architecture by moving data between the available processors.
- **Functional Specialization:** When we achieve a good match between the available hardware architectures and the requirements of an application, it is possible to improve the performance of a single hardware platform that accelerates every computing kernel in a complex software system.

Processor Coupled With Accelerator

Heterogeneous computing tries to improve the performance of applications by executing computing intensive kernels in accelerators, in order to maximize the data processing throughput (Gelado et al., 2010).

11

Modern cluster supercomputers consist of thousands of compute nodes. Each node is powered by general-purpose high-performance multicores, such as the Intel Xeon, the AMD Opteron or the IBM Power7. Hybrid cluster architectures have attached co-processors such as GPUs, FPGAs or Cell BEs.

Examples of successful heterogeneous computing systems include: (1) the Roadrunner supercomputer, the first supercomputer that reached a sustained performance of 1 petaflop (Top500.org, 2008] by combining 6,120 Opteron multicores with 12,240 Cell Broadband Engines; and (2) The Tianhe-1A supercomputer, which became the fastest TOP500 supercomputer in November 2010 (Top500.org, 2010) by combining 14,336 Xeon multicores with 7,168 NVIDIA GPUs.

The Chinese Tianhe-1A system, the TOP500 most powerful super-computer as of November 2010 with 2.57 petaflop/s, used 7,168 NVIDIA Tesla GPUs accompanied by 14,336 Xeon processors (HPC Wire, 2010). On the other hand, the Nebulae system[3] at the National Supercomputing Centre in Shenzhen and the Tsubame 2.0 system[4] at the Tokyo Institute of Technology also exploited NVIDA GPUs. As of June 2011, 14 systems of the TOP500 used NVIDIA or ATI chips (Top500.org, 2011).

Current fastest TOP500 heterogeneous supercomputers include the Piz Daint Cray XC50, which combines Xeon E5-2690v3 multicore processors with NVIDIA Tesla P100 GPUs to reach 9.77 petaflop/s (8th. position as of November 2016); and the Titan Cray XK7 which combines Opteron 6274 multicore processors with NVIDIA K20x GPUs to reach 17.59 petaflop/s (3rd. position as of November 2016).

Processor and Accelerator Embedded Into the Same Die

Multicore architectures featuring specialized accelerators are getting an increasing amount of attention. Major microprocessor manufacturers are starting to recognize the advantages of combining different types of processing elements into a heterogeneous architecture (Blake et al., 2009).

The heterogeneous computing approach is becoming pervasive and represents a tendency in the microprocessor industry. Take the examples of: (1) the Intel Sandy Bridge and the AMD Fusion architectures, that integrate a CPU with a GPU, a video decoding engine, and a SIMD accelerator into the same die; and (2) the Intel E600C series, which integrates a CPU and a FPGA to provide support to real-time embedded applications.

Heterogeneous multicore architectures comprise a general-purpose processor and fine-grained accelerators attached as functional units in the same chip or package as the CPU. Processor and accelerators are tightly coupled and share access to system memory. The on-chip system memory controller deals with memory requests coming from both general-purpose CPUs and accelerators.

Processor With GPU

Early Intel and AMD architectures integrate a x86 CPU with a GPU to accelerate graphics-intensive and visually rich applications such as high-definition (HD) video playing and modern 3D computer video games.

Intel Sandy Bridge processors, such as the Intel iCore7, include an on-chip GPU and an on-chip video transcoding hardware engine. Even though the GPU does not have a dedicated graphics memory, the GPU and the transcoding engine share the L3 cache with the general-purpose x86 cores. Further memory requirements are covered by accessing the system DRAM. The GPU, the video transcoding hardware, the x86 cores and the L3 cache are interconnected using a ring-based bus. In addition, Sandy Bridge chips integrate the SIMD AVX extensions to the x86 ISA. Like the Intel Sandy Bridge architecture, AMD Fusion processors combine multiple x86 cores, a GPU, a video transcoding hardware engine, and a SIMD engine. Likewise, the cores, the SIMD engine and the video transcoding hardware engine attach to the same high-speed bus, and have direct access to the main system memory (Brookwood, 2010).

Processor With FPGA

A Field Programmable Gate Array or FPGA is an array of logic blocks of different types (general logic, memory, multiplier blocks) surrounded by a programmable routing network that can be reconfigured on the fly to implement any digital design. The array is surrounded by programmable I/O blocks that allow the FPGA to interact with the exterior (Kuon et al., 2008). The attraction of FPGAs is their electrical efficiency given their potential computing power and its singular flexibility. More on acceleration of general-purpose applications using FPGAs can be found in (Herbordt et al., 2007).

Initiatives, such as the Intel E600C series (Intel, 2010a) and the Microsemi SmartFusion (Microsemi, 2017) processors, migrate a FPGA closer to the main CPU. The Intel E600C processor is a configurable Intel Atom CPU packaged with an Altera FPGA. On the other hand, the Microsemi SmartFusion processor combines an ARM Cortex, a FPGA and programmable analog components. This kind of architecture is geared towards applications such as industrial machines, portable medical equipment and communications devices (Intel, 2010b).

Intel has predicted that by 2020 30% of datacenter servers will be equipped with FPGAs, accelerating tasks such as machine learning, encryption, compression, network acceleration, and scientific computing.

LOAD DISTRIBUTION FOR GRAPH HETEROGENEOUS COMPUTING: OPPORTUNITIES

Given the advantages of the heterogeneous computing approach, we pose the following question: can we take advantage of different hardware architectures to efficiently solve problems that arise when we analyze large complex networks?

Heterogeneous computing is the idea of breaking down a task in such a way that different architectures do part of the work at the same time or in a synchronized manner. Given a platform that includes a CPU and a GPU, a fundamental problem is to decide how to partition and then distribute the graph between the CPU and the GPU to maximize performance.

Most conventional scientific graph partitioning algorithms produce equivalent partitions and focus to reduce communication costs by minimizing the edge cut (Chamberlain, 1998). A related and well-studied problem in Network Science is community detection, which seeks to find groups of nodes having dense intra-connections and sparse inter-connections.

Balanced and community detection algorithms focus on reducing the number of edges crossing groups. However, there is evidence (Gharaibeh et al., 2013, Gharaibeh et al., 2012) that graph partitioning algorithms should instead focus on fitting the capabilities of different parallel architectures and reduce the computation time of partitions, in order to benefit from the heterogeneous computing approach.

For example, Gharaibeh et al. (2013) argue that partitions should provide different degrees of parallelisms and maximize the utilization of the processors, yet they must lead to homogeneous parallelism to achieve balanced workload across the vertices of a partition. It is also stressed that a graph partitioner should focus on producing partitions that minimize computing time rather than communication time.

Current works place high-degree vertices in the CPU and low-degree vertices in the GPU (Gharaibeh et al., 2013; Gharaibeh et al., 2012; Nilakant and Yoneki, 2014) to achieve cache-friendliness and partition homogeneity.

However, to the best of our knowledge, besides the degree of nodes current works on graph heterogeneous computing do not fully exploit the information encoded in the topology inherent to complex networks to produce novel partitioning schemes for complex networks. Is it possible to exploit the topology of complex networks to better exploit multiple parallel architectures of different granularity?

BSP Graph Heterogeneous Computing

To overcome the limitations of individual parallel architectures, the High Performance Computing (HPC) industry is utilizing existing general-purpose CPUs combined with GPUs or tightly-coupled accelerators to improve the performance of data analytics on large volumes of data. This is known as *heterogeneous computing*.

Existing combinations of architectures in heterogeneous computing works for traversing complex networks include CPU + GPU (Gharaibeh et al., 2012; Gharaibeh et al., 2013; Hong et al., 2011, Zou et al., 2013; Banerjee et al., 2013; Munguia et al., 2012), CPU + AMD Accelerated Processing Units (Nilakant and Yoneki, 2014), and CPU + Intel Many Integrated Cores (Gao et al., 2014).

New Bulk Synchronous Process (BSP) platforms (Gharaibeh et al., 2012, Gharaibeh et al., 2013) are following a similar approach than industry-proven frameworks like Google Pregel, but applied to exploit the potential of HPC hybrid nodes that combine multi-cores and GPUs.

An example is that of Totem (Gharaibeh et al., 2012, Gharaibeh et al., 2013), that claims to minimize PCI-Express[5] communication overhead by batching data transfers in the communication step (Gharaibeh et al., 2012, Gharaibeh et al., 2013).

Gharaibeh et al., 2012 propose a heterogeneous parallel graph framework that runs in both CPU and GPU as a sequence of parallel super-steps, where each super-step is composed of the following phases (Figure 2):

1. **Partitioning Phase:** The graph is partitioned in as many partitions as the number of different processors.

15

Figure 2. The BSP CPU + GPU heterogeneous computing approach in (Gharaibeh et al., 2012; Gharaibeh et al., 2013)

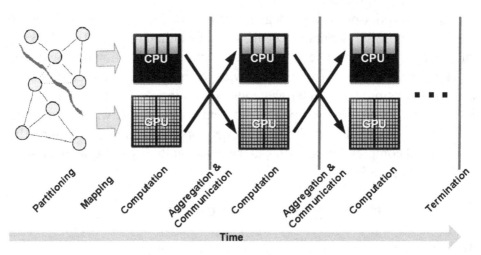

2. **Mapping Phase:** The graph partitions are assigned to the available processors. This mapping is static, i.e. does not change throughout the execution of the application.
3. **Computation Phase:** Each processor performs computation using local data and issue communication requests that are stored in a queue.
4. **Aggregation and Communication Phase:** Communication requests are aggregated and then exchanged among processors.

Under this new paradigm, the performance of BSP heterogeneous computing platforms like Totem depends on minimizing the computation time of partitions by increasing the suitability of partitions to processors. This represents a departure from conventional parallel techniques that focus on the balanced distribution of the graph among processors while minimizing communications.

The Measurement and Core of Complex Networks

Complex networks show patterns that suggest mechanisms that guide the formation of the network and that can be exploited for a variety of purposes. Much of the work in Network Science has been dedicated to the characterization of the structure of graphs in terms of *complex network metrics* (Costa et al., 2007). According to Brinkmeier (2004) complex network metrics enable:

- The representation of the essential properties of complex networks in a compact fashion. In this way, it is possible to focus on a set of statistics of interest instead of trying to decipher the structure of the whole graph.
- The differentiation among distinct classes of complex networks by measuring the set of invariant statistical properties that characterize the members of a particular graph class.
- The design of structure-aware algorithms capable of determining the elements of the graph that show a property of interest for a particular application domain.

For example, it has been reported that complex networks show a *core* (Carmi et al., 2007), integrated of highly connected hubs that represent the backbone of graphs. The k-core of a graph, a complex network metric, is the largest subgraph whose vertices have degree at least k (Dorogovtsev et al., 2006), and can be obtained efficiently by recursively pruning the vertices with degree smaller than k. The k-core decomposition defines a hierarchy of nodes that enables the differentiation between *core* and *peripheral* components of a graph.

Complex network metrics play an important role in the representation, characterization, classification and modeling of real-world graphs. However, there are very few works that try to exploit the structure of complex networks to design novel parallel algorithms that are better suited for modern architectures.

Is it possible to take advantage of the knowledge obtained by characterizing the topology of complex networks to guide the execution of topology-aware complex network algorithms?

Complex network properties, like the k-core decomposition, represent useful yet easy to calculate heuristics for designing a novel unbalanced complex network partition strategy for unbalanced load distribution in graph heterogeneous platforms.

Reduction of Networks and Graph Partitioning

Due to the massive size of real world complex graphs it is worth to consider mechanisms that reduce the size of this kind of structures. Reductive graph methods choose a subset of nodes from the original graph, trying to preserve a set of properties that characterize the graph. The "representative" subgraph should be small enough to be more manageable than the original one.

Reductive methods, start with the original graph and iteratively removes nodes or edges at random. Krishnamurthy et al. (2007) propose a set of reductive methods that reduce a percentage of the graph in stages. Examples of reductive methods are: deletion of random vertices, deletion of random edges, and contraction of random edges (Krishnamurthy et al., 2007). Reduction algorithms could easily fit into a multilevel approach for balanced graph partitioning, a key step for the achievement of the goals of the current thesis. In a multilevel scheme, the original graph is reduced into a series of successively coarser graphs, then partitioned at the coarsest graph, and finally uncoarsened.

Good results would allow us to design a load balancing strategy capable of distributing communities of a variety of sizes to heterogeneous architectures, such as multi-cores and GPUs. The communities then can be equally divided using a new multilevel approach for the balanced distribution of subgraphs to homogeneous processing elements (e.g. the cores of a multi-core CPU).

Is it possible to design graph reduction techniques that preserve non-redundant topological properties of real-world graphs for the balanced distribution of networks to homogeneous processing elements?

TOWARDS TOPOLOGY-AWARE LOAD BALANCING FOR GRAPH HETEROGENEOUS COMPUTING

The graph partitioning problem is relevant for any parallel processing strategy, and heterogeneous computing is not the exception. How to efficiently produce unbalanced partitions that fit the capabilities of different parallel architectures, reduce the computation time of partitions, and benefit from the heterogeneous computing approach?

Arguably, the most successful framework for solving the balanced graph partitioning problem on large scientific graphs is the multilevel approach (Buluc et al., 2013). Multilevel partitioning involves a coarsening phase, in which the original graph is reduced to obtain a hierarchy of coarsened and reduced graphs that preserve the structure of the original graph and that can be efficiently partitioned.

Current efforts on the multilevel graph partitioning method are mostly focused on balanced partitioning and on the partitioning of 3D FEM's, road maps, VLSI circuits, and data structures arising from linear programming problems. However, conventional coarsening algorithms are not suited for reducing complex networks (Abou-Rjeili and Karypis, 2006).

However, conventional coarsening algorithms are not suited for reducing complex networks. The reason is that real-world graphs, such as PPI, social and Web networks, show a very different structure than 3D meshes and grids found in scientific computing and modeling applications (Lumsdaine, 2007; Madduri, 2008). Graph partitioning techniques are needed that produce tasks with different sizes in order to exploit the computing power of different processors, such as multicores and GPUs (Shen and Zeng, 2005).

The coarsening stage of a multilevel partitioning algorithm should preserve the *natural* structure of complex networks, so that the partitioning can produce unbalanced groups of vertices that can be distributed to parallel architectures with different processing capabilities. However, conventional matching processes are inefficient when applied over high degree nodes recurrent in complex networks, causing the memory requirements for the storage of the hierarchy of coarse graphs to increment (Abou-Rjeili and Karypis, 2006).

To produce a coarsening process that (1) preserves the topology of complex networks and (2) that produces a low number of coarse levels, we have shown (Garcia-Robledo et al., 2016) that it is possible to preserve a number of non-redundant topological properties when coarsening complex networks by contracting links that preferentially connect nodes at very different k-shells. To demonstrate this, we propose a framework to produce graph coarsening algorithms that sequentially contract edges based on the k-core of the node ends, and successfully produce reduced version of complex network graphs that preserves graph properties like the scale-free degree distribution (Garcia-Robledo et al., 2016).

Therefore, we claim that it is possible to embed topology-aware coarsening strategy that preserves topological properties of complex networks into a multilevel-like partitioning algorithm that produces graph partitions that fit different architectures in a heterogeneous computing setup.

In this way, to efficiently solve a variety of problems in complex networks of the present and the future, it is necessary to design a novel parallel strategy that: (1) exploits the structure of the graph by using topological metrics and a partitioning strategy for complex networks; and (2) adopts a heterogeneous multi/many-core approach that combines the computing power of different parallel architectures, such as multicores and many-cores.

The way graphs are partitioning for load balancing has a direct impact on the performance of heterogeneous graph computing architecture. The mentioned fact and the size of real-world complex networks makes desirable to exploit heuristics guided by topological aspects inherent to complex networks, like their coreness and the heterogeneous centrality of their vertices. Next paragraphs describe the methodological approach used to support our claims and that is followed throughout this book:

Phase 1: *Study of a topology-aware coarsening approach for complex networks.*

The objective of Phase 1 is to study an algorithm for the coarsening of graphs that preserve non-redundant topological properties of complex networks by exploiting the notion of graph coreness. The k-core decomposition of graphs can be useful for identifying the most appropriate edges to contract in a graph coarsening strategy that preserves a variety of non-redundant graph properties, like the average degree, the average path length, the clustering coefficient and the scale-free degree distribution.

Phase 2: *Study of the influence of graph topology on multi/many-core performance.*

The objective of Phase 2 is to evaluate the behavior of multi-cores and many-cores on complex networks with different structure. This is to be achieved by observing the performance of BFS on multi-core CPUs and GPUs, when varying the topology of synthetic graphs. The obtained results will be used for the design of the unbalanced complex network partitioning algorithm by considering how BFS performs differently on networks with different structural properties.

Phase 3: *Design of a load-balance partitioning scheme for complex networks.*

The objective of Phase 3 is to design and study an unbalanced partitioning algorithm for complex networks that exploits the core of real-word graphs and a coarsening strategy. The partitioning strategy is expected to produce unbalanced partitions that increase the performance of a BSP heterogeneous computing framework.

Phase 4: *Evaluation of the load-balance partitioning scheme on a heterogeneous computing platform.*

The objective of Phase 4 is to evaluate the performance increase of an existing BSP graph heterogeneous computing platform when exploiting the unbalanced complex network partitioning algorithm designed at Phase 3 and the insights obtained for the unbalanced distribution of complex networks. The evaluation includes the comparison of the designed partitioning algorithms to state-of-the-art partitioning algorithms while performing BFS traversals on a benchmark of large real-world and synthetic complex networks.

Therefore, we seek to contribute by developing a methodology that guides the design of multilevel-like complex network load balance approach with a focus on the partitioning of real-world graphs, all in all considering the structure of complex networks in all stages of the methodology. The objective is to design and study a partitioner that produce different degrees of parallelisms and maximize the utilization of the processors while minimize computing time (rather than communication time).

With such a load-balancing strategy, we try to better leverage the combined parallelism offered by multi-cores and GPUs to accelerate graph traversals (breadth-first searches) on complex networks to overcome the poor data locality, memory contention problems, unbalancing issues, and low arithmetic loads that are limiting the performance of individual parallel architectures on graph analysis applications.

CONCLUSION

Networks Science is a new field devoted to the study of complex networks: graphical models of large physical, biological, technological, and sociological phenomena. To process real-world networks, CPUs can be combined with GPUs, in an approach known as heterogeneous computing. A fundamental problem in heterogeneous computing is to decide how to partition the graph to distribute it between the CPU and the GPU.

On the one hand, the performance of new Bulk Synchronous Parallel (BSP) heterogeneous platforms depends on minimizing the computation time of partitions. On the other hand, the characterization of the topology of complex networks through metrics like the k-core decomposition provides insights that can be exploited for a variety of purposes. This work presents a novel topology-aware approach for partitioning complex networks with applications in graph heterogeneous computing.

REFERENCES

Abou-Rjeili, A., & Karypis, G. (2006). Multilevel Algorithms for Partitioning Power-Law Graphs. *Proceedings of the 20th IEEE International Parallel & Distributed Processing Symposium (IPDPS'06)*, 124–124.

Abts, D., & Kim, J. (2011). *High Performance Datacenter Networks: Architectures, Algorithms, and Opportunities*. Morgan & Claypool Publishers.

Almasi, G., & Gottlieb, A. (1989). *Highly Parallel Computing*. Benjamin-Cummings Publishing.

Alpert, J., & Hajaj, N. (2008). *We Knew the Web Was Big*. Retrieved 28 April, 2017, from http://googleblog.blogspot.com/2008/07/we-knew-web-was-big.html

Amdahl, G. (1967). Validity of the Single Processor Approach to Achieving Large Scale Computing Capabilities. In *Proceedings of the April 18-20, 1967, Spring Joint Computer Conference*, (pp. 483–485). ACM. doi:10.1145/1465482.1465560

Angeloudis, P., & Fisk, D. (2006). Large Subway Systems as Complex Networks. *Physica A*, *367*(15), 553–558. doi:10.1016/j.physa.2005.11.007

Banerjee, D., Sharma, S., & Kothapalli, K. (2013). Work Efficient Parallel Algorithms for Large Graph Exploration. *Proceedings of the 20th Annual International Conference on High Performance Computing (HiPC'13)*, 433–442. doi:10.1109/HiPC.2013.6799125

Blake, G., Dreslinski, R., & Mudge, T. (2009). A Survey of Multicore Processors. *IEEE Signal Processing Magazine*, *26*(6), 26–37. doi:10.1109/MSP.2009.934110

Brinkmeier, M. (2004). Network Statistics. In U. Brandes & T. Erlebach (Eds.), *Network Analysis: Methodological Foundations* (pp. 293–317). Springer.

Brodtkorb, A., Dyken, C., Hagen, T., Hjelmervik, J., & Storaasli, O. (2010). State-Of-The-Art in Heterogeneous Computing. *Scientific Programming*, *18*(1), 1–33. doi:10.1155/2010/540159

Brookwood, N. (2010). *AMD Fusion Family of APUs: Enabling a Superior, Immersive PC Experience*. Whitepaper.

Buluc, A., Meyerhenke, H., Safro, I., Sanders, P., & Schulz, C. (2013). *Recent Advances in Graph Partitioning.* arXiv:13113144 [csDS]

Carmi, S., Havlin, S., Kirkpatrick, S., Shavitt, Y., & Shir, E. (2007). A Model of Internet Topology Using K-Shell Decomposition. *Proceedings of the National Academy of Sciences of the United States of America, 104*(27), 11150–11154. doi:10.1073/pnas.0701175104 PMID:17586683

Chamberlain, B. (1998). *Graph Partitioning Algorithms for Distributing Workloads of Parallel Computations. Technical report.* University of Washington.

Committee On Modeling Simulation And Games. (2010). *The Rise of Games and High Performance Computing for Modeling and Simulation.* Author.

Committee on Network Science for Future Army Applications. (2005). *Network Science.* National Academies Press.

Costa, L., Rodrigues, F., Travieso, G., & Boas, P. (2007). Characterization of Complex Networks: A Survey of Measurements. *Advances in Physics, 56*(1), 167–242. doi:10.1080/00018730601170527

Dehne, F., & Yogaratnam, K. (2010). *Exploring the Limits of GPUs With Parallel Graph Algorithms.* arXiv:10024482v1 [csDC]

Dorogovtsev, S., Goltsev, A., & Mendes, J. (2006). K-Core Organization of Complex Networks. *Physical Review Letters, 96*(4), 040601. doi:10.1103/PhysRevLett.96.040601 PMID:16486798

Flake, G., Lawrence, S., Giles, C., & Coetzee, F. (2002). Self-Organization and Identification of Web Communities. *Computer, 35*(3), 66–70. doi:10.1109/2.989932

Freeman, L. (1979). Centrality in Social Networks Conceptual Clarification. *Social Networks, 1*(3), 215–239. doi:10.1016/0378-8733(78)90021-7

Gao, T., Lu, Y., Zhang, B., & Suo, G. (2014). Using the Intel Many Integrated Core to Accelerate Graph Traversal. *International Journal of High Performance Computing Applications, 28*(3), 255–266. doi:10.1177/1094342014524240

Garcia-Robledo, A., Diaz-Perez, A., & Morales-Luna, G. (2016). Characterization and Coarsening of Autonomous System Networks: Measuring and Simplifying the Internet. In Advanced Methods for Complex Network Analysis, (pp. 148–179). IGI Global.

Gebali, F. (2010). *Algorithms and Parallel Computing*. Wiley.

Geer, D. (2005). Chip Makers Turn to Multicore Processors. *Computer*, *38*(5), 11–13. doi:10.1109/MC.2005.160

Gelado, I., Stone, J., Cabezas, J., Patel, S., Navarro, N., & Hwu, W. (2010). An Asymmetric Distributed Shared Memory Model for Heterogeneous Parallel Systems. In ACM SIGARCH Computer Architecture News - ASPLOS '10, (pp. 347–358). ACM. doi:10.1145/1736020.1736059

Gharaibeh, A., Costa, L., Elizeu, S., & Ripeanu, M. (2013). On Graphs, GPUs, and Blind Dating: A Workload to Processor Matchmaking Quest. *Proceedings of the 27th IEEE International Symposium on Parallel & Distributed Processing (IPDPS'13)*, 851–862. doi:10.1109/IPDPS.2013.37

Gharaibeh, A., Lauro, C., Elizeu, S., & Matei, R. (2012). A Yoke of Oxen and a Thousand Chickens for Heavy Lifting Graph Processing. *Proceedings of the 21st International Conference on Parallel Architectures and Compilation Techniques (PACT'12)*, 345–354. doi:10.1145/2370816.2370866

Girvan, M., & Newman, M. (2002). Community Structure in Social and Biological Networks. *Proceedings of the National Academy of Sciences of the United States of America*, *99*(12), 7821–7826. doi:10.1073/pnas.122653799 PMID:12060727

Guida, M., & Maria, F. (2007). Topology of the Italian Airport Network: A Scale-Free Small-World Network With a Fractal Structure? *Chaos, Solitons, and Fractals*, *31*(3), 527–536. doi:10.1016/j.chaos.2006.02.007

Gustafson, J. (1988). Reevaluating Amdahl's Law. *Communications of the ACM*, *31*(5), 532–533. doi:10.1145/42411.42415

Hendrickson, B., & Berry, J. (2008). Graph Analysis With High-Performance Computing. *Computing in Science & Engineering*, *10*(2), 14–19. doi:10.1109/MCSE.2008.56

Herbordt, M., VanCourt, T., Gu, Y., Sukhwani, B., Conti, A., Model, J., & DiSabello, D. (2007). Achieving High Performance With FPGA-based Computing. *Computer*, *40*(3), 50–57. doi:10.1109/MC.2007.79 PMID:21603088

Holme, P., Kim, B., Yoon, C., & Han, S. (2002). Attack Vulnerability of Complex Networks. *Physical Review E: Statistical, Nonlinear, and Soft Matter Physics, 65*(5), 056109. doi:10.1103/PhysRevE.65.056109 PMID:12059649

Hong, S., Oguntebi, T., & Olukotun, K. (2011). Efficient Parallel Graph Exploration on Multi-Core CPU and GPU. *Proceedings of the 2011 International Conference on Parallel Architectures and Compilation Techniques (PACT'11)*, 78–88. doi:10.1109/PACT.2011.14

HPC Wire. (2010). *China Breaks Ground on New Supercomputer Center.* Retrieved 28 April, 2017, from https://www.hpcwire.com/2010/11/30/china_breaks_ground_on_new_supercomputer_center/

Intel. (2010b). *New Configurable Processor for Embedded Markets.* Retrieved 28 April, 2017, from https://newsroom.intel.com/chip-shots/chip-shot-new-configurable-processor-for-embedded-markets/

Intel. (2010a). *Intel Expands Customer Choice With First Configurable Intel Atom-Based Processor.* Retrieved 28 April, 2017, from https://newsroom.intel.com/news-releases/intel-expands-customer-choice-with-first-configurable-intel-atom-based-processor/

Keyes, D., Sameh, A., & Venkatakrishnan, V. (1997). Parallel Numerical Algorithms: An Introduction. In ICASE/LaRC Interdisciplinary Series in Science and Engineering, (vol. 4, pp. 1–16). Dordrecht: Kluwer Academic Publishers.

Kirk, D., & Wen-mei, W. (2010). *Programming Massively Parallel Processors: A Hands-On Approach.* Morgan Kaufmann.

Koschützki, D., & Schreiber, F. (2008). Centrality Analysis Methods for Biological Networks and Their Application to Gene Regulatory Networks. *Gene Regulation and Systems Biology, 2*(1), 193–201. PMID:19787083

Krishnamurthy, V., Faloutsos, M., Chrobak, M., Cui, J., Lao, L., & Percus, A. (2007). Sampling Large Internet Topologies for Simulation Purposes. *Computer Networks, 51*(15), 4284–4302. doi:10.1016/j.comnet.2007.06.004

Kuon, I., Tessier, R., & Rose, J. (2008). *FPGA Architecture: Survey and Challenges.* Now Publishers Inc.

Lumsdaine, A., Gregor, D., Hendrickson, B., & Berry, J. (2007). Challenges in Parallel Graph Processing. *Parallel Processing Letters*, *17*(1), 5–20. doi:10.1142/S0129626407002843

Madduri, K. (2008). *A High-Performance Framework for Analyzing Massive Complex Networks* (PhD thesis). Georgia Institute of Technology.

Mattson, T. (2009). *How to Sound Like a Parallel Programming Expert: Part 1. Technical report*. Intel.

Memon, N., Larsen, H., Hicks, D., & Harkiolakis, N. (2008). Detecting Hidden Hierarchy in Terrorist Networks: Some Case Studies. *Proceedings of the 6th IEEE ISI PAISI, PACCF, and SOCO International Workshops on Intelligence and Security Informatics (PAISI, PACCF & SOCO'08)*, 477–489. doi:10.1007/978-3-540-69304-8_50

Microsemi. (2017). *SmartFusion Intelligent Mixed Signal FPGA Textbar System-On-Chip (SoC) Solutions - Actel*. Retrieved 28 April, 2017, from https://www.microsemi.com/products/fpga-soc/soc-fpga/smartfusion

Milo, R., Shen-Orr, S., Itzkovitz, S., Kashtan, N., Chklovskii, D., & Alon, U. (2002). Network Motifs: Simple Building Blocks of Complex Networks. *Science*, *298*(5594), 824–827. doi:10.1126/science.298.5594.824 PMID:12399590

Munguia, L., Bader, D., & Ayguade, E. (2012). Task-Based Parallel Breadth-First Search in Heterogeneous Environments. *Proceedings of the 19th International Conference on High Performance Computing (HiPC'12)*, 1–10. doi:10.1109/HiPC.2012.6507474

National Center for Biotechnology Information. (2017). *GenBank Release Notes*. Retrieved 28 April, 2017, from ftp://ftp.ncbi.nih.gov/genbank/gbrel.txt

Nilakant, K., & Yoneki, E. (2014). On the Efficacy of APUs for Heterogeneous Graph Computation. *Proceedings of the 4th Workshop on Systems for Future Multicore Architectures (SFMA'14)*, 2–7.

Page, L., Brin, S., Motwani, R., & Winograd, T. (1999). The PageRank Citation Ranking: Bringing Order to the Web. *World Wide Web Internet and Web Information Systems*, *54*(2), 1–17.

Pereira-Leal, J., Enright, A., & Ouzounis, C. (2004). Detection of Functional Modules From Protein Interaction Networks. *Proteins*, *54*(1), 49–57. doi:10.1002/prot.10505 PMID:14705023

PhysOrg.com. (2009). *Scientists Use World's Fastest Supercomputer to Model Origins of the Unseen Universe*. Retrieved 28 April, 2017, from https://phys.org/news/2009-10-scientists-world-fastest-supercomputer-unseen.html

Radatz, J. (1997). *The IEEE Standard Dictionary of Electrical and Electronics Terms* (6th ed.). IEEE.

Rauber, T., & Runger, G. (2010). *Parallel Programming: For Multicore and Cluster Systems*. Springer-Verlag. doi:10.1007/978-3-642-04818-0

Reinders, J. (2007). *Intel Threading Building Blocks: Outfitting C++ for Multi-Core Processor Parallelism*. O'Reilly Media.

ScienceDaily. (2009). *Scientists Use World's Fastest Supercomputer to Create the Largest HIV Evolutionary Tree*. Retrieved 28 April, 2017, from https://www.sciencedaily.com/releases/2009/10/091027161536.htm

ScienceDaily. (2017). *Supercomputer*. Retrieved 28 April, 2017, from https://www.sciencedaily.com/terms/supercomputer.htm

Shen, Y., & Zeng, G. (2005). An Unbalanced Partitioning Scheme for Graph in Heterogeneous Computing. *Proceedings of the 2005 Grid and Cooperative Computing (GCC'05)*, 1167–1172. doi:10.1007/11590354_139

Shlomi, T., Segal, D., Ruppin, E., & Sharan, R. (2006). QPath: A Method for Querying Pathways in a Protein-Protein Interaction Network. *BMC Bioinformatics*, *7*(199). PMID:16606460

Singh, R., Xu, J., & Berger, B. (2008). Global Alignment of Multiple Protein Interaction Networks With Application to Functional Orthology Detection. *Proceedings of the National Academy of Sciences of the United States of America*, *105*(35), 12763–12768. doi:10.1073/pnas.0806627105 PMID:18725631

Stark, D. (2011). *Advanced Semantics for Accelerated Graph Processing* (PhD thesis). Louisiana State University.

Sweney, M. (2010). *Mark Zuckerberg: Facebook 'Almost Guaranteed' to Reach 1 Billion Users*. Retrieved 28 April, 2017, from https://www.theguardian.com/media/2010/jun/23/mark-zuckerberg-facebook-cannes-lions

The Council on Competitiveness. (2009). *Grand Challenge Case Study: Crude Oil Catalysts. Technical report*. Council on Competitiveness.

Top500.org. (2008). *TOP500 June 2008 News*. Retrieved 28 April, 2017, from https://www.top500.org/lists/2008/06/

Top500.org. (2010). *China Grabs Supercomputing Leadership Spot in Latest Ranking of World's Top 500 Supercomputers*. Retrieved 28 April, 2017, from https://www.top500.org/news/lists/2010/11/press-release/

Top500.org. (2011). *Highlights - June 2011 Textbar TOP500 Supercomputing Sites*. Retrieved 28 April, 2017, from https://www.top500.org/lists/2011/06/highlights/

Trobec, R., Vajtersic, M., & Zinterhof, P. (2009). *Parallel Computing: Numerics, Applications, and Trends*. Springer. doi:10.1007/978-1-84882-409-6

Vajda, A. (2011). *Programming Many-Core Chips*. Springer-Verlag. doi:10.1007/978-1-4419-9739-5

Wen-mei, W., Keutzer, K., & Mattson, T. (2008). The Concurrency Challenge. *IEEE Design & Test of Computers*, *25*(4), 312–320. doi:10.1109/MDT.2008.110

Xie, X., Fang, X., Hu, S., & Wu, D. (2010). Evolution of Supercomputers. *Frontiers of Computer Science in China*, *4*(4), 428–436. doi:10.1007/s11704-010-0118-z

Yazdani, A., & Jeffrey, P. (2011). Complex Network Analysis of Water Distribution Systems. *Chaos (Woodbury, N.Y.)*, *21*(1), 016111. doi:10.1063/1.3540339 PMID:21456853

Zou, D., Dou, Y., Wang, Q., Xu, J., & Li, B. (2013). Direction-Optimizing Breadth-First Search on CPU-GPU Heterogeneous Platforms. *Proceedings of the 10th IEEE International Conference on High Performance Computing and Communications & IEEE International Conference on Embedded and Ubiquitous Computing (HPCC/EUC'13)*, 1064–1069. doi:10.1109/HPCC.and.EUC.2013.150

ENDNOTES

1   A random graph is a graph where the occurrence of edges depends on a given probability distribution.

2   A 3D mesh is a graph representing a 3D surface, usually integrated by triangles or polygons.

3   TOP500 third place with 1.27 petaflop/s as of November 2011.

4   TOP500 fourth place with 1.19 petaflop/s as of November 2011.

5   High-speed serial computer expansion bus used to connect GPU cards (and other kinds of expansion cards) to the server motherboard.

Chapter 2

Core Kernels for Complex Network Analysis

ABSTRACT

The emergence of Network Science has motivated a renewed interest in classical graph problems for the analysis of the topology of complex networks. For example, important centrality metrics, such as the betweenness, the stress, the eccentricity, and the closeness centralities, are all based on BFS. On the other hand, the k-core decomposition of graphs defines a hierarchy of internal cores and decomposes large networks layer by layer. The k-core decomposition has been successfully applied in a variety of domains, including large graph visualization and fingerprinting, analysis of large software systems, and fraud detection. In this chapter, the authors review known efficient algorithms for traversing and decomposing large complex networks and provide insights on how the decomposition of graphs in k-cores can be useful for developing novel topology-aware algorithms.

CHARACTERIZING THE TOPOLOGY OF COMPLEX NETWORKS

Network Science was initiated in the late 1950's and early 1960's with the works of Erdös and Rényi (1959) on random graphs. However, during late 1990's interest in complex networks exploded with the seminal works of Watts and Strogatz on small-world networks (Watts and Strogatz, 1998) and Barabási and Albert on scale-free graphs (Barabási and Albert, 1999).

DOI: 10.4018/978-1-5225-3799-1.ch002

They showed that complex networks encode intriguing properties in their topology that reveal important details of their functional organization and the underlying real-world phenomena.

Many complex network metrics have been proposed in literature (Newman, 2003; Costa et al., 2007) to characterize the topology of complex networks.

Complex network metrics can be roughly grouped into two classes: structural and scaling metrics. On the one hand, structural metrics summarize information about the global structure of the graph, or the local organization or importance of vertices. On the other hand, the scaling of some structural metrics with the degree of vertices can reveal non-trivial high-level properties of graphs, such the scale-free form of the graph degree distribution.

Complex network metrics give information about individual elements of a graph, for example, the importance of a vertex in terms of its degree, vertex distance to other nodes, or the properties of a vertex neighborhood. Complex network metrics can also give information about the whole graph; for example, the longest shortest path distance between any two vertices (diameter), the maximum number of neighbors of any vertex, or how much the degree distribution follows a scale-free form. Finally, the scaling with the degree of some metrics, such as the clustering or the rich-club coefficient, reveals, for example, if a degree distribution follows a scale-free form or the assortativity of a graph.

Degree Metrics

Let A be the adjacency matrix of a graph G with n vertices and m edges, where:

$$A_{uv} = \begin{cases} 1, & \text{if}\{u, v\} \in E \\ 0, & \text{otherwise} \end{cases}.$$

The *degree* k_u of a vertex $u \in V$ is the number of nearest neighbors[1] of u. Formally, $k_u = \sum_{u \in V} A_{uv}$. Let n_k be the number of vertices of degree k in G, such that $\sum_k n_k = n$. Let $P(k) = n_k / n$ be the *degree distribution of G*. $P(k)$ denotes the fraction of vertices in a graph that have degree k.

Let $\langle k \rangle$ denote the *average degree* over all the vertices of G:

$$\langle k \rangle = \frac{1}{n} \sum_{u \in V} k_u. \tag{1}$$

A metric derived from the degree of vertices is the *maximum degree* k_{max}:

$$k_{max} = \max_{u \in V} \{k_u\}. \tag{2}$$

Another degree metric is the average degree of the nearest neighbors of vertex u, $k_n(u)$, or *neighbor degree* for short, which is defined as follows:

$$k_n(u) = \frac{\sum_{v \in N_u} k_v}{|N_u|}. \tag{3}$$

The Sparseness of Complex Networks

Complex networks, random graphs, and 3D meshes are all sparse. They show a remarkably low number of edges $m \ll m_{max}$, where $m_{max} = \binom{n}{2}$ is the maximum number of possible edges in a simple undirected graph. Graph sparsity can be also defined in terms of the *graph density*:

$$d = m / m_{max}, \tag{4}$$

where $d \in [0,1]$ and $d \ll 1$ holds for sparse graphs.

Erdös and Rényi (1959) considered the space of all graphs of n vertices and m edges, and a uniform selection among them chooses just one. Each graph has the same probability to be selected. Simultaneously, Gilbert studied a model for random graphs where two vertices u, v are connected with probability p, being u, v chosen independently at random. For large values of n, both Erdös-Rényi and Gilbert models of random graphs tend to produce a degree distribution $P_{n,p}(k)$ that closes to a Poisson distribution

$$P(k) \rightarrow_n \frac{(np)^k}{k!} e^{-np}.$$

Graphs encountered in scientific computing, such as 3D meshes, are regular, i.e. their degree distribution is relatively uniform due to the geometric constraints of the underlying meshes. Good aspect ratios needed for the convergence of numerical methods in meshes cause an overall degree regularity (Abou-Rjeili and Karypis, 2006). This means that random and regular graphs tend to be homogeneous in terms of the vertex degree, as most of the vertex degrees in random graphs and 3D meshes are close to the average degree $\langle k \rangle$.

Unlike random and scientific computing graphs, complex networks present the combined properties of random but highly clustered graphs with a few quantity of vertices having the largest number of vertices. Complex networks tend to be heterogeneous in terms of the vertex degree. Likewise, complex networks from a variety of application domains share characteristics that differentiate them from random and regular networks: small-worldliness, scale-freeness, assortativity, and rich-clubs.

The following sections explain each of the above mentioned complex network properties.

Scale-Free Networks

Barabási and Albert (1999) found that the degree distribution $P(k)$ of many real-world networks obey a power law, in which the number of vertices of degree k is proportional to $k^{-\alpha}$, with $\alpha \in [2, 3]$. This contrasts with Erdös-Rényi random graphs, which present a Poisson degree distribution.

A power-law distribution implies that a network has only a few vertices with very high degree, called hubs (vertices with many neighbors), and most of the vertices have a low degree (vertices with very few neighbors). Observe in Table 1 a low average degree $\langle k \rangle \ll n$ but a high maximum degree k_{max} in complex networks, suggesting that the majority of nodes hold a low degree, yet hubs are present. Networks with a power-law degree distribution are known as *scale-free networks*.

A graph is scale-free if the degree distribution $P(k)$ decreases with k following a power-law form (Barabási et al., 2000). If we measure the Pearson correlation between k and the degree distribution $P(k)$, being both the metrics in a logarithmic scale, we can decide on the linearity of the degree distribution on a log-log plot and hence the presence of the power-law phenomenon.

Let $COR(Y, Z)$ denote the Pearson correlation coefficient between sequences Y and Z. Recall that $k_{max} = \max_{u \in V}\{k_u\}$. Let $K = \left(k_{min}, ..., k_{max}\right)$

Table 1. Measurements of real-world complex networks. Measurements were performed on the undirected version of the giant component of each graph. $n =$ *number of vertices,* $m =$ *number of edges,* $d =$ *density,* $\langle CC \rangle =$ *avg. clustering coefficient,* $\langle k \rangle =$ *avg. degree,* $k_{max} =$ *maximum degree,* $\langle L \rangle =$ *average shortest-path length,* $D =$ *diameter. Density values are rounded to four decimals*

Complex Network	Type	n	m	d	$\langle CC \rangle$	$\langle k \rangle$	k_{max}	$\langle L \rangle$	D
usairport_2010	Infrastructure	1,572	17,214	0.0139	0.64	21.90	314	3.12	8
YeastS	Protein	2,224	6,609	0.0027	0.20	5.94	64	4.38	11
SciMet	Citation	2,678	10,368	0.0029	0.20	7.74	164	4.18	12
openflights	Routes	2,905	15,645	0.0037	0.59	10.77	242	4.10	14
Kohonen	Citation	3,704	12,673	0.0018	0.30	6.84	740	3.67	12
CA-GrQc	Collaboration	4,158	13,422	0.0016	0.66	6.46	81	6.05	17
EPA.gov	Web	4,253	8,897	0.0010	0.14	4.18	175	4.50	10
EVA	Companies	4,475	4,652	0.0005	0.09	2.08	552	7.53	18
power	Infrastructure	4,941	6,594	0.0005	0.11	2.67	19	18.99	46
California	Web	5,925	15,770	0.0009	0.12	5.32	199	5.03	13
as20000102	Internet	6,474	12,572	0.0006	0.40	3.88	1,458	3.71	9
Zewail	Citation	6,640	54,173	0.0025	0.34	16.32	331	3.85	10
Erdös02	Collaboration	6,927	11,850	0.0005	0.40	3.42	507	3.78	4
Wiki-Vote	Wikipedia	7,066	100,736	0.0040	0.21	28.51	1,065	3.25	7
Lederberg	Citation	8,212	41,430	0.0012	0.36	10.09	1,103	4.41	16
CA-HepTh	Collaboration	8,638	24,806	0.0007	0.58	5.74	65	5.95	18
PGPgiantcompo	Users	10,680	24,316	0.0004	0.44	4.55	205	7.49	24
oregon2_010526	Internet	11,461	32,730	0.0005	0.49	5.71	2,432	3.56	9
Reuters911	News	13,308	148,035	0.0017	0.39	22.25	2,265	3.12	10
foldoc	Linguistics	13,356	91,471	0.0010	0.34	13.70	728	3.87	8
CA-AstroPh	Collaboration	17,903	196,972	0.0012	0.67	22.00	504	4.19	14
CA-CondMat	Collaboration	21,363	91,286	0.0004	0.70	8.55	279	5.35	15
as-22july06	Internet	22,963	48,436	0.0002	0.35	4.22	2,390	3.84	11
ASEdges9_2008	Internet	23,113	234,125	0.0009	0.70	20.26	7,409	2.79	6
as-caida20071105	Internet	26,475	53,381	0.0002	0.33	4.03	2,628	3.88	17
Email-Enron	Email	33,696	180,811	0.0003	0.71	10.73	1,383	4.03	13
2010_01_AS	Internet	33,796	94,394	0.0002	0.38	5.59	2,634	3.82	10
Cit-HepPh	Citation	34,401	420,784	0.0007	0.30	24.46	846	4.33	14
p2p-Gnutella31	p2p	62,561	147,878	0.0001	0.01	4.73	95	5.94	11
Wordnet3	Linguistics	75,606	119,564	< 0.0001	0.06	3.16	543	6.71	19
soc-Epinions1	Social	75,877	405,739	0.0001	0.26	10.69	3,044	4.31	15
soc-sign-Slashdot	Social	81,867	497,672	0.0001	0.09	12.16	2,546	4.07	13

be the sequence of the different vertex degrees in G, where $k_{min} = \min_{u \in V} \{k_u\}$. Let $\log(S) = \big(\log(y) \mid y \in S\big)$ return a sequence with the logarithm of each element in S.

The scaling of $P(k)$ with k can be summarized as follows:

$$P(k)_k = \mathrm{COR}\Big(\log\big(K\big), \log\big(\big(P(k) \mid k \in K\big)\big)\Big), \tag{5}$$

where $P(k)_k \in [-1,1]$. As $P(k)_k$ approaches -1 a scale-free degree distribution is more likely. Note that $P(k)_k$ is also known as the *straightness coefficient* (Costa et al., 2007).

Small-World Networks

Let d_{uv} be the length of the shortest (geodesic) path between two vertices $u, v \in V$. The *average shortest path length* $\langle L \rangle$ is the average of all d_{uv} in G (Costa et al., 2007):

$$\langle L \rangle = \frac{1}{n(n-1)} \sum_{u \neq v} d_{uv}. \tag{6}$$

Let $e_{uv} = \{u, v\}$ be an edge connecting vertices u and v, and $N_u = \{v \mid e_{uv} \in E\}$ be the neighborhood of vertex v, defined as the set of vertices adjacent to v. Let $E_u = \{e_{vw} \in E \mid v, w \in N_u\}$ be the set of edges that connect the neighbors of vertex u. The *clustering coefficient* of a vertex u, $CC(u)$, is the ratio of the number of edges among the neighbors of u to the maximum possible number of edges among them:

$$CC(u) = \frac{2E_u}{k_u(k_u - 1)}. \tag{7}$$

A metric μ that is defined either for an individual node or an individual edge, such clustering coefficient $CC(u)$, can be averaged over all nodes or edges to obtain a single measurement $\langle \mu \rangle$ for the whole graph. In this way, the *average clustering coefficient* $\langle CC \rangle$ is the average of $CC(u)$ over all nodes.

Watts and Strogatz (1998) found that the six-degree of separation phenomenon (Milgram, 1967) can be observed in real-world networks. In other words, they found that the majority of the vertex pairs in complex networks are only a few steps away, in spite of their elevated number of vertices. This property can be mathematically characterized by $\langle L \rangle$, which grows logarithmically with n in a variety of real-world graphs.

Observe in Table 1 that complex networks are sparse (low d) and that $\langle L \rangle \ll n$ holds. Likewise, a variety of complex networks show an important quantity of 3-cycles or triangles, which results in an elevated average clustering coefficient $1 / n \ll \langle CC \rangle < 1$, i.e. remarkably greater that the expected $\langle CC \rangle$ of a random network and lesser than the $\langle CC \rangle$ of a complete graph. Networks that show a very small average path length and a high clustering coefficient are known as *small-world networks*.

The *diameter* D of a graph is another distance-based metric, and is defined as the length of the longest shortest path in G:

$$D = \max_{u \neq v}\{d_{uv}\}. \tag{8}$$

Centrality of Nodes

Centrality metrics try to quantify the intuitive idea that some vertices and edges are more *important* than others. This kind of metrics assign a numerical value to each vertex or edge, in order to establish an ordering of relevance of the elements in the graph. Distance centrality metrics are defined in terms of the distances or shortest paths between pairs of vertices, and they are compute-intensive. Distance centrality metrics include the betweenness centrality, the central point dominance, and the closeness centrality.

In a real-world graph, the larger the number of shortest paths in which a vertex participates, the more the importance of that vertex. It is possible to quantify the importance of a node u in terms of its *vertex betweenness centrality* $nBc(u)$, defined as:

$$nBc(u) = \sum_{v,w \in V, v \neq w} \frac{\sigma(u, v, w)}{\sigma(v, w)}, \tag{9}$$

where $\sigma(u, v, w)$ is the number of shortest paths between v and w that pass through u, for all $v, w \in V$, $v \neq w$; and $\sigma(v, w)$ is the total number of shortest paths between v and w, for all $v, w \in V$, $v \neq w$. In other words, $nBc(u)$ is the proportion of shortest paths that pass through u. The *edge betweenness centrality* $mBc(e)$ is a similar metric that measures the proportion of shortest paths that passes through an edge e:

$$mBc(e) = \sum_{v,w \in V, v \neq w} \frac{\sigma(u, e, v)}{\sigma(v, w)}, \tag{10}$$

where $\sigma(e, v, w)$ is the number of shortest paths between v and w that pass through edge e, for all $v, w \in V$, $v \neq w$. The *central point dominance CPD* is defined in terms of the vertex betweenness centrality as follows:

$$CPD = \frac{1}{n - 1} \sum_{u \in V} (nBc_{max} - nBc(u)), \tag{11}$$

where $nBc_{max} = \max_{u \in V} \{nBc(u)\}$.

The *closeness centrality* of vertex u, $Cc(u)$, is inversely proportional to the sum of the distances of u to every other vertex in the graph.

$$Cc(u) = \frac{1}{\sum_{v \in V} d_{uv}}. \tag{12}$$

Finally, the *eigenvector centrality* $Xc(u)$ of a vertex u is based on the idea than the centrality of u is the result of the combination of the centralities of its neighbors. Let λ be a constant. We have:

$$Xc(u) = \frac{1}{\lambda} \sum_{v=1}^{n} A_{uv} Xc(v).$$

Previous equation can be rephrased $\lambda X = AX$, where X is the eigenvector of A, corresponding to the largest eigenvalue λ. A famous eigenvector-based centrality is PageRank, a Web ranking algorithm used by Google in their search engine (Page et al., 1999). Similarly to the eigenvector centrality,

PageRank is based on the notion that the centrality of a Web page recursively depends on the centrality of the Web pages linking to it.

Assortative Mixing

Empirical evidence suggests that complex networks present non-trivial correlations in their interconnection patterns, i.e. they present some degree of *assortative mixing*. For example, in some graphs modeled after artificial phenomena, such as Autonomous System Networks (ASN's), highly connected vertices tend to preferentially connect to weakly connected ones and vice versa. The degree-degree correlation of such networks is negative or *disassortative*.

In social networks, on the other hand, weakly connected vertices tend to preferentially connect to other weakly connected vertices, and strongly connected vertices tend to connect to other strongly connected ones. The degree-degree correlation of such graphs is positive or *assortative*. Degree correlations may have an impact in the percolation phenomena, resilience and robustness, spreading processes, and communication efficiency of complex networks (Newman, 2002; Angeles et al., 2007; Pastor-Satorras et al., 2001).

The assortative mixing of graphs can be characterized by using the *assortative coefficient* as_r, which measures the correlation between the degrees of the vertices at the ends of the graph edges (Newman, 2002):

$$as_r = \frac{m^{-1}\sum_{i}^{m} k_{v_i^a} k_{v_i^b} - \left[m^{-1} \sum_{i}^{m} \frac{1}{2}(k_{v_i^a} + k_{v_i^b}) \right]^2}{m^{-1}\sum_{i}^{m} \frac{1}{2}(k_{v_i^a}^2 + k_{v_i^b}^2) - \left[m^{-1} \sum_{i}^{m} \frac{1}{2}(k_{v_i^a} + k_{v_i^b}) \right]^2}, \tag{13}$$

where $k_{v_i^a}$ and $k_{v_i^b}$ are the degrees of the vertices at the ends of the ith edge $e_i = \{v_i^a, v_i^b\}$.

Club of Rich Vertices

The rich-club phenomena refers to the fact that, in some complex networks, the richest vertices (high-degree vertices or hubs) tend to be more connected to each other than low-degree vertices. It is said that the richest vertices form a *club*. Specifically, a graph has a rich-club when nodes with degree greater than a given k tend to be more densely connected than vertices of degree smaller than k. The existence of a rich-club in a graph can be assessed by the *rich-club coefficient* $\phi(k)$. Let $m_{>k}$ be the number of edges connecting the $n_{>k}$ vertices that have degree greater than k. The rich-club coefficient $\phi(k)$ is defined as:

$$\phi(k) = \frac{2m_{>k}}{n_{>k}(n_{>k}-1)}. \tag{14}$$

The rich-club coefficient $\phi(k)$ resembles the clustering coefficient in that it expresses how close are the vertices of the rich-club to form a complete graph. The presence of a rich-club in real-world networks may reveal high-level properties related to influential vertices. For example, rich-clubs in ASN's reveal an architecture where important Internet providers are strongly interconnected to form the transit backbone of the Internet (Zhou and Mondragon, 2004).

On the Correlation of Complex Network Properties

These presented complex network properties are not trivially related (Colizza et al., 2006). For example, an assortative network does not always have a rich-club structure. Likewise, disassortative networks may have a strongly connected rich-club: hub vertices have a high number of edges, and only a few of these edges are needed to provide strong connection to the other hubs (Zhou and Mondragon, 2007).

On the other hand, uncorrelated scale-free networks are always small-world, but this is not necessarily true for correlated scale-free graphs (Small et al., 2008). Furthermore, the well-known graph model of Albert and Barabási (Barabási et al., 2000) produces scale-free graphs that are neither assortative nor disassortative (Newman, 2002).

Previously, we have present a methodology for the identification of metric correlation patterns and evaluation of non-redundant complex network metrics on the topology of the Internet (Garcia-Robledo et al., 2016). We find crisp relations among sets of complex network metrics on Autonomous System Networks. The distance and density metrics were highly correlated. Likewise, metrics related to the dominance of the most important vertex also showed strong linear dependencies. These correlation patterns may reflect specific and important details about the Internet topology. In addition, size-dependent metrics, even when normalized to be size-independent, still played an important role in expressing the *essence* of the structure of the Internet.

Distance-based global and centrality metrics, such as the diameter, the betweenness centrality, and the central point dominance, are computing intensive. As it will be further developed, their calculation in large sparse graphs involves as many full BFS traversals as the number of nodes in the ASN, requiring from hours to months in modern architectures if parallelism is not exploited, or if repeated measurements are needed. Correlation patterns can be useful to substitute compute intensive metrics with highly correlated metrics that are considerably faster to calculate.

We also find that scaling metrics summarize important properties of complex networks, such as the scale-freeness, the hierarchical clustering, and the assortativity. Scaling metrics proved to be useful for characterizing ASN's, by showing to be (linearly) independent from any of the other studied metrics across different ASN datasets.

The effect of the absence of highly redundant metrics on the characterization of complex networks can be assessed in tasks such as clustering, classification, and PCA (Principal Component Analysis) visualizations. With the identification of highly-correlated complex network metrics, future studies can reduce redundancy and focus on those metrics that explain different aspects of networks. Even different graph ensembles of the same real-world phenomenon (e.g. ASN's) might differ significantly. Thus, correlation patterns should be studied for each dataset separately.

Towards a Formal Definition of a Complex Network

There is not a universally accepted formal definition of complex network beyond the definition of graph. This hampers the formal definition of the class of complex networks addressed in this book. Nonetheless, it is possible to mention that this book deals with connected undirected graphs that show the followings properties: relatively large number of vertices and edges, low density (sparsity), small-world, scale-free, and modeled after real-world phenomena, like the topology of the Internet.

Thus, for the purposes of this work, a *complex network* $G = (V, E)$ is defined as an undirected graph with vertex set V and edge set $E \subset V^{(2)}$, with: (1) $n = |V|$ and $m = |E|$ in the order of hundreds, thousands or millions, (2) low average degree $\langle k \rangle \ll n$, (3) low density $d \ll 1$, (4) scale-free degree distribution $P(k) \sim k^{-\alpha}$, (5) low average path length $\langle L \rangle \ll n$, and (6) high average clustering coefficient $1 / n \ll \langle CC \rangle < 1$.

TRAVERSING THE STRUCTURE OF COMPLEX NETWORKS

BFS is an intuitive search strategy that discovers the vertices of a graph by levels. Starting from a given vertex, BFS discovers all vertices at distance 1 from that vertex, then all vertices at distance 2, and so on. BFS is being used for calculating shortest-path-based metrics on complex networks due to its efficiency on sparse graphs. Both the Graph500 (Murphy et al., 2010) and GreenGraph500 (Feng and Cameron, 2007) projects, that evaluate the capacity of state-of-the-art large-scale systems to solve data intensive problems.

Visitor Breadth-First Search

Algorithm in Figure 1 shows the basic Single-Source BFS (SS-BFS) algorithm, called the visitor SS-BFS algorithm. It starts from a given vertex and uses a queue to store intermediate results as it traverses the graph. In the first step,

Figure 1. Single-Source BFS (SS-BFS) algorithm

Input: $G = (V, E), n, s$ // G is a graph with n nodes, s is the source vertex
Output: None
    $visited[i] \leftarrow 0$ **for** $i \in \{1, ..., n\}$
    $q \leftarrow$ NewQueue()
    QueuePush(q, s)
    while not QueueEmpty(q) **do**
        $u \leftarrow$ QueuePop(q)
        $visited[u.index] \leftarrow 1$
        $N_u \leftarrow$ GetNeighbors(G, u)
        for $v \in N_u$ **do**
            if $visited[v.index] = 1$ **then**
                continue
            end if
            QueuePush(q, v)
        end for
    end while

the visitor BFS algorithm enqueues the root vertex s. In the second step, it dequeues a vertex v and visits it. Then, it enqueues the nearest neighbors of v that have not yet been visited. If the queue is empty, then every vertex in the graph has been visited and the traverse is done. If the queue is not empty, there are still unvisited vertices, so repeat from the second step.

Time complexity of visitor BFS is $O(n + m)$, since every vertex and every edge is visited in the worst case.

All-Sources Breadth-First Search (AS-BFS)

All-Sources BFS (AS-BFS) is a highly recurrent kernel in complex network applications. AS-BFS consists of performing as many full BFS traversals as the number of vertices in the network, each BFS starting from a different source vertex. AS-BFS is the core of variety of global and centrality metrics that enable, for example, the evaluation of general aspects of the topology of large networks and the determination of the importance of a particular vertex.

AS-BFS algorithms can be used to calculate shortest-path-based metrics, such as the average path length $\langle L \rangle$, the diameter D, the betweenness centrality nBc, and the central point dominance CPD. These topological metrics have been used, for example, for the analysis of the errors caused by attacks to the structure of a national airport network (Chi and Cai, 2004), for the analysis of the vulnerability of the Internet at the ASN level (Albert et al., 2000), to identify key proteins in protein-protein networks (Koschutzki and Schreiber, 2008), and to identify the most relevant agents (e.g. leaders) in terrorist social networks (Yang, 2008).

AS-BFS performs as many full BFS traversals as the number of vertices n. Thus, time complexity of visitor AS-BFS is $O(n^2 + nm) \approx O(nm)$.

Example of AS-BFS Application: Graph Diameter

Algorithm in Figure 2 shows how to use the visitor AS-BFS algorithm to calculate the graph diameter D. Algorithm in Figure 2 is very similar to the SS-BFS algorithm in Figure 1, with the difference that the former performs n BFS's (outer for loop) and that it keeps a record of the current longest distance registered between any source to any other node. This distance is then returned as the diameter D of the graph.

Time complexity for calculating D by using the visitor approach is the same as visitor AS-BFS: $O(n^2 + nm)$.

Figure 2. All-Sources BFS (AS-BFS) algorithm for calculating the graph diameter D

Input: $G = (V, E), n$
Output: D // D is the diameter of G
    $D \leftarrow 0$
    for $s \in V$ **do**
        $visited[i] \leftarrow 0$ **for** $i \in \{1, ..., n\}$
        $dist[i] \leftarrow -1$ **for** $i \in \{1, ..., n\}$
        $dist[s.index] \leftarrow 0$
        $q \leftarrow$ NewQueue()
        QueuePush(q, s)
        while not QueueEmpty(q) **do**
            $u \leftarrow$ QueuePop(q)
            $visited[u.index] \leftarrow 1$
            $du \leftarrow dist[u.index]$
            if $du > D$ **then**
                $D \leftarrow du$
            end if
            $N_u \leftarrow$ GetNeighbors(G, u)
            for $v \in N_u$ **do**
                if $visited[v.index] = 1$ **then**
                    continue
                end if
                $dist[v.index] \leftarrow du + 1$
                QueuePush(q, v)
            end for
        end while
    end for
    return D

FINDING THE CORE OF COMPLEX NETWORKS

An important step to understand the structure of a complex network is to discover how dense connections are built, from simpler dyads or cliques to larger well-connected clusters. A widely used and easy-to-calculate definition of node clusters is that of k-cores.

The k-core of a graph is its largest subgraph whose vertices have degree at least k (Dorogovtsev et al., 2006). Formally, a k-core of a graph $G = (V, E)$ is a subgraph H induced by $V_H \subseteq V$, if and only if $\forall u \in V_H : k_u \geq k$ and H is a maximum subgraph with this property (Batagelj and Zaversnik, 2011). A node $u \in V$ is said to belong to the k-shell if and only if it belongs to the

k-core but not to the $(k+1)$-core. It is said that if u is in the k-shell, then u has a shell index of k (Dorogovtsev et al., 2006).

The k-core decomposition identifies internal cores and decomposes the networks layer by layer, revealing the structure of the different k-shells from the innermost to the outermost one. The k-core can be obtained efficiently, by recursively pruning the vertices with degree smaller than k in $O(m)$ time (Batagelj and Zaversnik, 2011). This renders the calculation of k-cores efficient in large sparse graphs.

The k-core decomposition has been successfully applied in a variety of application domains that include: the identification of the core of the Internet (Carmi et al., 2007), large graph visualization and fingerprinting (Alvarez-Hamelin et al., 2008), analysis of large software systems (Zhang et al., 2010), and fraud detection (Wang and Chiu, 2005). As stated by Batagelj and Zaversnik (2011): "the cores, because they can be efficiently determined, are one among few concepts that provide us with meaningful decompositions of (very) large networks."

The Batagelj-Zaversnik Algorithm

The k-core decomposition algorithm is computed by repeatedly removing the minimum degree vertices from the graph. This implies sorting all the remaining vertices by their degree at each step of the decomposition.

Batagelj and Zaversnik, 2011 designed an efficient algorithm based on bin-sort. The algorithm uses an array to store the vertices in sorted order of degree, and another array to store the position of each vertex in the sorted array. When a vertex is removed from the graph, the degree of its neighbors is decremented. Then, each neighbor is moved to the appropriate position in the sorted array and its position is updated in the other array. In this way, the algorithm avoids sorting the vertices by degree at each step (Dasari et al., 2014). Time complexity of the Batagelj and Zaversnik algorithm is $O(\max(n, m)) \approx O(m)$ (Batagelj and Zaversnik, 2011).

Algorithm in Figure 3 lists the Batagelj-Zaversnik k-core decomposition algorithm as presented by Dasari et al., 2014. The *deg* array store the degrees of the vertices sorted by degree. Sorted order is stored in the *vert* array. The *pos* array keeps the position of a vertex in the vert array[2]. The *bin* array is initialized such that *bin i* contains the index of the first vertex with degree i in the vert array. Consequently, *vert* array will be divided into chunks of vertices, where chunk i represent the vertices with degree i. The algorithm

Figure 3. Batagelj-Zaversnik algorithm for the k-core decomposition as presented by Dasari et al. (2014)

Input: $deg, vert, pos, bin$
Output: updated deg array with the k-shell indexes for all nodes
for $i = 0$ to $n - 1$ **do**
    $v \leftarrow vert[i]$
    for each neighbor u of node v **do**
        if $deg[u] > deg[v]$ **then**
            $du \leftarrow deg[u]$
            $pu \leftarrow pos[u]$
            $pw \leftarrow bin[du]$
            $w \leftarrow vert[pw]$
            if $u \neq w$ **then**
                $pos[u] \leftarrow pw$
                $pos[w] \leftarrow pu$
                $vert[pu] \leftarrow w$
                $vert[pw] \leftarrow u$
            end if
            $bin[du] \leftarrow bin[du] + 1$
            $deg[u] \leftarrow deg[u] - 1$
        end if
    end for
end for

processes the vertices in *vert* array in order by decrementing the degree of each of its neighbors and moving them to the appropriate chunks in the *vert* array (Dasari et al., 2014).

APPLICATION OF THE DECOMPOSITION OF GRAPHS: COARSENING INTERNET NETWORKS

The massive size of complex networks introduces the need for graph coarsening mechanisms that reduce the size of real-world graphs for faster processing, gaining insight into the structure of graphs, and assisting the visualization process when the sizes of graphs are too large for a meaningful graphical representation. Graph coarsening methods combine connected nodes by contracting edges to shrink the graph while preserving graph properties of interest.

In a graph G, the contraction of an edge $e \in \{a, b\}$ is the replacement of vertices a and b with a new vertex w such that edges incident to the new vertex w are the edges that were incident with vertices u or v. The contraction of an edge that connects a high-degree vertex to a low-degree vertex will result in the high-degree node with some extra edges incident to it. Think of it as a giant vertex that "suctions" a very small one, remaining almost "unaltered", in terms of its previous degree. Can we exploit the notion of "suction" of vertices to maintain "unaltered" degree-based properties of a graph?

The concept of *coreness* is a natural notion of the importance of nodes in real-world complex networks. In (Garcia-Robledo et al., 2016) we show how a graph coarsening approach based on the contraction of edges and the k-core decomposition can be useful to obtain coarse and reduced versions of complex networks while preserving well-known topological properties.

Let us consider the graph coarsening problem. If $\{u, v\} \in E$ the corresponding edge contraction substitutes the vertices u and v by a new vertex v_{new}, and its neighborhood $N_{v_{new}}$ is the union $(N_u \cup N_v) - \{u, v\}$. Parallel edges, resulting from the combination of vertices with common neighbors, are removed to keep the graph simple.

Let $M(G) = \{\mu_1(G), \mu_2(G), ...\}$ be a set of topological properties of G that want to be preserved. The problem of producing graphs of smaller size that preserve the properties of the original one can be stated as follows:

Problem: Graph Representative Coarsening Problem (GRCP)
Instance: A graph $G = (V, E)$ of n vertices and m edges.
Solution: A sequence of h graphs $G_1', G_2', ..., G_h'$ of decreasing size $n > n_1' > ... > n_h'$ and $m > m_1' > ... > m_h'$, obtained by means of *edge contractions*, such that $M(G_i') \approx M(G_{i-1}') \approx M(G)$.

The idea is that the solutions of a problem for G_i' can be efficiently extended to that for G_{i-1}' and vice versa. Nodes at low k-shell indexes represent peripheral nodes (Carmi et al., 2007).

Minimizing the Impact of Edge Contractions on the Graph Topology

Let G_i'' denote the graph G after i contractions. G_1'' has one less vertex than G:

$$|V_1''|=|V|-1,\tag{15}$$

where V_i'' denote the vertex set of graph G_i''. One can see that the maximum number of edge contractions is $|V|-1$. Thus, the graph $G_{|V|-1}''$, i.e. the graph after $|V|-1$ contractions, is the empty graph with one vertex.

Recall that k_u denotes the degree of vertex u and that N_u denotes the neighbors of u. The contraction of an edge $\{u,v\}$ can introduce parallel edges when vertices u and v have common neighbors, i.e. when $N_u \cap N_v \neq \varnothing$. Let $Q_{uv} = N_u \cap N_v$ be the set of common neighbors of nodes u and v. Let $q_{uv} = |Q_{uv}|$. Let the term "simplification" denote the removal of loops and parallel edges in a pseudo-graph. The number of remaining edges after one contraction and after the simplification of the resulting graph is:

$$|E_1''|=|E|-q_{uv}-1,\tag{16}$$

where E_i'' denote the edge set of graph G_i''. The new vertex v_{new} will be incident to the edges of u and v, excluding the contracted edge and the edges that are "vanished" when the graph was simplified. It is possible to express the degree of v_{new} in terms of the degrees of u, v, and the number of common neighbors q_{uv} as follows:

$$k_{v_{new}} = (k_u -1)+(k_v -1)-q_{uv} = k_u +k_v -q_{uv} -2.\tag{17}$$

One way of minimizing the impact of an edge contraction on the topology of a complex network is to perform contractions that result in the minimum number of vanished edges. As shown in Equation 17, the number of removed edges is affected by the number of common neighbors between the contracting nodes.

Intuitively, to reduce the size of a graph without affecting its structure one should remove the nodes that are unimportant in terms of the structure of the graph. In this context, one would want to combine nodes whose combination result in the most important nodes affected the least.

As shown in Equation 17, this can be achieved if the difference between the degrees k_u and k_v is high. Think of combining hubs, i.e. high-degree vertices present in scale-free complex networks, with low-degree vertices. This would result in the same hub and a non-important node removed. Non-important or peripheral vertices might have a low degree and a low number of common vertices with core or important ones.

By bringing together the considerations mentioned above, we claim that the identification of core and peripheral vertices enables the finding of high-degree vertices connected to low-degree vertices, with a low number of common neighbors. The combination of such vertices can reduce the size of the network while minimizing the impact on the graph topology.

The Contract *k*-Shell Edge Framework

The Contract k-shell Edge (CKE) graph coarsening framework (Garcia-Robledo et al., 2016) exploits the organization of nodes induced by the k-core decomposition. The term "framework" is used here to denote a coarsening scheme the k-shell visitation algorithm can be substituted to obtain different instances of CKE coarsening algorithms. The CKE framework exploits the following intuition: contracting edges connecting nodes at very different k-shells should not impact the global properties of complex networks.

Algorithm in Figure 4 contains the main CKE coarsening framework algorithm. The input is a graph G, the k-shell visitation algorithm π, a vertex centrality algorithm γ, and the final number of nodes n_{final}. Algorithm in Figure 4 returns a coarsened graph with n_{final} nodes. In each iteration, the

Figure 4. The Contract k-shell Edge (CKE) framework algorithm (Garcia-Robledo et al., 2016)

Input: $G = (V, E), \pi, n_{final}$ // π is the node visitation algorithm
Output: coarse graph G' with n_{final} nodes
   $S \leftarrow$ ShellDecomposition(G)
   $G' \leftarrow G$ // $G' = (V', E')$, where $V' = V, E' = E$
   while True **do**
      $k \leftarrow$ NextShell(S, π)
      $v \leftarrow$ NextVertexAtShell(k, S)
      $u \leftarrow$ SelectNeighbor(v, G', S)
      $G', S \leftarrow$ ContractEdge($\{u, v\}, G', S$)
      if $|V'| = n_{final}$ **then**
         return G'
      end if
   end while

CKE framework visits a single node at a given k-shell. Each time a vertex v is visited, a neighbor u of v located at the farthest k-shell is selected, and the edge $\{u,v\}$ is contracted. The CKE framework keep visiting vertices and contracting edges until the number of nodes reaches n_{final}.

The invoked functions by the CKE framework are:

- $S \leftarrow \text{ShellDecomposition}(G)$: Given G, returns the k-shell decomposition set S, where S_i denotes the k-shell index of vertex i

- $k \leftarrow \text{NextShell}(S,\pi)$: Given the k-shell decomposition set S, returns the next non-empty k-shell index, according to the shell visitation algorithm π.

- $v \leftarrow \text{NextVertexAtShell}(k,S)$: Given S, it returns the next existing vertex v at the k-shell. Vertices are returned cyclically, as if they were arranged in a circular list in arbitrary order.

- $u \leftarrow \text{SelectNeighbor}(v,G,S)$: Given v, G and S, returns the neighbor $u \in N_v$ of v at the farther k-shell, so that $u = \max \arg_{u \in N_v}\{|S_v - S_u|\}$.

  If there is a tie among different neighbors of v, an arbitrary tied neighbor is returned.

- $G',S' \leftarrow \text{ContractEdge}(\{u,v\},G,S)$: Given G, returns a new graph G' with $|V|-1$ vertices, where the edge $\{u,v\} \in E$ has been contracted. G' is simplified. Given S, it also returns the updated S' set that include the k-shell index of the new combined vertex v_{new} and the inherited k-shell indexes. Let w be the vertex $w = \max \arg_{w \in \{u,v\}}\{S_w\}$, i.e. the vertex with the largest k-shell index between u and v. v_{new} "inherits" the k-shell index and the centrality of w, such that $S'_{v_{new}} = S_w$.

Let $k^{\max} = \max S$ be the highest k-shell index of any vertex in G. Four different CKE algorithms π based on the CKE framework are studied in this section: CKE-Orbit, CKE-Spiral, CKE-Star, and CKE-Wheel. The difference among the CKE algorithms is the k-shells visitation algorithm π, that defines the order in which the k-shells are explored:

- **CKE-Orbit:** Visits all the nodes at the $k^{\max}$-shell. Then, it starts all over again by visiting all the nodes at the $k^{\max}$-shell one more time, repeating the procedure until the number of nodes reaches n_{final}.

- **CKE-Spiral:** Starts by visiting all the nodes at the k^{max}-shell. Then, it visits all the nodes at the $(k^{max}-1)$-shell, and so on. When CKE-Spiral reaches the 1-shell, it starts all over again at the k^{max}-shell, repeating the procedure until the number of nodes reaches n_{final}.

- **CKE-Star:** Starts by visiting a single node at the k^{max}-shell. In the next iteration, it visits a single node at the $(k^{max}-1)$-shell, and so on. When CKE-Star reaches the 1-shell, it starts all over again by visiting the next node at the k^{max}-shell, repeating the procedure until the number of nodes reaches n_{final}.

- **CKE-Wheel:** Starts by visiting all the nodes at the k^{max}-shell. Then, it visits a single node at the remaining k-shells, in decreasing order of the k-shells. When CKE-Wheel reaches the lowest k-shell, it starts all over again and visits all the nodes at the k^{max}-shell again, repeating the procedure until the number of nodes reaches n_{final}.

The most compute intensive functions is ShellDecomposition(G), which needs $O(m)$ time, as discussed previously. Note that the k-core decomposition is performed only once, at the beginning of the CKE algorithm. ContractEdge($\{u,v\}, G, S$) makes sure that the new vertex *inherits* the k-shell index of one of the contracting vertices, so there is no need to calculate the decomposition and the centrality again. The inheritance of the k-shell index also guarantees that there will be always at least a non-empty k-shell.

Besides the k-core decomposition, the next more expensive computation is the single-edge contraction, which, depending on the graph representation can be done in up to $O(n)$ time. CKE algorithms perform up to $n - n_{final}$ edge contractions. CKE algorithms run in $O(n(n - n_{final}) + m)$ time. Thus, theoretical time for the CKE algorithms depends mainly on the efficiency of the single-edge contraction operation and the desired final number of nodes n_{final}.

Coarsening of an Autonomous System Network

An Autonomous System is a group of dozens to millions of host IP addresses (routing prefixes) that share common routing policies. AS's interact with each other through a massive network of thousands of links to form an AS Network (ASN). An ASN communicates millions of host IP addresses across the world. From a technological perspective, the measurement of the Internet can be considered a big data problem that involves topology measurements for the discovery (and inference) of AS connections that, viewed as a whole, reveal important details of the functional organization and the evolution of the Internet (Cho, 2012).

The characterization of the structure of ASN's is a key step for: the optimization of Internet paths by analyzing existing infrastructure deficiencies, the evaluation of the effect of AS links on the evolution of the Internet topology, the generation of synthetic routing tables for simulating lookup algorithms, the design and evaluation of improved Internet topology generators, and the simplification of ASN's for simulation purposes (Krishnamurthy et al., 2007; Winick and Jamin, 2002; CAIDA, 2016).

Table 2 contains actual measurement values for a variety of complex network metrics on the largest ASN instance of the RV/RIPE dataset (January, 2010). The January 2010 ASN is scale-free, as it shows a high and negative degree distribution scaling $P(k)_k$, a large maximum degree k_{max}, and a small average degree $\langle k \rangle$. It is also small-world, showing a small average path length $\langle L \rangle$ and a high average clustering coefficient $\langle CC \rangle$. It is slightly disassortative, with a negative assortative coefficient as_r, and it presents a rich-club of core vertices. Finally, the ASN shows central nodes with high central point dominance CPD, high average vertex betweenness centrality $\langle nBc \rangle$, and high average neighbor degree $\langle k_n \rangle$.

The root-mean-square deviation (RMSD) of a complex network metric μ on a graph G can be used to measure the average deviation of the metric from its original value $\mu(G)$ during a graph reduction process. Given the RMSD, the RMSD percentage (RMSDP) is calculated to quantify the percentage of deviation of a given metric up to a given point of the graph coarsening process. Formally, we define the RMSDP as follows:

$$RMSDP = 100 \times \frac{RMSD}{\mu(G)}. \tag{18}$$

To compare the main four main CKE strategies and find a single strategy that best preserves most of the metrics, Table 3 shows the RMSDP's for the CKE algorithms that do not exploit centrality metrics, at 30% of remaining nodes reduction. In Table 3, CKE-Orbit appears as the algorithm that produced the lowest RMSDP's for 8 out of 11 metrics. In the remaining metrics, it appeared in the second place after CKE-Wheel, which is, as previously

Table 2. Values for different complex network metrics evaluated on the RV/RIPE (January 2010) ASN graph

Metric μ	Symbol	$\mu(G)$
Nodes	n	33,796
Edges	m	94,394
Average degree	$\langle k \rangle$	5.59
Maximum degree	k_{max}	2,654
Degree distribution scaling	$P(k)_k$	-0.93
Average path length	$\langle L \rangle$	3.82
Average clustering coefficient	$\langle CC \rangle$	0.38
Assortativity coefficient	as_r	-0.02
Rich-club coefficient	$\phi(k)$	0.74
Central point dominance	CPD	0.14
Average betweenness centrality	$\langle nBc \rangle$	47,668.27
Average neighbor degree	$\langle k_n \rangle$	504.71

mentioned, just a variation of CKE-Orbit. An exception was the rich-club coefficient metric, that was better preserved by CKE-Star.

With the CKE strategy, it is also possible to preserve the scaling of different metrics on the RV/RIPE ASN. For example, it was observed that the scaling curve of the log-log degree distribution $P(k)_k$ preserved its magnitude with an RMDP deviation of only 0.6% after reducing 70% of the graph using the CKE-Orbit algorithm. This confirms that coarse graphs preserved the scale-free property of the original ASN. Results with CKE-Wheel suggested that contracting edges outgoing from vertices at different k-cores can be

Table 3. RMSDP for the four CKE strategies at a 30% of remaining nodes (70% of graph size reduced)

Metric μ	Symbol	CKE-Orbit	CKE-Spiral	CKE-Star	CKE-Wheel
Average betweenness centrality	$\langle nBc \rangle$	**43.76**	51.18	49.82	47.79
Central point dominance	CPD	**9.51**	37.33	41.83	38.41
Average degree	$\langle k \rangle$	19.41	18.8	21.09	**10.07**
Average path length	$\langle L \rangle$	**6.44**	16.12	14.78	12.26
Average clustering coefficient	$\langle CC \rangle$	**36.82**	72.11	78.02	62.05
Maximum degree	k_{max}	19.91	30.03	22.1	**9.66**
Assortativity coefficient	as_r	**316.45**	573.16	550.09	550.01
Degree distribution scaling	$P(k)_k$	**0.6**	1.34	2.58	1.79
Average neighbor degree	$\langle k_n \rangle$	**9.84**	111.71	74.63	56.81
Rich-club coefficient	$\phi(k)$	250.04	175.01	**36.15**	79.97

advantageous for better preserving metrics like the average and the maximum degree.

Unlike simple random coarsening algorithms, the CKE approach is able to produce representative coarse graphs in a single run. The presented results on a collection of size-independent and size-dependent metrics can be useful to select the appropriate CKE algorithm when it is desired to preserve a specific complex network metric or topological property.

CONCLUSION

This chapter listed graph topological properties shared by complex networks, such as the small-worldliness, scale-freeness, assortativity, rich-clubs, and the k -core decomposition. Likewise, well-known complex networks metrics that explain specific aspects of complex networks were also described. Finally, visitor and algebraic algorithms for BFS were presented.

Metrics that are size-independent or that can be normalized are of special interest in this chapter, as they enable studies involving complex networks of different size.

Due to its efficiency on sparse graphs, BFS is adequate for calculating distance-based complex network metrics, such as the betweenness centrality, on large graphs. However, even when a single BFS takes only $O(n + m)$ time, complex network applications usually require as many as the total number of vertices. This renders BFS-based applications unfeasible on complex networks with thousands to billions of nodes if parallelism is not exploited.

The k-core decomposition, which can be calculated efficiently in time $O(m)$, produces an onion-like organization of graphs, being the nodes at the inner levels (core levels) better interconnected than the nodes at the outer (peripheral) ones.

Four graph reduction strategies were described for coarsening the topology of complex networks: CKE-Orbit, CKE-Spiral, CKE-Star, and CKE-Wheel. CKE coarsening strategies exploit the following intuition: contracting edges connecting nodes at very different k-shells should not impact the global properties of complex networks. The authors showed that the contraction of edges joining core and peripheral vertices is a powerful tool to reduce ASN's while preserving size-independent and size-dependent complex network metrics alike, as well as high-level properties of real-world networks, such as the scale-free distribution.

Unlike simple random coarsening algorithms, the CKE approach is able to produce representative coarse graphs in a single run. The presented results on a collection of complex network metrics can be useful to select the appropriate CKE algorithm when it is desired to preserve a specific complex network metric or topological property.

Next chapters will describe how to exploit the k-core decomposition to design heuristics that solve two problems related to the processing of large complex networks: graph coarsening and unbalanced graph partitioning.

REFERENCES

Abou-Rjeili, A., & Karypis, G. (2006). Multilevel Algorithms for Partitioning Power-Law Graphs. *Proceedings of the 20th IEEE International Parallel & Distributed Processing Symposium (IPDPS'06)*, 124–124.

Albert, R., Jeong, H., & Barabási, A. (2000). Error and Attack Tolerance of Complex Networks. *Nature*, *406*(6794), 378–382. doi:10.1038/35019019 PMID:10935628

Alvarez-Hamelin, J., Dall'Asta, L., Barrat, A., & Vespignani, A. (2008). K-Core Decomposition: A Tool for the Visualization of Large Scale Networks. *Networks and Heterogeneous Media*, *3*(2), 371–393. doi:10.3934/nhm.2008.3.371

Angeles, M., Pastor-Satorras, R., & Vespignani, A. (2007). Correlations in Complex Networks. In G. Caldarelli (Ed.), *Structure and Dynamics of Complex Networks* (pp. 35–66). From Information Technology to Finance and Natural Science.

Barabási, A., Albert, R., & Jeong, H. (2000). Scale-Free Characteristics of Random Networks: The Topology of the World-Wide Web. *Physica A*, *281*(1-4), 69–77. doi:10.1016/S0378-4371(00)00018-2

Barabási, A., & Albert, R. (1999). Emergence of Scaling in Random Networks. *Science*, *286*(5439), 509–512. doi:10.1126/science.286.5439.509 PMID:10521342

Batagelj, V., & Zaversnik, M. (2011). An O(m) Algorithm for Cores Decomposition of Networks. *Advances in Data Analysis and Classification*, *5*(2), 129–145. doi:10.1007/s11634-010-0079-y

The CAIDA AS Relationships Dataset. January 2004 to November 2007. (n.d.). Retrieved from http://www.caida.org/data/as-relationships/

Carmi, S., Havlin, S., Kirkpatrick, S., Shavitt, Y., & Shir, E. (2007). A Model of Internet Topology Using K-Shell Decomposition. *Proceedings of the National Academy of Sciences of the United States of America*, *104*(27), 11150–11154. doi:10.1073/pnas.0701175104 PMID:17586683

Chi, L., & Cai, X. (2004). Structural Changes Caused by Error and Attack Tolerance in Us Airport Network. *International Journal of Modern Physics B*, *18*(17–19), 2394–2400. doi:10.1142/S0217979204025427

Cho, K. (2012). Internet Measurement and Big Data. *Internet Infrastructure Review*, *15*, 31–34.

Colizza, V., Flammini, A., Serrano, M., & Vespignani, A. (2006). Detecting Rich-Club Ordering in Complex Networks. *Nature Physics*, *2*(2), 110–115. doi:10.1038/nphys209

Costa, L., Rodrigues, F., Travieso, G., & Boas, P. (2007). Characterization of Complex Networks: A Survey of Measurements. *Advances in Physics*, *56*(1), 167–242. doi:10.1080/00018730601170527

Dasari, N. S., Desh, R., & Zubair, M. (2014). Park: An efficient algorithm for k-core decomposition on multicore processors. In *Big Data (Big Data), 2014 IEEE International Conference on*, (pp. 9–16). IEEE.

Dorogovtsev, S., Goltsev, A., & Mendes, J. (2006). K-Core Organization of Complex Networks. *Physical Review Letters*, *96*(4), 040601. doi:10.1103/PhysRevLett.96.040601 PMID:16486798

Erdös, P., & Rényi, A. (1959). On Random Graphs, I. *Publicationes Mathematicae (Debrecen)*, *6*, 290–297.

Feng, W., & Cameron, K. (2007). The Green500 List: Encouraging Sustainable Supercomputing. *Computer*, *40*(12), 50–55. doi:10.1109/MC.2007.445 PMID:21603088

Garcia-Robledo, A., Diaz-Perez, A., & Morales-Luna, G. (2016). Characterization and coarsening of autonomous system networks: Measuring and simplifying the internet. In *Advanced Methods for Complex Network Analysis* (pp. 148–179). IGI Global. doi:10.4018/978-1-4666-9964-9.ch006

Koschützki, D., & Schreiber, F. (2008). Centrality Analysis Methods for Biological Networks and Their Application to Gene Regulatory Networks. *Gene Regulation and Systems Biology*, *2*(1), 193–201. PMID:19787083

Krishnamurthy, V., Faloutsos, M., Chrobak, M., Cui, J., Lao, L., & Percus, A. (2007). Sampling Large Internet Topologies for Simulation Purposes. *Computer Networks*, *51*(15), 4284–4302. doi:10.1016/j.comnet.2007.06.004

Milgram, S. (1967). The Small World Problem. *Psychology Today*, *1*(1), 61–67.

Murphy, R., Wheeler, K., Barrett, B., & Ang, J. (2010). *Introducing the Graph 500. Technical report*. Cray Users Group at Sandia National Laboratories.

Newman, M. (2002). Assortative Mixing in Networks. *Physical Review Letters*, *89*(20), 208701. doi:10.1103/PhysRevLett.89.208701 PMID:12443515

Newman, M. (2003). The Structure and Function of Complex Networks. *SIAM Review*, *45*(2), 167–256. doi:10.1137/S003614450342480

Page, L., Brin, S., Motwani, R., & Winograd, T. (1999). The PageRank Citation Ranking: Bringing Order to the Web. *World Wide Web Internet and Web Information Systems*, *54*(2), 1–17.

Pastor-Satorras, R., Vázquez, A., & Vespignani, A. (2001). Dynamical and Correlation Properties of the Internet. *Physical Review Letters*, *87*(25), 258701. doi:10.1103/PhysRevLett.87.258701 PMID:11736611

Small, M., Xu, X., Zhou, J., Zhang, J., Sun, J., & Lu, J. A. (2008). Scale-Free Networks Which Are Highly Assortative but Not Small World. *Physical Review. E*, *77*(6), 066112. doi:10.1103/PhysRevE.77.066112 PMID:18643341

Wang, J., & Chiu, C. (2005). Detecting Online Auction Inflated-Reputation Behaviors Using Social Network Analysis. *Proceedings of the 2005 Annual Conference of the North American Association for Computational Social and Organizational Science (NAACSOS'05)*, 1–9.

Watts, D., & Strogatz, S. (1998). Collective Dynamics of 'Small-World' Networks. *Nature*, *393*(6684), 440–442. doi:10.1038/30918 PMID:9623998

Winick, J., & Jamin, S. (2002). *INET-3.0: Internet Topology Generator. Technical report*. University of Michigan.

Yang, C. (2008). Knowledge Discovery and Information Visualization for Terrorist Social Networks. In H. Chen & C. Yang (Eds.), *Intelligence and Security Informatics: Techniques and Applications* (pp. 45–64). Springer. doi:10.1007/978-3-540-69209-6_3

Zhang, H., Zhao, H., Cai, W., Liu, J., & Zhou, W. (2010). Using the K-Core Decomposition to Analyze the Static Structure of Large-Scale Software Systems. *The Journal of Supercomputing*, *53*(2), 352–369. doi:10.1007/s11227-009-0299-0

Zhou, S., & Mondragon, R. (2004). The Rich-Club Phenomenon in the Internet Topology. *IEEE Communications Letters*, *8*(3), 180–182. doi:10.1109/LCOMM.2004.823426

Zhou, S., & Mondragon, R. (2007). Structural Constraints in Complex Networks. *New Journal of Physics*, *9*(6), 173. doi:10.1088/1367-2630/9/6/173

ENDNOTES

[1]   If not explicitly stated otherwise, the term "nearest neighbors" of vertex u refers to the vertices adjacent to u.

[2]   If $vert\, i = v$ then $pos\, v = i$.

Chapter 3
Accelerated Network Traversal Using Multi/Many-Cores

ABSTRACT

New BSP platforms like TOTEM are following a similar approach to Big Data industry-proven frameworks but applied to exploit the potential of HPC heterogeneous nodes that combine multi-cores and GPUs. The performance of platforms under this new paradigm depends on minimizing the computation time of partitions by increasing the suitability of partitions to processors. However, there is a lack of studies on the suitability of parallel architectures for processing different families of graphs, including small-world and scale-free networks. In this chapter, the authors show how to characterize the performance of multi/many-cores when traversing synthetic networks of varying topology in order to reveal the suitability of multi-cores and GPUs for processing different families of graphs.

INTRODUCTION

AS-BFS is a recurrent kernel in many shortest-path-based metrics for the analysis of the topology of complex networks, such as the average path length, the diameter, and the graph eccentricity.

The variety of AS-BFS-related problems on complex networks introduces large amounts of processing times, revealing the need for parallel strategies that exploit the features of modern hardware accelerators, such as GPUs, in order to speed up the analysis of large and evolving networks.

DOI: 10.4018/978-1-5225-3799-1.ch003

In spite of the numerous efforts to speedup visitor BFS, current results show that it has been difficult to leverage the massive parallelism of GPUs to accelerate the processing of real-world graphs. Current results show that speedups heavily depend on the graph instances, and that there exist real-world instances where the GPU implementation is slower than its CPU counterpart (Harish and Narayanan, 2007; Luo et al., 2010).

There are works that exploit the duality between linear algebra and graph traversals (Kepner and Gilbert, 2011). Sparse matrix operations provide a rich set of data-level parallelism, which suggests that SpMV-based algebraic formulations of BFS might be more appropriate for the GPU data-parallel architecture (Qian et al., 2012). In this sense, Qian et al. (2012) propose an algebraic BFS algorithm for GPU that overcomes the irregular data access patterns on Electronic Design Automation (EDA) applications. Even when SpMV is considered as a challenging problem due to the insufficient data locality and the lack memory access predictability on real-world sparse matrices (Qian et al., 2012; Goumas et al., 2009), it still offers higher arithmetic loads and clearer data-access patterns than the visitor approach.

In this chapter, we present a methodology to characterize the performance of AS-BFS on multi/many-cores, by comparing implementations of AS-BFS for multi-core CPUs and GPUs on synthetic scale-free, regular, and random graphs. The performance of the visitor and SpMV AS-BFS approaches on multi-core and GPU is studied by varying the degree distribution, the density, and the diameter of sparse and dense graphs.

MULTI-CORE CPU VS GRAPHICS PROCESSOR UNIT

The semiconductor industry has diverged into two separated paths: the multi-core and the many-core approaches (Wen-mei et al., 2008). CPU and GPU design philosophies are contrasting: CPUs integrate a few full-featured cores and advanced control logic, whereas GPUs are powered by many small cores in order to achieve higher throughputs.

Multi-Core CPUs

During the past decade several physical factors, such as the memory wall, the power wall, overheating and excessive path delays, forced the industry to change the path of technological development of processors (Koch, 2005).

Instead of increasing the clock speed and the instruction throughput, major microprocessor vendors such as Intel and AMD turned to offering parallel machines in the form of hyper-threaded single-chip multi-core processors (Sutter, 2005). Multiple cores can share components and need less power to function. In addition, multicores perform more work in the same clock cycle, which enable them to run at lower frequency, addressing the overheating problem and the excessive consumption of power (Usmail, 2010).

Multicore processors are pervasive in many segments of the industry, including signal processing, the embedded market, and the ultramobile industry, as the need for more performance, general-purpose programmability and energy consumption reduction has grown. Modern multicore processors can be coarsely grouped based on the market segment for which they are designed (Gonzalez et al., 2010):

1. **Server Multicores:** Are found in powerful systems such as enterprise data centers and supercomputers, and typically are shared by a large amount of users. These multicores present the larger number of cores from all the groups. Recently, the HPC community is specially concerned with energy consumption and heat dissipation issues because centers are now consuming more energy than heavy manufacturing in the United States. Examples of HPC multicores are the Intel Xeon, the AMD Opteron, the IBM Power7 and the Oracle Sparc VIIIfx.
2. **Desktop Multicores:** Are found in commodity desktop machines used at home and offices. In such systems, computing power and the noise of cooling are important parameters. Examples of general-purpose multicores are the Intel Core i7 Extreme Edition and the AMD Phenom II.
3. **Mobile Multicores:** Are found in laptops computers. These devices operate using a battery, thus energy consumption is the most important parameter, along with basic computing power. Examples of mobile cores are the Intel Core i7 Mobile, Intel Core 2 Duo Mobile, AMD Turion X2 Mobile and the AMD Athlon Neo.
4. **Ultramobile Multicores:** Are found in mobile devices such as tablets and smartphones. In such devices energy consumption is of vital importance. Event thought computing power is of secondary importance, ultramobile devices now run data-intensive applications such as video, videogames and Internet browsing. These applications demand increased computational performance but lower cost and power consumption

(Karam et al., 2009). Examples of ultramobile cores are the Intel Atom, the NVIDIA Tegra, the ARM Cortex, and the Texas Instruments OMAP.

5. **Embedded Multicores:** Are found in everyday devices: cars, digital signal processors (DSPs), videogame consoles, consumer electronics, wireless and network devices, etc. Usually these multicore processors have very reduced size. Due to they are used in very different types of devices, important parameters may vary. Energy efficiency and reduced cost are two common parameters. Several vendors manufacture multicore DSP platforms and embedded multicores such as Freescale, MIPS and ARM.

Implementations of multicore processors are numerous and diverse. However, many multicore processors share common attributes such as (Gebali, 2010): (1) general-purpose programmable cores, (2) special-purpose accelerator cores, (3) a cache hierarchy, and (4) an interconnection network.

Performance of multicores in applications such as audio and video processing can be boosted by exploiting the existing SIMD extensions (also known as Vector Processing Units or VPUs) supported by major multicore systems. SIMD extensions are additional ISA instructions that improve performance for common operations as specialized hardware can do operations like a vector transpose in one instruction (Blake et al., 2009). For example, Intel has extended its x86 ISA with the Streaming SIMD Extensions (SSE), the SSE2, the SSE3, the SSE4 (HD Boost), and the Advanced Vector Extension (AVX), AVX2 and AVX-512. AMD introduced 3DNow! and support for SSE through SSE4 as well as support for AVX.

Existing multicore software tools used to develop multicore-capable software take the forms of languages and libraries. Native APIs such as Pthreads provide direct and low-level access to system threads and lock mechanisms to synchronize threads and protect critical sections of code. They are ready to be used from the C programming language. Higher-level libraries such as OpenMP try to help non-experts in parallel programming to easily parallelize their code by means of the use of loop-parallel directives and common parallel design patterns.

On the one hand, Pthreads is a set of functions and data structures that handle most of the actions required by threads: creating and terminating threads, waiting for threads to complete, and locking/synchronization mechanisms. The subroutines which comprise the Pthreads API can be grouped into four major groups:

- **Management of the Thread Infrastructure:** Includes functions to create, detach and join threads, among other thread management operations. It also includes functions to set/query thread attributes (joinable, scheduling, etc.)
- **Mutex Functions:** Includes functions to create, destroy, lock and unlock mutex regions. In addition, mutex attribute functions that set or modify attributes associated with mutex regions are also provided.
- **Synchronization:** Includes routines that manage read/write locks and barriers.
- **Condition Variables:** Includes functions to create, destroy, wait and signal condition variables (routines that address communications between threads that share a mutex). Functions to set/query condition variable attributes are also supported.

On the other hand, OpenMP extends the C, C++ and Fortran languages with function calls, environments and pragmas for high-level shared memory programming. It was soon clear that the real contribution of OpenMP are its pragmas, which allows to easily transform a sequential program into a high-performance parallel application without a complete restructuring of the original serial code. Pragmas are used define data-parallel regions of code, e.g. loops which work can be parallelized and distributed among a number of threads. The OpenMP runtime library is in charge of the underlying threading mechanisms needed to actually implement parallelism (thread creation, synchronization, etc.).

Many-Core Graphics Processing Units

This category of architecture is usually represented by processors such as GPUs that target a specific domain. An exception is the Intel Xeon Phi Many Integrated Core (MIC) processor that integrates a large number of full-featured general-purpose processors for high-performance and signal processing purposes.

GPUs were initially designed as graphics accelerators. Starting in the 1980s, GPUs were shipped as multiple chip devices. By the 1990s, single-chip GPUs became widely available in the market thanks to companies like Intel, S3, 3Dfx, NVIDIA, ATI, and Matrox. GPU capabilities rapidly evolved from simple pixel-drawing functions to the full 3D pipeline: transforms, lighting, rasterization, texturing, depth testing, and display (NVIDIA, 2009a).

Since 2003, GPUs has been used to accelerate non-graphical applications. Early efforts exploited 3D graphic programming application interfaces (APIs) such as DirectX, OpenGL, and Cg to port data parallel algorithms to GPUs. This technique is called GPGPU, short for general purpose GPU programming (Kirk and Wen-mei, 2010). Graphic APIs abstract the underlying GPU to allow the programmer to write GPU programs using a C-like programming language and graphics-specific structures such as vertexes and fragments.

Even though GPGPU applications achieved remarkable performance speedups, programmers that used graphics APIs to develop general purpose applications faced several problems (NVIDIA, 2009b):

- They needed vast knowledge of graphic APIs and GPU architecture.
- Programs had to be expressed in terms of vertex coordinates, textures and shader programs, increasing the complexity of the problem.
- Lack of basic programming features, such as random R/W to memory, greatly restricted GPU programming.
- Lack of double precision support caused that many scientific applications couldn't be implemented on GPUs.

Only a few programmers had the necessary skills to master GPGPU programming, and performance improvements could only be achieved for a limited set of applications. However, in 2007 NVIDIA, a major mainstream graphics card manufacturer, released the Compute Unified Device Architecture (CUDA) along with the G80 branch of GPUs. With CUDA, programmers no longer need to deal with graphic APIs to leverage GPU computing power. Instead, programmers now interact with a general purpose and more familiar C/C++ environment (Kirk and Wen-mei, 2010). This technique is known as GPU computing.

Theoretical peak performance of modern GPUs is in the order of teraflops (1×10^{12} floating-point operations per second). This make GPUs attractive to accelerate many compute-intensive algorithms that are likely to be benefited from this kind of architecture (Brodtkorb et al., 2010). GPUs are based on the idea of stream multiprocessors (SMs). An SM is a type of SIMD machine integrated of Shader Processors (SP, or Unified Shader, or CUDA Core) and Special Function Units (SFU). SPs are simple processors whose ISA is designed to deal with data streams and execute a massive number of threads (Gebali, 2010).

CUDA C is the standard CUDA programming language. It consists of a minimal set of extensions to the C language and a runtime library that exposes hardware features of the GPU that are not accessible in conventional 3D graphics APIs like OpenGL or DirectX (NVIDIA, 2010). NVIDIA development tools include the CUDA C/C++ compiler, GPU debugging & profiling tools, GPU-accelerated math libraries (CUBLAS, CUFFT, CUSPARSE, CURAND) and GPU-accelerated performance primitives.

Nowadays, the popularity of GPUs to accelerate general purpose algorithms has increased since GPUs offer massive parallelism, huge memory bandwidth, and a general-purpose instruction set. Parallel architectures such as CUDA greatly facilitate GPU programming and CPU/GPU cooperation.

GPUs have been successfully applied to accelerate a wide variety of intensive-compute scientific and industrial algorithms in areas such as bioinformatics, computational structural mechanics, computational electromagnetics, computational finance, computational fluid dynamics, data mining, electronic design automation, computer vision, medical imaging and weather modeling, among other fields.

Multi-Core CPUs vs. GPUs

In both multi-core and many-core approaches, the number of cores doubles with each generation (Kirk and Wen-mei, 2010). However, since 2003, GPUs have exceeded CPU's floating-point performance. As of 2009, the ratio between GPU's and multi-core CPU's peak floating-point calculation throughput is about 10 to 1 (Kirk and Wen-mei, 2010). This gap is mainly due to the following factors (Kirk and Wen-mei, 2010):

1. Differences in the design philosophy: CPUs are designed to optimize the execution of a single thread in parallel or even in an out-of-order fashion by including sophisticated control logic and large cache memories that do not contribute to the peak calculation speed.
2. Memory bandwidth: CPUs have to satisfy requirements from legacy operating systems, applications, and I/O devices that make memory bandwidth more difficult to increase.

Unlike CPUs, GPUs have fewer legacy constraints and a simpler memory model, which enable GPUs to achieve higher memory bandwidth. Take as an example the difference between a high-end four-core Intel Xeon E3-1280 with 21 GB/s of memory bandwidth and a NVIDIA Tesla C2070 with 144 GB/s of memory bandwidth.

In summary, CPU and GPU design philosophies are contrasting: CPUs integrate a few full-featured cores and advanced control logic, whereas GPUs are powered by many small cores in order to achieve higher throughputs.

RELATED WORK

There is a list of known factors that difficult the design of efficient parallel algorithms for graphs: data-driven computations, unstructured problems, poor locality and low arithmetic load (Lumsdaine, 2007). Current results show that speedups heavily depend on the graph instances, and that there exist real-world instances where the GPU implementation is slower than its CPU counterpart (Harish and Narayanan, 2007; Luo et al., 2010).

A number of GPU-accelerated BFS algorithms in literature are visitor/level-synchronous: each level is visited in parallel, preserving the sequential ordering of BFS frontiers (Merrill et al., 2012). The level-synchronous approach is an extension of the well-known visitor BFS algorithm (Cormen et al., 2009).

The visitor level-synchronous Parallel Random-Access Machine (PRAM) strategy (Arjomandi and Corneil, 1975) executes in parallel the examination of the neighborhoods of the vertices in the current frontier to determine, also in parallel, the subset of the nearest neighbors that will be explored in the next frontier. The performance of level-synchronous strategies is strongly influenced by the diameter D of graphs. For example, the work of Hong et al. (2011) shows very large overheads on a road network with high diameter and average search depth Merrill et al. (2012).

One technique to reduce the impact of diameter is to reduce the inter-level synchronization overhead. For example, Luo et al. (2010) implement a hierarchical kernel organization where an inter-block synchronization mechanism synchronizes threads across blocks by global memory communication. Liu et al. (2012) use an inter-block synchronization technique to decrease the level-synchronous launch overhead by first evaluating the frontier size: if it surpasses a given threshold, a new thread configuration is prepared for the next kernel invocation. Merrill et al. (2012), on the other hand, propose prefix-sums to replace atomic operations for determining enqueue offsets.

Many real-world graphs are small-world and scale-free, which means that their effective diameter is very low. However, it is not yet fully understood how changes in the diameter of graphs affects the performance of level-synchronous AS-BFS implementations on GPU.

The degree distribution is another property that influences BFS performance. The vertex-level parallelism, where the GPU spans as many tasks as vertices in the current BFS barrier, leads to load imbalance on graphs with a small quantity of hubs (very high-degree nodes), such as scale-free graphs. For example, the implementation of Luo et al. (2010) is slower than the CPU on synthetic scale-free graphs. Likewise, the GPU kernels of Harish and Narayanan (2007) are slow on scale free-graphs due to non-uniform loop lengths induced by hubs, which causes more lookups to the device memory.

Taking into account that algorithms like BFS are memory bounded, it is important that partitions are cache-friendly. In this sense, some works (Gharaibeh et al., 2013; Gharaibeh and Elizeu, 2013; Chhugani et al., 2012) have suggested the use of bit-vectors to compactly represent visited nodes can lead to improved performance on CPUs. Cache-friendliness is achieved by Gharaibeh et al., (2013) by placing high-degree vertices in CPU and low-degree vertices in the GPU. In this way, the bit-vector size of the CPU partition shrinks and the chances for it to fit the cache are increased.

Nilakant and Yoneki (2014) also observe an increased performance when placing low-degree nodes on the GPU and large-degree nodes on the CPU for BFS. In addition, it is suggested that homogeneity of the node degrees placed on the GPU might help to minimize thread divergence on GPUs (Nilakant and Yoneki, 2014).

The study of Shi and Zhang (2011) shows the effect of the preferential attachment on the performance of various GPU-accelerated AS-BFS-based centrality metrics on synthetic scale-free graphs. However, besides works like the one of Shi and Zhang (2011), there is little work on the study of the isolated influence of specific graph properties, like the degree distribution or the density, on the performance of GPU implementations.

What is the influence of the graph topology on the performance of different architectures like multi-core CPUs and GPUs when accelerating the traversal of large graphs? Which kind of graphs are more appropriate for being processed on multi-core CPUs? Which kind of graphs are more appropriate for GPUs?

This chapter is devoted to answer these questions.

PARALLEL AS-BFS ON MULTI-CORES AND GPU

The visitor and the algebraic AS-BFS approaches provide different levels of parallelism. On the one hand, the visitor approach provides a coarse-grain parallelism level that lead to load balance on modern multi-cores. On the other hand, GPUs can benefit from the more structured parallelism and from higher arithmetic loads provided by the SpMV algebraic approach.

This section describes visitor and algebraic algorithms for accelerating AS-BFS on multi-core CPUs and GPUs.

AS-BFS Parallel Granularity Levels

The AS-BFS visitor approach offers three levels of parallelism:

1. **Coarse-Grain Parallelism:** The parallel algorithm spans n concurrent tasks. Each task consists of a full SS-BFS traversal. All tasks proceed in parallel with no synchronization operations. This level of parallelism is conductive to load balance.
2. **Medium-Grain Parallelism:** For a BFS barrier in an SS-BFS, the parallel algorithm spans as many tasks as vertices in the barrier. Thus, each task consists of exploring the neighborhood of a single vertex in the current BFS barrier. The exploration of all vertices in the barrier can proceed totally in parallel if there are no shared neighbors between any two vertices. In the presence of common neighbors, synchronization operations may be required. This level of parallelism is conductive to load imbalance on graphs with a small quantity of hubs (very high-degree nodes), such as scale-free graphs.
3. **Fine-Grain Parallelism:** For each BFS barrier in an SS-BFS, the parallel algorithm spans as many tasks as the edges outgoing from the vertices in the current barrier. Thus, each task consists of the exploration of one edge, i.e. one neighbor of one vertex in the current BFS barrier. The level of parallelism depends on the distribution of edges between any two BFS barriers. Fine-grain parallelism is conductive to load balance even on scale-free graphs.

The algorithm of Harish and Narayanan (2007) is an example of medium-grain parallelism: every vertex is exhaustively examined on the GPU to determine those belonging to the current frontier. The strategy of Shi and

Zhang (2011) is an example of fine-grain parallelism, since it exhaustively checks every edge on the GPU to determine in parallel the ones that are located at the current frontier.

On the other hand, the algebraic AS-BFS approach offers three levels of parallelism:

1. **Coarse-Grain Parallelism:** The parallel algorithm spans n concurrent tasks. Each task consists of a full SS-BFS traversing of the graph. All n tasks can proceed in parallel, with no synchronization operations. Thus, each processor performs an independent sequence of SpMV's. This level of parallelism is conductive to load balance.
2. **Medium-Grain Parallelism:** The exploration of each barrier in an SS-BFS is accelerated by parallelizing the SpMV. The level of parallelism depends on the matrix format.
3. **Fine-Grain Parallelism:** Each dot-product involved in a single SpMV is accelerated by specialized hardware.

The selection of the appropriate parallel granularity depends on the target parallel hardware architecture.

Parallel AS-BFS on Multi-Core CPUs

For AS-BFS on multi-core CPUs, the coarse-grain parallelism, that distributes the SS-BFS's among the available cores, is the most appropriate strategy: given the low number of cores, a finer strategy would introduce large parallel overheads.

AS-BFS by Vertex Visitation on Multi-Core CPUs

The algorithm in Figure 1 shows the pseudocode for the coarse-grained visitor AS-BFS parallel algorithm. It is the classical queue-based SS-BFS in a for loop that iterates n times. The for loop is parallelized by distributing the n SS-BFS's among the available cores.

As explained previously, a visitor SS-BFS takes $O(n + m)$ time, since every vertex and every edge is visited in the worst case. AS-BFS performs as many SS-BFS traversals as the number of vertices n. Thus, time complexity of the algorithm in Figure 1 is $O(n(n + m)) = O(n^2 + nm)$.

Figure 1. Visitor AS-BFS algorithm for CPU multi-core

> **Input:** $G = (V, E), n$
> **Output: None**
>   **for** $s \in V$ **in parallel do**
> $visited[i] \leftarrow 0$ **for** $i \in \{1, ..., n\}$
> $q \leftarrow \text{NewQueue}()$
> $\text{QueuePush}(q, s)$
>   **while not** $\text{QueueEmpty}(q)$ **do**
> $u \leftarrow \text{QueuePop}(q)$
> $visited[u.index] \leftarrow 1$
> $N_u \leftarrow \text{GetNeighbors}(G, u)$
>   **for** $v \in N_u$ **do**
>   **if** $visited[v.index] = 1$ **then**
>   **continue**
>   **end if**
> $\text{QueuePush}(q, v)$
>   **end for**
>   **end while**
>   **end for**

AS-BFS by SpMVs on Multi-Core CPUs

The algorithm in Figure 2 shows the pseudocode for the coarse-grained SpMV AS-BFS parallel algorithm. It is the SpMV SS-BFS algorithm in a for loop that iterates n times. The for loop is parallelized by distributing the n SS-BFSs among the available cores.

Figure 2. Algebraic AS-BFS algorithm for CPU multi-core

> **Input:** A, n // A is the adjacency matrix of G
> **Output: None**
> $A' \leftarrow A + I_n$ // I_n is the identity matrix of order n
>   **for** $i \in \{1, ..., n\}$ **in parallel do**
> $x[j] \leftarrow 0$ **for** $j \in \{1, ..., n\}$
> $x[i] \leftarrow 1$
> $zeros \leftarrow \infty$
>   **while** $zeros > 0$ **do**
> $y \leftarrow A'x$ // SpMV
> $zeros \leftarrow \text{CountZeros}(y)$
> $\text{SwapPointers}(x, y)$
>   **end while**
>   **end for**

The algorithm for an SpMV SS-BFS in the algorithm in Figure 1 is as follows. Let A be the $n \times n$ symmetric adjacency matrix of G. Let $A' = A + I_n$ be the augmented adjacency matrix, where I_n is the $n \times n$ identity matrix.

Let x and y be two vectors of length n filled with zeros. x and y are called the traversal vectors. At the beginning, $x[s] \leftarrow 1$, where s is the position of the source vertex. Vector y is the SpMV $y = A'x$. After the ith SpMV, the neighbors at distance i from vertex s will be stored as non-zeros in y. Unvisited nodes will remain as zeros. SwapPointers() exchanges the pointers of x and y, so that the next SpMV can reuse the memory allocated for x and y. CountZeros() counts the number of zeros in y. The algorithm iterates until there are no zeros in y, i.e. until it visits all the vertices in G.

If the adjacency matrix is sparse, as in the case of complex networks, large-scale SpMVs can be most efficiently solved if non-zero elements of the matrix are not stored. This is achieved by representing the matrix by using a sparse matrix format. There are many methods for efficiently storing sparse matrices. The COO, CSR and CSC representations are the most general formats: they make no assumptions on the sparsity structure of the matrix nor the spatial distribution of the non-zeros. In addition, they do not store any unnecessary elements.

Let us briefly explain these sparse matrix compression formats:

- **COO (Coordinate):** It uses three arrays: *row*, *column* and *data*. In the *row* and *column* arrays the indexes of the rows and the columns are stored. In a third array, *data*, we store the values of the non-zero elements of the matrix. The *data* array is not needed if we are storing sparse adjacency matrices for unweighted graphs: we know that all the *data* values will be 1.
- **CSR (Compressed Sparse Row):** It is very similar to the COO format. It uses three arrays: *prow*, *column* and *data*. In the *column* and *data* arrays, we store the indexes of the columns and the values of the non-zero elements of the matrix, respectively. In the *prow* array, we store the locations in the *data* vector that start a row, reading the matrix in a row-wise fashion: left-to-right, top-to-bottom. In other words, the CSR format is the COO format but with the *row* vector compressed.
- **CSC (Compressed Sparse Column):** Analogous to the CSR format, the CSC format is very similar to the COO format. It uses three arrays: *row*, *pcolumn* and *data*. In the *row* and *data* arrays, we store the indexes of the rows and the values of the non-zero elements of the

matrix, respectively. In the *pcolumn* array, we store the locations in the *data* vector that start a column, reading the matrix in a column-wise fashion: top-to-bottom, left-to-right. In other words, the CSC format is the COO format but with the *column* vector compressed.

The CSR representation of A' can be used to require $O(2m + n)$ time for a single SpMV, where $2m + n$ is the number of non-zeros in A'. In each SS-BFS, the algorithm performs as many SpMV's as the number of BFS barriers, which is upper bounded by D. Thus, an SS-BFS can be expected to take $O(D(2m + n))$, and the algorithm in Figure 1 to take $O(D(2nm + n^2))$ time, since AS-BFS requires n SS-BFS's.

Parallel AS-BFS on GPUs

There are two levels of parallelism that are appropriate for GPUs: (1) medium-grain: for each BFS frontier, the exploration of all vertices in the frontier can proceed totally in parallel if there are no shared neighbors between any two vertices; and (2) fine-grain: for each BFS frontier, the exploration of the edges going from the current frontier to the next one are traversed in parallel.

Visitor Approach for AS-BFS on GPUs

Algorithms in Figures 3 and 4 show the pseudocode of the fine-grained AS-BFS strategy for GPUs, as proposed by Shi and Zhang (2011).

Figure 3. Visitor AS-BFS algorithm for GPU (FrontierBFSKernel) (Shi and Zhang, 2011)

Input: $a_1, a_2, dist, continue, depth$
Output: Updated *continue* and *dist*
for each thread i **in parallel do**
    $u \leftarrow a_1[i]$
    $w \leftarrow a_2[i]$
    if $dist[u] = depth$ **then**
        if $dist[w] = -1$ **then**
            $continue \leftarrow$ True
            $dist[w] \leftarrow depth + 1$
        end if
    end if
end for

Figure 4. Visitor AS-BFS algorithm for GPU (host) (Shi and Zhang, 2011)

> **Input:** a_1, a_2, n // a_1, a_2 is the graph edge list
> **Output: None**
> **for** $i \in \{1, ..., n\}$ **do**
> $depth \leftarrow 0$
> $dist[j] \leftarrow -1$ **for** $j \in \{1, ..., n\}$
> $dist[i] \leftarrow 0$
> $continue \leftarrow$ True
>   **while** *continue* **do**
>   **run on GPU:** FrontierBFSKernel($a_1, a_2, dist, continue, depth$)
> $depth \leftarrow depth + 1$
>   **end while**
> **end for**

The algorithm in Figure 3 shows the pseudocode for the GPU kernel FrontierBFSKernel(). The kernel accelerates the examination of all edges in the current SS-BFS frontier. Vectors $a_1[i]$ and $a_2[i]$ store the vertices to which the ith edge is incident to, so the length of both arrays is $O(m)$. Vector l stores the distance between the source vertex and every other vertex. In each kernel invocation, threads are distributed among all m edges of G. Each thread examines if its edge connects the current BFS frontier to the next frontier. If so, it raises a flag (*continue*) to indicate that there is a new BFS frontier that must be explored in the next kernel invocation.

The algorithm in Figure 4 shows the pseudocode for the AS-BFS, that invokes FrontierBFSKernel(). It performs as many SS-BFS's as the total number of vertices in the CPU (host), sequentially. For each SS-BFS, it invokes FrontierBFSKernel() on the GPU as many times as the number of BFS frontiers.

The performance of the algorithm in Figure 4 is affected mostly by the number of GPU kernel calls. In each SS-BFS, the algorithm performs as many kernel calls as the number of BFS barriers, which again is upper bounded by $O(D)$. Since AS-BFS performs n SS-BFS's, the algorithm in Figure 4 performs $O(nD)$ kernel calls.

Algebraic Approach for AS-BFS on GPUs

For running the algebraic approach on GPUs, the exploration of the frontiers in each SS-BFS can be accelerated by parallelizing the SpMV.

The algorithm in Figure 5 shows a pseudocode for the medium-grain algebraic AS-BFS parallel algorithm. As the reader may notice, the strategy is very similar to the fine-grain visitor algorithm for GPU: a full BFS is performed for each vertex $s \in V$, sequentially. However, this time the SpMV's (SpMVKernel()) and the zero-counting (CountZerosKernel()) are accelerated on GPU. SwapPointersKernel() simply interchanges the pointers of the x and y vectors in the device, to reuse the allocated space and the intermediate data produced in the device during the whole AS-BFS calculation.

Similarly to the algorithm in Figure 4, the performance of the algorithm in Figure 4 is mainly affected by the number of kernel calls. In each SS-BFS, the algorithm invokes the SpMVKernel(), SwapPointersKernel(), and CountZerosKernel() kernels. Since in an SS-BFS the algorithm performs as many kernel calls as the number of BFS barriers, an SS-BFS needs $O(3D)$ kernel calls. Given that the algorithm in Figure 5 performs n SS-BFS's, the total number of kernel calls is $O(3nD)$.

COMPARISON OF MULTI-CORES AND GPU WHEN PERFORMING AS-BFS

To methodologically study: (1) the suitability of multi-core CPUs and GPUs for processing different kinds of graphs and (2) the influence of the topology of graphs on parallel performance, this section shows the performance of the

Figure 5. Algebraic AS-BFS algorithm for GPU (host)

Input: A, n // A is the adjacency matrix of G, n is the number of nodes
Output: None
    $A' \leftarrow A + I_n$ // I_n is the identity matrix of order n
    for $i \in \{1, ..., n\}$ **do**
        $x[j] \leftarrow 0$ **for** $j \in \{1, ..., n\}$
        $x[i] \leftarrow 1$
        $zeros \leftarrow \infty$
        while $zeros > 0$ **do**
            run on GPU: $y \leftarrow$ SpMVKernel(G, x)
            run on GPU: $zeros \leftarrow$ CountZerosKernel(y)
            run on GPU: SwapPointersKernel(x, y)
        end while
    end for

visitor and the SpMV approaches on sparse and dense graphs with varying diameter, degree distribution, and edge density on both multi-core and GPU.

Implementations

For the implementations of visitor and algebraic AS-BFS for multi-core CPUs, the coarse-grained algorithms previously described were used. For the implementation of visitor AS-BFS for GPUs, the algorithm by Shi and Zhang (2011) was used. The algorithm by Shi and Zhang (2011) leads to load balance on scale-free graphs.

For the implementation of the SpMV approach for GPUs, the two-phase scheme (SpMV and zero-counting) was used. The similarities between the selected strategies for visitor and algebraic AS-BFS on GPUs enabled a fair comparison between the two algorithmic approaches.

Experimented Graphs

The r-regular, Gilbert, and the Barabási-Albert random graph models were used to create uncorrelated random graphs with regular, Poisson, and scale-free degree distribution, respectively.

Random Graph Models

Examples of homogeneous graphs are regular graphs encountered in scientific computing, like 3D meshes. A simple model of such graphs are the r-regular graphs, where every vertex is connected to r other vertices. The degree distribution of an r-regular graph is $P(k) = 1$ for $k = r$.

Random graphs are also homogeneous graphs. A Gilbert exponential random graph (Gilbert, 1959) is a graph of n vertices in which two vertices u and v are connected with equal probability p, being u and v chosen independently. It is known that the degree distribution of Gilbert graphs follows a Poisson law $P(k) \approx \dfrac{(np)e^{-np}}{k!}$ when $n \to \infty$. Gilbert random graphs present small diameter $D \approx \dfrac{\log n}{\log pn}$ (Chung and Lu, 2001).

Recall that complex networks modeled after real-world phenomena, such as the Internet topology, Web graphs, and social networks, tend to be heterogeneous in terms of the vertex degree. Their degree distribution $P(k)$ obey a power law.

A well-known model of scale-free graphs is that of Barabási-Albert (Barabási et al., 2000). A Barabási-Albert graph is the result of a random graph process where, at any given instant, the probability that a new vertex v is connected to an existing vertex u is proportional to k_u. The degree distribution of a Barabási-Albert graph follows a power law $P(k) \approx k^{-3}$ (Bollob and Riordan, 2004). Bollob and Riordan (2004) showed that the diameter D of Barabási-Albert graphs is ultra-small: asymptotically $\log n / \log \log n$.

A summary of the properties of the experimented models can be found in Table 1.

Random Graph Datasets

Three datasets of graphs with different degree distribution were considered in the experiments: (1) *Regular graphs:* set of 21 sparse and dense r -regular, to experiment with graphs with very large diameter. (2) *Exponential graphs:* set of 21 sparse and dense Gilbert random graphs with Poisson (exponential decaying) degree distribution. *(3) Scale-free graphs*: set of 21 sparse and dense Barabási-Albert random graphs with scale-free degree distribution.

Each graph dataset was, in turn, composed of the following two subsets: (1) a subset of 10 sparse graphs of 40,000 vertices with 10 different densities $d \in [6 \times 10^{-4}, 6 \times 10^{-3}]$, and (2) a subset of 11 dense graphs of 3,000 vertices

Table 1. Summary of the used random graph models used for experimentation

Distribution	Model	Degree Distribution $P(k)$	Diameter D	Diameter Type
Regular	r -regular	1 for $k = r$	$O(n / r)$	Large
Exponential	Gilbert	$\dfrac{(np)^k e^{-np}}{k!}$	$\log n / \log pn$	Small
Scale-free	Barabási-Albert	k^{-3}	$\log n / \log \log n$	Ultra-small

with 11 different densities $d \in [1 \times 10^{-2}, 1]$. In spite of the difference in the number of vertices in both graph subsets, the number of edges of the sparse graphs were comparable. The multi-core CPU and GPU visitor and SpMV implementations were run 10 times for each of the 63 graphs. Average runtimes in milliseconds are reported.

Figure 6 shows the average graph diameter for the non-regular (exponential and scale-free) and the regular sparse and dense graphs. Note that the diameter of the regular graphs was several orders of magnitude larger than the diameter of the non-regular graphs. Likewise, note that the difference between the diameter of exponential and scale-free sparse graphs was of 1.

A summary of the topology of the experimented graphs can be found in Table 2.

Figure 6. Variation of the diameter with the graph density of the sparse and dense experimented graphs

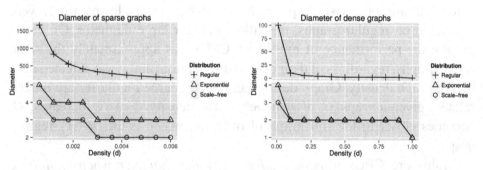

Table 2. Summary of the properties of the synthetic graph datasets used for experimentation

Degree Distribution $P(k)$	Regular		Exponential		Scale-Free	
Sparsity	Sparse	Dense	Sparse	Dense	Sparse	Dense
Graphs	10	11	10	11	10	11
Nodes n	40,000	3,000	40,000	3,000	40,000	3,000
Density d order interval	$[10^{-4}, 10^{-3}]$	$[10^{-2}, 1]$	$[10^{-4}, 10^{-3}]$	$[10^{-2}, 1]$	$[10^{-4}, 10^{-3}]$	$[10^{-2}, 1]$

Hardware Platform

Experiments were performed on the Xiuhcoatl Hybrid Supercomputing Cluster hosted at Cinvestav-IPN. The multi-core CPU implementations ran on AMD Opteron 6274 (Interlagos) processors at 2.2 GHz and 64 GB of RAM, using 16 cores. The GPU implementations ran on NVIDIA C2070 (Fermi) GPUs with 448 CUDA cores at 1.15 GHz and 6GB GDDR5 of DRAM. GPU experiments were single-GPU.

Multi-Core CPUs vs. GPUs: Visitor AS-BFS Approach

In the following paragraphs, a reduction in execution time means a performance improvement, whereas an increasing in execution time means a performance detriment. Figure 7 contains the observed multi-core CPU performance when exploiting the visitor approach.

Multi-core CPUs were most affected by the degree regularity and density when exploiting the visitor approach. On sparse graphs, lowest times were registered on regular graphs, regardless of their large diameter. On dense graphs, the performance of multi-core CPUs was approximately the same for all graphs, regardless of their degree distribution; and it was affected only by the graph density. Graph density and node degree regularity are indeed related: given a graph G of n nodes, as the density d of G increases, G becomes closer to the full graph of order n, which is an $(n-1)$-regular graph.

Multi-core CPUs *were not affected by the diameter when exploiting the visitor approach*. Again, Figure 7 shows that in sparse graphs the best

Figure 7. Multi-core CPU performance when exploiting the visitor approach on sparse and dense graphs

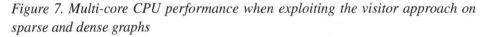
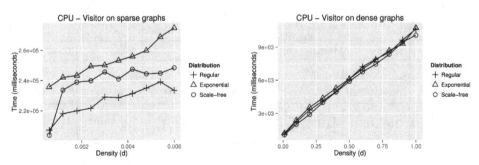

performance was observed in regular graphs, regardless of its large diameter, which was up to two orders of magnitude larger than the diameter of exponential and scale-free graphs.

In contrast, the GPU performance was mostly affected by the graph diameter. Figure 8 contains the observed GPU performance when exploiting the visitor approach. In the sparse dataset, best performance was observed on scale-free graphs (smaller diameter), followed by exponential (2nd largest diameter) and then regular (largest diameter) graphs.

Thus, the lower the diameter of graphs, the better the GPU performance. This is caused by the cost of kernel re-launchings. A graph with ultra-small diameter, like scale-free graphs, minimizes the diameter and thus the number of kernel re-launchings.

The effect of the diameter in GPUs performance is most noticeable in regular graphs: the GPU performance improves with the density in both sparse and dense graphs. This GPU performance improvement, however, is not primarily the effect of an increasing density, but the effect of the reduction of the graph diameter as the density approaches 1.

In summary, when exploiting the visitor approach:

- Multi-core CPUs were mostly affected by the degree regularity (sparse graphs) and density (dense graphs).
- Multi-core CPUs were not affected by the diameter (neither on sparse nor dense graphs).
- In contrast, the GPU performance was mostly affected by the graph diameter (in both sparse and dense graphs).

Figure 8. GPU performance when exploiting the visitor approach on sparse and dense graphs

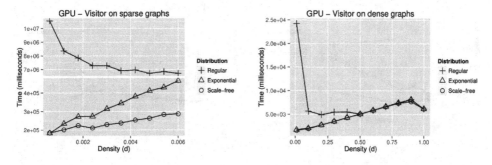

Multi-Core CPUs vs. GPUs: SpMV AS-BFS Approach

Figure 9 contains the observed multi-core CPU's performance when exploiting the SpMV approach. Figure 10 contains the observed GPU performance.

When running SpMV, the multi-core CPU's performance was primarily affected by the graph diameter. In this regard, SpMV on multi-core CPUs holds similarities with visitor/algebraic AS-BFS on GPU. As in the case of visitor on GPUs, best performance was observed on scale-free graphs, followed by exponential and regular graphs. Regular graphs showed one order of magnitude larger execution times than non-regular graphs due to their large diameter.

Figure 9. Multi-core CPU performance when exploiting the SpMV approach on sparse and dense graphs

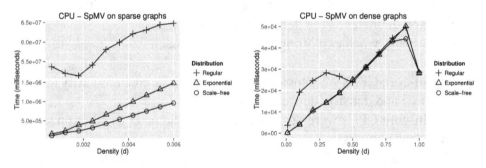

Figure 10. GPU performance when exploiting the SpMV approach on sparse and dense graphs

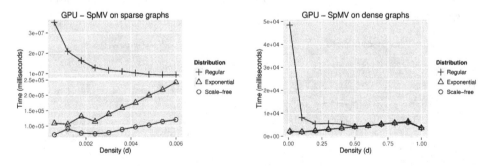

The similarity between algebraic AS-BFS on multi-core CPUs and visitor/algebraic AS-BFS on GPUs was expected. All these implementations perform synchronizations in each BFS frontier.

Furthermore, a small difference in diameter between exponential and scale-free graphs have a non-negligible effect on the SpMV performance on both multi-core and GPU, and this effect is amplified with increasing edge density in sparse non-regular graphs. The SpMV approach was more efficient on scale-free graphs than exponential graphs, again due to the diameter difference.

However, when running SpMV AS-BFS's, multi-core CPUs were less influenced by the diameter than GPUs. Unexpectedly, the performance decreased for SpMV for multi-core CPUs on sparse graphs, whereas it increased for visitor GPU on the same kind of graphs. This was observed in spite of the theoretical SpMV time complexity $O(D(n^2 + nm))$ that is directly affected by the diameter. When comparing the two algorithmic approaches on multi-core CPUs, the visitor approach performed better than SpMV in every kind of graph. This was most noticeable on regular sparse graphs, where multi-core visitor was around 200x faster than multi-core SpMV due to the elevated number of SpMVs induced by the large diameter of this kind of graphs. It was concluded that the algebraic approach is generally unsuitable for multi-core CPUs.

In contrast, on GPU, the SpMV approach improved on the visitor performance on sparse/dense non-regular and dense regular graphs. The higher arithmetic load induced by SpMV on GPUs showed to have a beneficial influence on performance on low-diameter graphs. In general, it was observed that the SpMV approach is suitable for GPUs on low-diameter graphs, where high arithmetic loads exceed the kernel re-launching overhead.

In summary, when exploiting the SpMV approach:

- The multi-core CPU performance was primarily affected by the graph diameter, similarly to GPUs when running both the algebraic and the visitor approaches.
- However, multi-core CPUs were less influenced by the diameter than GPUs.
- Multi-core CPUs were generally unsuitable for running the SpMV approach, while the GPU was benefited from higher arithmetic loads.

Influence of the Graph Topology on Multi-Core CPUs and GPUs

Table 3 summarizes the observations on the influence of the graph topology on multi-core CPUs and GPUs when varying the density, diameter and degree regularity of graphs.

For multi-core CPUs, density and regularity are the main factors affecting performance: the more regular the graphs, the more the performance when running the visitor approach. In contrast, multi-core CPUs are unsuitable for running SpMV-based traversals.

On GPUs, the diameter is the main factor affecting performance, regardless of the algorithmic approach. GPUs seem to better exploit the high arithmetic loads induced by SpMVs, though.

To compare the computing power of multi-core CPUs and GPUs when running AS-BFS, Table 4 shows average multi-core CPUs and GPUs speedups over an efficient single-core visitor CPU implementation, when varying the density and degree regularity of graphs. 16-core CPUs and GPUs showed comparable performance.

Table 3. Influence of the graph topology on multi-core CPUs and GPUs when varying the density, diameter and degree regularity of graphs. All the four graph datasets are covered: sparse regular, sparse non-regular, dense regular and dense non-regular.

Processor	Approach	Sparse		Dense	
		Regular	Non-regular	Regular	Non-regular
CPU	Visitor	Regularity and density	Regularity and density	Density	Density
	SpMV	Diameter and density	Diameter and density	Diameter and density	Diameter and density
GPU	Visitor	Diameter	Diameter and density	Diameter and density	Diameter and density
	SpMV	Diameter	Diameter and density	Diameter and density	Diameter and density

Table 4. Multi-core CPU and GPU speedup over single-core visitor CPU when varying the density and degree regularity of graphs. All the four graph datasets are covered: sparse regular, sparse non-regular, dense regular and dense non-regular. The algorithmic approach with the highest speedup is reported in each cell. Speedups are shown in intervals, from the least dense to the densest graph in the corresponding graph dataset.

Processor	Sparse		Dense	
	Regular	Non-regular	Regular	Non-regular
CPU	Visitor 1.97x to 4.28x	Visitor 3.99x to 6.88x	Visitor 5.85x to 7.27x	Visitor 6.9x to 8.07x
GPU	Visitor 0.04x to 0.14x	SpMV 8.1x to 11.83x	SpMV 4.87x to 12.83x	SpMV 9.57x to 13.97x

In general, the GPU running the SpMV approach showed better performance than the multi-core CPU running the visitor approach, but the performance difference was not very noticeable. Table 4 also shows that GPUs and multi-core CPUs behaved differently when running the same algorithmic approach on regular graphs: GPUs proved to be unsuitable for high-diameter regular sparse graphs (the single-core CPU implementation was faster).

CONCLUSION

This chapter showed how structural properties present in complex networks influence the performance of level-synchronous AS-BFS strategies in the following (decreasing) order of importance: (1) whether the graph is regular or non-regular (due to the huge difference of the diameter), (2) whether the graph is scale-free or not (due to the ultra-small diameter of power-law graphs), and (3) the graph density.

Multi-core CPUs are mostly affected by the degree regularity and density when exploiting the visitor approach. This suggests that, in a heterogeneous computing context, a load balance strategy should produce and assign regular and dense graph partitions for the CPU.

In addition, it was found that multi-core CPUs and GPUs are suitable for complementary kinds of graphs. GPUs performed notably better on non-regular sparse graphs. This contrasts with multi-core CPUs, that performed better than GPUs on large-diameter regular graphs.

The processing of AS-BFS-related algorithms on real-world graphs can be potentially benefited from a topology-driven hybrid approach that combines CP's and GPUs, by considering the presented evidence that CPUs and GPUs behave differently on graphs with different structural properties.

REFERENCES

Arjomandi, E., & Corneil, D. (1975). Parallel Computations in Graph Theory. *Proceedings of the 16th Annual Symposium on Foundations of Computer Science (FOCS'75)*, 13–18. doi:10.1109/SFCS.1975.24

Barabási, A., Albert, R., & Jeong, H. (2000). Scale-Free Characteristics of Random Networks: The Topology of the World-Wide Web. *Physica A*, *281*(1-4), 69–77. doi:10.1016/S0378-4371(00)00018-2

Blake, G., Dreslinski, R., & Mudge, T. (2009). A Survey of Multicore Processors. *IEEE Signal Processing Magazine*, *26*(6), 26–37. doi:10.1109/MSP.2009.934110

Bollobás, B., & Riordan, O. (2004). The Diameter of a Scale-Free Random Graph. *Combinatorica*, *24*(1), 5–34. doi:10.1007/s00493-004-0002-2

Brodtkorb, A., Dyken, C., Hagen, T., Hjelmervik, J., & Storaasli, O. (2010). State-Of-The-Art in Heterogeneous Computing. *Scientific Programming*, *18*(1), 1–33. doi:10.1155/2010/540159

Chhugani, J., Satish, N., Kim, C., Sewall, J., & Dubey, P. (2012). Fast and Efficient Graph Traversal Algorithm for CPUs: Maximizing Single-Node Efficiency. *Proceedings of the 26th IEEE International Parallel and Distributed Processing Symposium (IPDPS'12)*, 378–389. doi:10.1109/IPDPS.2012.43

Chung, F., & Lu, L. (2001). The Diameter of Random Sparse Graphs. *Advances in Applied Mathematics*, *26*(4), 257–279. doi:10.1006/aama.2001.0720

Cormen, T., Leiserson, C., Rivest, R., & Stein, C. (2009). *Introduction to Algorithms* (3rd ed.). The MIT Press.

Gebali, F. (2010). *Algorithms and Parallel Computing*. Wiley.

Gharaibeh, A., Costa, L., Elizeu, S., & Ripeanu, M. (2013). On Graphs, GPUs, and Blind Dating: A Workload to Processor Matchmaking Quest. *Proceedings of the 27th IEEE International Symposium on Parallel & Distributed Processing (IPDPS'13)*, 851–862. doi:10.1109/IPDPS.2013.37

Gharaibeh, A., & Elizeu, S. (2013). *Efficient Large-Scale Graph Processing on Hybrid CPU and GPU Systems*. arXiv:13123018 [csDC]

Gilbert, E. (1959). Random Graphs. *Annals of Mathematical Statistics, 30*(4), 1141–1144. doi:10.1214/aoms/1177706098

Gonzalez, A., Latorre, F., & Magklis, G. (2010). Processor Microarchitecture: An Implementation Perspective. *Synthesis Lectures on Computer Architecture, 5*(1), 1–116. doi:10.2200/S00309ED1V01Y201011CAC012

Goumas, G., Kourtis, K., Anastopoulos, N., Karakasis, V., & Koziris, N. (2009). Performance Evaluation of the Sparse Matrix-Vector Multiplication on Modern Architectures. *The Journal of Supercomputing, 50*(1), 36–77. doi:10.1007/s11227-008-0251-8

Harish, P., & Narayanan, P. (2007). Accelerating Large Graph Algorithms on the GPU Using CUDA. *Proceedings of the 14th International Conference on High Performance Computing (HiPC'07)*, 197–208. doi:10.1007/978-3-540-77220-0_21

Hong, S., Kim, S., & Oguntebi, T. (2011). Accelerating CUDA Graph Algorithms at Maximum Warp. *Proceedings of the 16th ACM Symposium on Principles and Practice of Parallel Programming (PPoPP'11)*, 267–276. doi:10.1145/1941553.1941590

Karam, L., AlKamal, I., Gatherer, A., Frantz, G., Anderson, D., & Evans, B. (2009). Trends in Multicore DSP Platforms. *IEEE Signal Processing Magazine, 26*(6), 38–49. doi:10.1109/MSP.2009.934113

Kepner, J., & Gilbert, J. (2011). *Graph Algorithms in the Language of Linear Algebra*. SIAM. doi:10.1137/1.9780898719918

Kirk, D., & Wen-mei, W. (2010). *Programming Massively Parallel Processors: A Hands-On Approach*. Morgan Kaufmann.

Koch, G. (2005). *Discovering Multi-Core: Extending the Benefits of Moore's Law*. Whitepaper.

Liu, G., An, H., Han, W., Li, X., Sun, T., & Zhou, W. (2012). *FlexBFS: A Parallelism-Aware Implementation of Breadth-First Search on GPU*. Academic Press.

Lumsdaine, A., Gregor, D., Hendrickson, B., & Berry, J. (2007). Challenges in Parallel Graph Processing. *Parallel Processing Letters*, *17*(1), 5–20. doi:10.1142/S0129626407002843

Luo, L., Wong, M., & Wen-mei, H. (2010). An Effective GPU Implementation of Breadth-First Search. *Proceedings of the 47th Design Automation Conference (DAC'10)*, 52–55. doi:10.1145/1837274.1837289

Merrill, D., Garland, M., & Grimshaw, A. (2012). Scalable GPU Graph Traversal. *Proceedings of the 17th ACM SIGPLAN Symposium on Principles and Practice of Parallel Programming (PPoPP'12)*, 117–128.

Nilakant, K., & Yoneki, E. (2014). On the Efficacy of APUs for Heterogeneous Graph Computation. *Proceedings of the 4th Workshop on Systems for Future Multicore Architectures (SFMA'14)*, 2–7.

NVIDIA. (2009a). *NVIDIA's Fermi: The First Complete GPU Computing Architecture*. Whitepaper.

NVIDIA. (2009b). *NVIDIA's Next Generation CUDA Compute Architecture*. Fermi: Whitepaper.

NVIDIA. (2010). *NVIDIA CUDA C Programming Guide 32*. Author.

Qian, H., Deng, Y., Wang, B., & Mu, S. (2012). Towards Accelerating Irregular EDA Applications With GPUs. *Integration, the VLSI Journal*, *45*(1), 46–60.

Shi, Z., & Zhang, B. (2011). Fast Network Centrality Analysis Using GPUs. *BMC Bioinformatics*, *12*(149), 1–7. PMID:21569426

Sutter, H. (2005). The Free Lunch Is Over: A Fundamental Turn Toward Concurrency in Software. *Dr. Dobb's Journal*, *30*(3), 202–210.

Usmail, C. (2010). *Examination of Multi-Core Architectures. Technical report*. DTIC Document. doi:10.21236/ADA533388

Wen-mei, W., Keutzer, K., & Mattson, T. (2008). The Concurrency Challenge. *IEEE Design & Test of Computers*, *25*(4), 312–320. doi:10.1109/MDT.2008.110

Section 2

Chapter 4
Partitioning of Complex Networks for Heterogeneous Computing

ABSTRACT

The most fundamental problem in BSP parallel graph computing is to decide how to partition and then distribute the graph among the available processors. In this regard, partitioning techniques for BSP heterogeneous computing should produce computing loads with different sizes (unbalanced partitions) in order to exploit processors with different computing capabilities. In this chapter, three major graph partitioning paradigms that are relevant to parallel graph processing are reviewed: balanced graph partitioning, unbalanced graph partitioning, and community detection. Then, the authors discuss how any of these paradigms fits the needs of graph heterogeneous computing where the suitability of partitions to hardware architectures plays a vital role. Finally, the authors discuss how the decomposition of networks in layers through the k-core decomposition provides the means for developing methods to produce unbalanced graph partitions that match multi-core and GPU processing capabilities.

INTRODUCTION

Processing complex networks has proven to be an important challenge, in that it requires current High Performance Computing (HPC) platforms to support a new set of novel graph computing applications. The HPC industry is utilizing clusters of computers, multi-core CPUs and CPUs combined with application-specific accelerators, such as GPUs, to improve the performance of graph algorithms on large networks.

DOI: 10.4018/978-1-5225-3799-1.ch004

There is a list of publicly available libraries that exploit homogeneous parallel processing, i.e. the use of a single HPC parallel architecture (e.g. a multi-core server or a HPC cluster integrated of computing nodes with the same characteristics) to power the processing of large networks modeled after real-world phenomena.

The first problem in parallel graph computing is to decide how to partition and then distribute the graph among the available processors.

In homogeneous computing, the balanced graph partitioning problem consists of finding the best way to divide the vertices of a graph into a predefined number of partitions, such that the following conditions are met: (1) the number of vertices among partitions are balanced and (2) the number of edges crossing partitions (edge cut) is minimized (Chamberlain, 1998).

Since the performance of a homogeneous system is determined by the slowest processor, workload imbalance can affect the overall system performance. However, in heterogeneous computing graph partitioning techniques should produce computing loads with different sizes (unbalanced partitions) in order to exploit processors with different computing capabilities, such as multi-cores and GPUs (Shen and Zeng, 2005).

Gharaibeh et al. (2012) and Gharaibeh et al. (2013) show that it is possible to render communication overhead negligible in kernels like BFS and PageRank by aggregating communications in a CPU + GPU heterogeneous computing context. It is also suggested that the graph partitioner should focus on producing partitions that minimize computing time rather than communications. *What kind of partitions should new graph partitioning techniques produce to fit the capabilities of different parallel architectures, reduce the computation time of partitions, and benefit from the heterogeneous computing approach?*

In this chapter, three paradigms of complex network partitioning are reviewed: the balanced complex network partitioning where the number of partitions is known, the unbalanced partitioning of complex networks where the number of partitions is known, and the unbalanced partitioning of complex networks where the number of partitions is unknown (community detection).

PARTITIONING AND MAPPING FOR PARALLEL COMPUTING

The main goal of graph parallel computing, and of any parallel application in general, is to obtain a high-performance algorithm that solve a problem faster while keeping programming effort and resource requirements of the program low. To achieve this we must care about several factors related to both parallel software and parallel infrastructure, such as the partitioning and the distribution of the work among available processors, as well as the impact of the communications and synchronizations in the performance of the parallel application.

In the first steps, we have to split the computation into a collection of tasks in order to expose enough concurrency to keep processes busy most of the time, but no so much concurrency to avoid that the overhead of task management exceeds benefits of decomposition. In the last steps, we determine mechanisms to assign tasks to processes. Goals are: balance the workload (computation, I/O, communication) among processes, reduce interprocess communication, and reduce overhead due to assignment operations.

Partitioning and Communication

The general approach for parallelizing an application is to first partition the problem in as many tasks as we can in order to obtain a fine-grained decomposition of the data. The idea is to expose opportunities for parallelism at an early stage, ignoring target hardware and software details (e.g. parallel architecture, number of processors, parallel programming paradigm, etc.). Goals in this first step are: divide data and operations on small tasks of comparable size, avoid redundant computations in tasks, and, if possible, yield several alternative partitions.

Once we have a set of small tasks, we care about the communication patterns between them. The objectives in the next step are to avoid introducing unnecessary communication operations and yield tasks that perform the same number of communications. Tasks may incur into different communication patterns:

- In local communication, each task communicates with a small amount of other tasks (e.g. neighbors).
- In global communication, each task has to communicate with a large amount of tasks.

Agglomeration and Mapping

Once we have considered the communication patterns, we care about target platform issues, performance requirements and implementation costs. In the agglomeration step we combine tasks to yield lesser tasks of greater size in order to decrease communication costs and increase useful computation time. Goals of this step are: decrease communication costs by increasing granularity of computation and communication, retain flexibility with respect to scalability and posterior mapping decisions, and yield tasks with similar computation and communication costs.

Communication costs are proportional to the amount of data to be transferred. In addition, communication and task creation also have startup costs. Having a large amount of tasks may impact negatively on performance due to excessive communication and startup costs. Amount of communication performed for a unit of computation decreases as task size increases.

The last step is to assign each task to physical processors, maximizing processor utilization and minimizing communication costs. This activity is called *mapping*. Goals of the mapping step are: place tasks that are able to run concurrently on different processors to increase concurrency and place tasks that communicate frequently on the same processor to increase locality. Mapping of tasks to processors should achieve two objectives: (1) reducing the amount of time that processes spend interacting, and (2) reducing the total amount of time that some processes spend idle. However, these two objectives often conflict with each other.

Partitioning and Mapping in Graph Computing

Graphs are widely used to model data loads and dependencies in parallel processing. Any parallel computation (either for graph processing or not) can be expressed as a set of vertices representing units of computation (load) and a set of edges encoding data dependencies (communications). Nodes and edges are weighted with the amount of work and data, respectively. In this way, graph partitioning can be employed to determine how to better distribute the work to achieve the best parallel performance. Specifically, the workload can be evenly distributed over the available processors by partitioning the vertices of the graph into equally weighted sets while minimizing the edges crossing between partitions to decrease communications.

In parallel graph processing, the nodes of the graph itself mirror the workload. However, as will be further developed, evenly distributing the number of nodes among the partitions might not be a solution if the processors do not have the same computing capabilities, even if the edge cut is minimum. The following sections describe partitioning strategies for graph computing for (1) when all the processors have the same capabilities (homogeneous computing) and (2) when the processors have different characteristics (heterogeneous computing).

BALANCED PARTITIONING OF COMPLEX NETWORKS

Homogeneous computing architectures are composed of multiple processors with the same characteristics interconnected by a high-speed network or multiple cores in the same system interconnected by a system bus. Multi-core computers and HPC cluster computers are examples of homogeneous computing architectures.

Multi-core processors have a few but complex cores with an on-chip hierarchy of large caches for supporting general-purpose and HPC applications. Cluster computers, on the other hand, are a group of dedicated machines connected via high-speed switched networks optimized for processing large-scale intensive calculations.

In cluster computing, processors cannot directly access the memory from others processors: the only available mechanism to communicate data among processes is to pass messages through the network. In this context, graph partitionings should minimize the number of crossing edges to minimize the number of messages passed among the nodes, since an elevated number of communications can have a negative impact in the parallel application performance.

In this section, existing algorithms for solving the balanced graph partitioning problem on complex networks are reviewed.

The Balanced Graph Partitioning Problem

The balanced graph partitioning problem deals with finding a balanced set of K vertex partitions, in such a way that the number of edges crossing the partitions is minimized. The following is a formal definition of the balanced graph partitioning problem for homogeneous computing.

Let $G = (V, E)$ be a graph. A vertex $\mathcal{K}_\mathcal{A}$-partition is a collection of $\mathcal{K}$ vertex sets $\mathcal{V} = \{\mathcal{P}_1, \mathcal{P}_2, ..., \mathcal{P}_\mathcal{K}\}$ such that $\bigcup_i \mathcal{P}_i = V$ and $\mathcal{P}_i \cap \mathcal{P}_j = 0$ whenever $i \neq j$, for all i. The vertex $\mathcal{K}_\mathcal{A}$-partition determines a map $\mathcal{W} : V \to \mathcal{V}$ such that $\forall v \in V : v \in \mathcal{W}(v)$, and an edge cut $E_\mathcal{V} = \{\{u, v\} \mid \mathcal{W}(u) \neq \mathcal{W}(v)\}$.

- **Problem:** The K-way Graph Balanced Partitioning Problem (KBGPP)
- **Instance:** A graph $G = (V, E)$ of n vertices, and a positive integer $\mathcal{K} \in \mathbb{Z}^+$.
- **Solution:** A vertex $\mathcal{K}_\mathcal{A}$-partition $\mathcal{V}_0 = \{\mathcal{P}_1, \mathcal{P}_2, ..., \mathcal{P}_\mathcal{K}\}$ such that $|\mathcal{P}_i| \approx \left\lceil \frac{\|V\|}{\mathcal{K}} \right\rceil$ for all i, and $\left|E_{\mathcal{V}_0}\right| = \min\left\{\left|E_\mathcal{V}\right| \mid \mathcal{V} \text{ is a } \mathcal{K}_\mathcal{A}\text{-partition}\right\}$.

Let $E_\mathcal{V}(i) = \{\{u, v\} \mid u \in \mathcal{P}_i, v \notin \mathcal{P}_i\}$ be the edges going from vertices in partition $\mathcal{P}_i$ to vertices in other partitions. From the KBGPP definition, it follows that the quality of a $\mathcal{K}_\mathcal{A}$-partition $\mathcal{V}$ is determined by: (1) the vertex balance, where $|\mathcal{P}_i|$ should be at most $\left\lceil \frac{\|V\|}{\mathcal{K}} \right\rceil$ for all i; and (2) the number of edges going to other partitions $|E_\mathcal{V}(i)|$, which should be the minimum for all i.

The KBGPP is NP-complete (Garey et al., 1976). KBGPP is relevant for the mapping of tasks to processors of a parallel machine. Given a graphical representation of the tasks and the communication requirements of a parallel computation, the solution of the balanced partitioning problem allows the balanced distribution of the load and the minimization of inter-processor communications.

Given the computational intractability of KBGPP, a variety of heuristics has been proposed to provide approximate solutions. Consider the example of the balanced bisection of graphs based on the network flow (Honghua-Yang and Wong, 1996). A flow network is a directed graph in which each edge $e \in E$ has a capacity $c(e) \geq 0$. Given two nodes $s, t \in V$, a flow s-t in G is a function $f : E \to \mathbb{R}_0^+$ such that: (1) $\forall e \in E$, $0 \leq f(e) \leq c(e)$; (2) $\forall u \in V \setminus \{s, t\}$ the sum of the outgoing flow from u is equals to the sum of the ingoing flow at u; and (3) the sum of the outgoing flow from s is equals to the sum of ingoing flow at t. A maximal flow in G is a flow of maximum value from s to t. According to the max-flow/min-cut theorem, it is possible to find the minimum cut that divides G in two partitions from the maximum flow of G. Although the bisection may not be perfectly balanced, it is possible to divide the largest partition by applying the max-flow/min-cut theorem recursively to eventually obtain a balanced partitioning.

Balanced Partitioning vs. Complex Networks

Solving KBGPP for complex networks is a challenging task (Lumsdaine, 2007; Madduri, 2008). Lang, (2004) and Lang (2005) show that the quality of the cut inversely varies with the cut balance in information graphs such as the Yahoo! IM service graph and a co-author DBLP graph. Likewise, Lang (2004) and Lang (2005) demonstrate than spectral methods produce poorly balanced partitions in the mentioned graphs. Additionally, Madduri (2008) experimentally showed that the size of the cut produced by Metis and Chaco while partitioning a scale-free graph is approximately two orders bigger than when partitioning an Euclidean graph.

Although graphs encountered in scientific computing are sparse like complex networks, their degree distribution is relatively uniform due to the geometric constraints of the underlying meshes. Good aspect ratios needed for the convergence of numerical methods in meshes cause an overall regularity in this kind of graphs (Abou-Rjeili and Karypis, 2006).

Multilevel Partitioning of Complex Networks

Arguably, the most successful heuristic for solving KBGPP on large scientific graphs is the multilevel graph partitioning approach (Buluc et al., 2013):

1. **Coarsening Phase:** The original graph G is reduced or *coarsened* into a series of successively coarser graphs $G'_1, ..., G'_h$.
2. **Partitioning Phase:** The coarsest graph G'_h is partitioned into $\mathcal{K}$ parts.
3. **Uncoarsening and Refinement Phase:** The partitioning of G'_h is interpolated to G'_{h-1} and refined; the process is repeated and terminated at G.

The multilevel approach for graph partitioning starts with an unweighted graph. Then, during the coarsening process, the graph is enriched with weights of the collapsed vertices and edges to preserve connectivity information that will help the balanced partitioning algorithm to produce high-quality partitions on the coarsest graph.

The multilevel approach is extensively used for partitioning graphs that arise in large scientific computations and implemented in variety software packages such as Jostle (Walshaw and Cross, 2007), Metis (Karypis and Kumar, 1998), and Scotch (Pellegrini and Roman, 1996).

However, there is little work on the multilevel partitioning of scale-free networks, like social, biological, and Web networks. Table 1 presents a summary of current efforts that present results on obtaining balanced partitions on scale-free networks using the multilevel approach.

Abou-Rjeili and Karypis (2006) propose a clustering-based coarsening scheme by allowing arbitrary-size sets of vertices to be collapsed together. According to Abou-Rjeili and Karypis (2006), the idea is to "allow the coarsening algorithms to identify clusters of highly connected vertices." The proposed random greedy techniques for graph coarsening define strategies for visiting the edges during the identification of clusters of vertices. The greedy techniques are combined with different edge ordering criteria, such as the vertex degree, weight, and a generalization of the concept of the vertex k-core.

Abou-Rjeili and Karypis (2006) experimented on Citation, DBLP, Actor, Google, and Internet networks at the router level, reporting better edge-cuts than the Metis package on these scale-free graphs. However, their solution

Table 1. Current multilevel works for partitioning scale-free networks

Author(s)	Networks	Coarsening	Observations
Abou-Rjeili and Karypis, 2006	Citations, DBLP, Actor, Google, PPI, Scan, Lucent	Globally greedy, globally random-locally greedy, K-core + local information	Beat Metis and Chaco Limited to two-way partitioning
Zhang *et al.*, 2011	Citations, DBLP, Actor, Google, PPI, Scan, Lucent	Based on the betweenness centrality	Beat Metis and spectral Betweeness is compute expensive on large graphs
Sanders and Schulz, 2012	DBLP, Citeseer, CAIDA router	Rating function based on local information GPA (Global Path Algorithm)	Do not provide comparison to widely-used packages or algorithms
Safro *et al.*, 2012	DBLP, Citeseer, CAIDA router	Algebraic distance between nodes AMG (Algebraic MultiGrid)	Do not provide comparison to widely-used packages or algorithms

95

only allows two-way partitioning (bisection) of networks, although they mention that their strategy can be generalized to $\mathcal{K}$-way partitioning.

The Girvan-Newman community detection algorithm (Girvan and Newman, 2002) is used by Zhang et al. (2011) to determine the set of edges that will be contracted in each phase of the coarsening stage. The contracting edges are those of maximum betweenness centrality that the Girvan-Newman algorithm eliminates in order to divide the graph into communities of highly connected vertices. As a result, the work of Zhang et al. (2011) follows a divisive hierarchical approach.

Zhang et al. (2011) experimented on Citations, DBLP, Actor, Google, PPI, and two router-level Internet networks. The betweenness-based partitioning algorithm outperforms the algorithm by Abou-Rjeili and Karypis (2006), the Metis package, and a spectral algorithm with respect to 6 benchmarks out of 7. Unfortunately, the calculation of the betweenness centrality is compute-intensive, even for relatively small graphs, which limits the applications of this approach.

There are other authors that not only focus their efforts on scientific graphs but also show results on real-world complex graphs. For example, the authors of KaFFPa (Sanders and Schulz, 2012) employ the Global Path Algorithm (GPA) matching algorithm, which visits the edges in order of decreasing weight to obtain a collection of paths and cycles. The collection is used later to find an optimal solution to the graph matching problem. The authors of KaFFPa experimented with graphs of the DIMACS graph partitioning and clustering challenge, such as DBLP, Citeseer, and CAIDA router networks. However, the authors do not provide a comparison neither to other algorithms or widely used packages for graph partitioning.

Safro et al. (2014) implemented an algebraic multi-grid (AMG) coarsening strategy. The authors experimented with graphs of the DIMACS graph partitioning and clustering challenge. However, as in the case of KaFFPa, the authors do not provide a comparison neither to other algorithms or widely used packages for graph partitioning.

UNBALANCED PARTITIONING OF COMPLEX NETWORKS

General-purpose processors are being combined with application-specific accelerators, like GPUs, or tightly-coupled accelerators, such as APUs and MICs, to improve the performance of graph algorithms on large real-world networks. This is called heterogeneous computing.

In heterogeneous computing, the power of different processors varies, so the size of the tasks to be scheduled should not be the same. In this section, works on the unbalanced graph partitioning problem of complex networks are reviewed.

The Unbalanced Graph Partitioning Problem

The unbalanced graph partitioning problem is to find the best way to divide the vertices of a graph into a predefined number of partitions, such that: (1) the number of vertices among partitions are distributed according to a partition balance set, and (2) the number of edges that cross partitions is minimized (Shen and Zeng, 2005).

Let $\{\beta_1, \beta_2, ..., \beta_K\}$, $\beta_i \in [0,1]$, be the partition balance set. A vertex $\mathcal{K}_B$-partition is a collection of $\mathcal{K}$ vertex sets $\mathcal{V} = \{\mathcal{P}_1, \mathcal{P}_2, ..., \mathcal{P}_K\}$ such that $\bigcup_i \mathcal{P}_i = V$, $\mathcal{P}_i \cap \mathcal{P}_j = 0$ whenever $i \neq j$, and $|\mathcal{P}_i| \approx \beta_i n$, for all i. The vertex $\mathcal{K}_B$-partition determines a map $\mathcal{W} : V \rightarrow \mathcal{V}$ such that $\forall v \in V : v \in \mathcal{W}(v)$, and an edge cut $E_\mathcal{V} = \{\{u,v\} \mid \mathcal{W}(u) \neq \mathcal{W}(v)\}$.

- **Problem:** K-way Graph Unbalanced Partitioning Problem (KGUPP) (Shen and Zeng, 2005)
- **Instance:** A graph $G = (V, E)$ of n vertices, a positive integer $\mathcal{K} \in \mathbb{Z}^+$, and the partition balance set $\{\beta_1, \beta_2, ..., \beta_K\}$.
- **Solution:** A vertex $\mathcal{K}_B$-partition $\mathcal{V}_0 = \{\mathcal{P}_1, \mathcal{P}_2, ..., \mathcal{P}_K\}$ such that $|\mathcal{P}_i| \approx \beta_i n$ for all i, and $|E_{\mathcal{V}_0}| = \min\{|E_\mathcal{V}| \mid \mathcal{V}$ is a $\mathcal{K}_B$-partition$\}$.

From the KUGPP definition, it follows that the quality of a $\mathcal{K}_B$-partition $\mathcal{V}$ is determined by: (1) the vertex balance, where $|\mathcal{P}_i|$ should be approximately $\beta_i n$ for all i; and (2) the number of edges going to other partitions $| E_\mathcal{V}(i) |$, which should be the minimum for all i.

There is little work on the unbalanced graph partitioning problem. Shen and Zeng (2005) propose a multilevel unbalanced graph partitioning algorithm for heterogeneous computing where the number of the partitions is equal to the number of processors and the size of each partition is set according to the computing power. The coarsening is based on a heavy edge matching algorithm. Partitioning stage is driven by an unbalanced partition growing algorithm. Refinement stage is based on the idea of decreasing edge-cuts of the Kernighan-Lin refinement algorithm. Unfortunately, the work is designed for regular scientific graphs like 2D FEM's, maps, and 2D dual graphs.

Unbalanced graph partitioning strategies, like the one by Shen and Zeng (2005), might be more suitable for the development of heterogeneous computing strategies than balanced partitioning algorithms. However, as in the case of balanced graph partitioning, algorithms that minimize the number of crossing edges might not be adequate in practice for heterogeneous computing platforms where the suitability of partitions to the processors is a key factor (Gharaibeh et al., 2013).

Community Detection

A related and well-studied problem is community detection on complex networks. Girvan and Newman (2002) found that a variety of complex networks show groups of tightly interconnected nodes or *communities* that might reveal important information on the functional role of nodes in the same community.

Thus, the community detection problem is to find communities or subsets of nodes that are well-connected inside each community but sparsely connected to nodes of other communities.

Let the connectivity of a vertex pair u, v, $\lambda(u, v)$, be the minimum number of edges that have to be removed to disconnect u and v. Let a vertex partition $\mathcal{P} \subseteq V$ be a community if, for all $u, v, w \in \mathcal{P}$ and $w' \in V - \mathcal{P}$, $\lambda(u, v) > \lambda(w, w')$ holds (Borgatti et al., 1990). In other words, a vertex subset $\mathcal{P}$ is a community if any pair of vertices in $\mathcal{P}$ has a higher connectivity than any pair of nodes consisting in a vertex inside $\mathcal{P}$ and a vertex outside $\mathcal{P}$.

A vertex $\mathcal{K}_c$-partition is a collection of $\mathcal{K}$ vertex sets $\mathcal{V} = \{\mathcal{P}_1, \mathcal{P}_2, ..., \mathcal{P}_\mathcal{K}\}$ such that $\bigcup_i \mathcal{P}_i = V$, $\mathcal{P}_i \cap \mathcal{P}_j = 0$ whenever $i \neq j$, and $\mathcal{P}_i$ is a community, for all i. The vertex $\mathcal{K}_c$-partition determines a map $\mathcal{W} : V \rightarrow \mathcal{V}$ such that $\forall v \in V : v \in \mathcal{W}(v)$, and an edge cut $E_\mathcal{V} = \{\{u, v\} \mid \mathcal{W}(u) \neq \mathcal{W}(v)\}$.

It is stated the following:

- **Problem:** The Graph Community Detection Problem (GCDP)
- **Instance:** A graph $G = (V, E)$ of n vertices.
- **Solution:** A vertex $\mathcal{K}_c$-partition $\mathcal{V}_0 = \{\mathcal{P}_1, \mathcal{P}_2, ..., \mathcal{P}_\mathcal{K}\}$ such that $\mathcal{P}_i$ is a community, for all i; and $\left|E_{\mathcal{V}_0}\right| = \min\left\{\left|E_\mathcal{V}\right| \mid \mathcal{V} \text{ is a } \mathcal{K}_c\text{-partition}\right\}$.

Note that, in contrast to the **KBGPP** and **KUGPP** problems, the number of partitions or communities $\mathcal{K}$ is not provided as input. The quality of a partitioning for the GCDP can be evaluated through the modularity index $\mathcal{Q}$ (Newman and Girvan, 2004):

$$\mathcal{Q} = \sum_{i=1}^{\mathcal{K}} \left[\frac{|\mathcal{L}_i|}{m} - \left(\frac{\sum\limits_{u \in \mathcal{P}_i} k_u}{2m} \right)^2 \right],$$

where $\mathcal{L}_i \subseteq E$ is the set of edges in community $\mathcal{P}_i$. $\mathcal{Q}$ measures the proportion of edges in E having both ends at vertices in community i (intra-community edges), subtracted from the proportion of edges in E having at least one end at a vertex inside community i (extra-community edges). Values approaching $\mathcal{Q} = 1$ denote a *strong* community detection partitioning. The problem of finding a $\mathcal{K}_c$-partition that maximizes $\mathcal{Q}$ is NP-hard (Brandes et al., 2007).

There is much work on the GCDP (Fortunato, 2010). Most common techniques include divisive hierarchical clustering, like those based on the current-flow betweenness (Brandes and Fleischer, 2005), the random-walk betweenness (Newman, 2005), the edge-clustering coefficient (Radicchi et al., 2004), and the information centrality (Fortunato et al., 2004); modularity minimization, such as agglomerative hierarchical clustering (Newman and Girvan, 2004), simulated annealing (Guimera and Amaral, 2005), and extreme optimization (Duch and Arenas, 2005); and eigenvector-based algorithms (Donetti and Munoz, 2004). Table 2 summarizes some works for these community detection paradigms.

Take the example of the Girvan-Newman algorithm, a greedy algorithm with $O(n^3)$ time complexity in sparse graphs. The Girvan-Newman is a hierarchical divisive clustering algorithm based on the removal of edges with largest centrality. The algorithm calculates the betweenness centrality of all edges. Then, the edge with highest edge betweenness centrality is removed and the betweenness of the affected edges are computed again. The algorithm repeats this procedure until all edges are removed. The output is a dendrogram that mirrors the hierarchical organization of communities in the network.

Divisive hierarchical clustering techniques determine the edge that has to be removed according to some edge centrality metric, allowing us to differentiate edges located between communities from edges inside communities. The

Table 2. Examples of four community detection paradigms: hierarchical clustering, modularity optimization, and spectral clustering

Paradigm	Description	Complexity
Hierarchical clustering	Detects and removes edges that connect vertices belonging to different communities, in such a way that the graph disconnects and each connected component represents a community. To detect community-crossing edges centrality metrics like the edge betweenness (Girvan and Newman, 2002), current flow betweenness, random walks betweenness (Newman, 2005), edge clustering coefficient (Radicchi et al., 2004), and information centrality (Fortunato et al., 2004) are used.	Flow and random walks betweenness algorithm by Girvan and Newman (2002) takes $O(n^3)$ in sparse graphs. Edge clustering coefficient approach (Radicchi et al. 2004) takes $O(m^4 n^2)$ in dense graphs and $O(n^2)$ in sparse graphs. Information centrality approach by (Fortunato et al. 2004) takes $O(m^3 n)$ in dense graphs and $O(n^4)$ in sparse graphs.
Modularity optimization	The maximum modularity problem is to find a partition of the vertex set V of disjoint subsets $\{\mathcal{P}_1, \mathcal{P}_2, ...\}$ $\{\mathcal{P}_1, \mathcal{P}_2, ...\}$ that maximizes the modularity index $\mathcal{Q}$ of the network. The problem is NP-hard (Brandes et al., 2007), thus greedy algorithms (Newman and Girvan, 2004) and heuristics like simulated annealing (Guimera and Amaral, 2005) and extreme optimization (Duch and Arenas, 2005) have been developed to produce approximate solutions.	Newman greedy algorithm in Newman and Girvan (2004) takes $O((m + n)n)$ in dense graphs and $O(n^2)$ in sparse graphs. The complexity of the SA algorithm by Guimera and Amaral (2005) depends on the SA parameters and it is difficult to estimate (Guimera and Amaral, 2005). Extreme optimization algorithm by Duch and Arenas (2005) takes $O(n^2 \log n)$.
Spectral clustering	Spectral clustering exploits the eigenvectors of the Laplace matrix by transforming the initial set of objects into vectors whose components are the elements of the eigenvectors. The representation induced by the eigenvectors makes the cluster properties clearer as the communities appear as well-separated group of vectors (Donetti and Munoz, 2004).	The bottleneck in algorithm by Donetti and Munoz (2004) is the calculation of the eigenvectors, which requires $O(n^3)$ time. If not all eigenpairs are required, the more efficient Lanczos method can be employed.

following paragraphs summarize some divisive hierarchical cluster algorithms for community detection:

- Brandes and Fleischer (2005) propose the current-flow betweenness centrality that conceives a graph as a network of electrical resistances. When applying an electrical potential difference (voltage) between two vertices, the edges transport a quantity of electric current calculated through the Kirchoff equations. The current flow betweenness is then the quantity of electric current that flows through a given edge or vertex.

- Newman (2005) proposes the random-walking betweenness, a metric that is equivalent to the current flow betweenness that measures the quantity of random walks between all pairs of vertices in a network that go through a given edge. Both the current flow betweenness and the random walk betweenness can be calculated in $O(n^3)$ time in sparse graphs.

- Radicchi et al. (2004) propose the edge clustering coefficient that measures the fraction of triangles or cycles of three edges in which a given edge participates. This only requires local information. The underlying idea is: edges inside a community participate in a larger quantity of 3-cycles than edges outside communities. The algorithm by Radicchi et al. (2004) takes $O(m^4 n^2)$ time in dense graphs and $O(n^2)$ in sparse graphs.

- Fortunato et al. (2004) propose the information centrality metric, based on the drop of efficiency of diffusion of information in a network due to the removal of a given edge. The algorithm has a temporal complexity of $O(m^3 n^2)$ in dense graphs, and a complexity of $O(n^4)$ in sparse graphs.

The modularity $\mathcal{Q}$ is arguably the most used metric in for evaluating the quality of the community partitioning of a graph, and has been exploited to design a family of algorithms for community detection that try to maximize the value Q of a graph. However, it has been shown that the problem of maximizing $\mathcal{Q}$ represents an NP-hard problem (Brandes et al., 2007), so a variety of greedy and meta-heuristic algorithms has been proposed:

- Newman and Girvan (2004) propose an agglomerative hierarchical clustering algorithm that starts with as many communities as nodes in the graph. Nodes are then aggregated in pairs in such a way that the aggregations produce a global increment of the modularity $\mathcal{Q}$. If $\mathcal{Q} = 0$, then the graph does not have a well-defined community partitioning. On the contrary, if $\mathcal{Q} \geq 0.3$, the graph has a non-trivial community partitioning. The algorithm of Newman and Girvan (2004) has a time complexity of $O(n^2 + nm)$ in dense graphs, and a complexity of $O(n^2)$ in sparse graphs.

- Guimera and Amaral (2005) propose a Simulated Annealing (SA) meta-heuristic algorithm for modularity maximization. The cost function is $U = -Q$. In every iteration, both random local updates (moving a vertex from one community to another) and global updates (combine or divide a community) take place. An update is accepted with probability $p = 1$ if $U_f \leq U_i$, where U_f is the cost after the update and U_i is the cost before the update. Otherwise, the update is accepted with probability $p = \exp\left(\dfrac{U_f - U_i}{T}\right)$, where T is the annealing temperature. The complexity of this algorithm depends on different parameters of the SA algorithm.

- Duch and Arenas (2005) propose an Extreme Optimization (EO) meta-heuristic algorithm for community detection. The algorithm evaluates the local modularity metric $q_i = e_{S(i)} - k_i a_{S(i)}$ for each vertex i, where $a_{S(i)}$ is the number of links that node i in community S has to other nodes inside S, k_i is the degree of node i and $e_{S(i)}$ is the fraction of links that have one or both vertices inside of the community where i is located. The algorithm starts with a random partitioning of the network into two communities. In each iteration the vertex with minimum q_i is changed to another community and q_i is computed again. The algorithm iterates until $Q = \sum_i^n q_i$ cannot be further enhanced. The complexity of this algorithm is $O(n^2 \log n)$.

Techniques based in the spectra of the Laplace matrix of the network use an eigenvector or a combination of several eigenvectors as a measure of similarity between nodes to detect communities. On the other hand, some community detection algorithms are inspired in models of physical phenomena studied in mechanic statistics such as the Potts model:

- Donetti and Munoz (2004) present a technique of agglomerative hierarchical clustering based on the specter of the Laplace matrix that arranges vertices in an H-dimensional space, where H is the number of eigenvectors of the Laplace matrix. The similarity metric is the angle between the vectors of two points in the space. This results in a dendrogram, and the partitioning with maximum modularity is selected from the dendrogram.

- Reichardt and Bornholdt (2006) propose a technique based on the Potts model in which spin variables (nodes) interact with other neighboring spin variables (links) and form spin clusters sharing the same state (communities) when the system reaches a ground state due to ferromagnetic interactions. The objective is to optimize the graph Hamiltonian $\mathcal{H}$, i.e. the energy of a system of Potts' spins of infinite range, given that the ground state of such a system corresponds to the graph community structure. Reichardt and Bornholdt (2006) approximate the ground state by means of a SA meta-heuristic.

SNAP, ParComm and SUPE-Net (Hou and Yao, 2010) are examples of works that exploit the community structure of networks for load distribution. CommPar is a load balancing strategy in distributed-memory parallel environments based on the community detection of social networks. The division of the graph is performed at two levels: (1) first communities are calculated by using the Infopar community detection algorithm (Rosvall and Bergstrom, 2008), (2) then, the METIS balanced partitioning technique is applied in order to divide each community uniformly and obtain the final mapping of partitions to processors. Unfortunately, the authors of CommPar do not perform a more exhaustive study on alternative community detection algorithms besides Inforpar.

Another work that considered the organization of communities for parallel computing is that of Madduri (2008). Madduri present a parallel hierarchical clustering that optimize the index of modularity Q. In the first steps, when the network is divided in big communities, the algorithm computes and approximates the edge betweenness. In the following steps, when the networks has been broken into smaller communities, the algorithm computes in parallel the exact edge betweenness centrality, turning the parallel granularity during the execution of the algorithm in a semi-automatic way.

Besides the works of Hou and Yao (2010) and Madduri (2008), there is a lack of authors that address the problem of load balancing for parallel computing of graphs by considering topological properties of real-world complex networks such as the community organization.

There are factors that make the application of community detection in heterogeneous computing not a straightforward task. In community detection, the number of clusters is unknown and produced by the algorithm. As in homogeneous partitioning, community detection focuses on reducing the number of edges crossing groups rather than producing partitions with specific topological properties. Additionally, most community detection algorithms are at least quadratic, which hampers their application on million-node complex networks.

PARTITIONING OF COMPLEX NETWORKS FOR HETEROGENEOUS COMPUTING

Suitability of Graph Partitions to Architectures

Heterogeneous computing seeks to improve the performance of graph applications by executing computing intensive kernels in both general-purpose processors and accelerators, in order to maximize the number of edges processed per second. Common combinations of architectures to accelerate graph applications in research literature include CPU + GPU (Gharaibeh et al., 2012; Gharaibeh et al., 2013; Hong et al., 2011; Zou et al., 2013; Banerjee et al., 2013; Munguia et al., 2012), CPU + APU's (Nilakant and Yoneki, 2014), and CPU + MIC's (Gao et al., 2014).

The BSP approach applied to graph heterogeneous computing minimizes CPU-GPU communication overhead by batching data transfers in the communication step (Gharaibeh et al., 2012; Gharaibeh et al., 2013). As stated by Gharaibeh et al., 2012: "adopting the BSP model allows to circumvent the fact that the GPUs are connected via the higher-latency PCI-Express bus."

In this way, graph partitioning is now focused on minimizing computation time rather than communication. Given this new paradigm of load distribution, *what kind of partitions should new graph partitioning techniques produce to fit the capabilities of different parallel architectures, reduce the computation time of partitions, and benefit from heterogeneous computing?*

Gharaibeh et al. (2013) and Gharaibeh and Elizeu (2013) argue that partitions should provide different degrees of parallelisms and maximize the utilization of the processors, yet they must lead to homogeneous parallelism to achieve balanced workload across the vertices of a partition. Gharaibeh et al. (2013) and Gharaibeh and Elizeu (2013) also show that it is possible to render communication overhead negligible in kernels like BFS and PageRank on scale-free graphs by exploiting aggregation techniques and a BSP parallel model. As a consequence, it is suggested that the graph partitioner should focus on producing partitions that minimize computing time rather than communication time.

Taking into account that algorithms like BFS are memory bounded, it is important that partitions are cache-friendly. In this context, Gharaibeh et al. (2013), Gharaibeh and Elizeu (2013), and Chhugani et al. (2012) suggest that the use of bit-vectors to compactly represent visited nodes can lead to improved performance on CPUs. Cache-friendliness is achieved by Gharaibeh et al. (2013) and Gharaibeh and Elizeu (2013) by placing high-degree vertices in CPU and low-degree vertices in the GPU. By placing high-degree vertices in GPU, the bit-vector size of the CPU partition shrinks and the chances for it to fit the cache are increased.

Nilakant and Yoneki (2014) also observe an increased performance when placing low-degree nodes on the GPU and large-degree nodes on the CPU for BFS. In addition, it is suggested that homogeneity of the node degrees placed on the GPU might help to minimize thread divergence on GPU's (Nilakant and Yoneki, 2014). Another factor is the bandwidth differences among different architectures. In this context, Zou et al. (2013) propose a simple formula to distribute nodes based on the bandwidth of CPUs and GPUs: $|V|*B_h / (B_h + B_d)$, where B_h and B_d are the bandwidths of the CPU and the GPU, respectively.

Unfortunately, many works fail to consider the suitability of different algorithms to different architectures in a graph heterogeneous computing setup. As shown in the previous chapter, multicores can process large diameter graphs (like very sparse regular graphs) considerably better that GPUs, with a difference of up to two orders of magnitude in time processing, regardless of the algorithmic approach.

Topology-Based Graph Partitioning

Table 3 shows that current works for graph heterogeneous computing (Gharaibeh et al., 2012; Gharaibeh and Elizeu, 2013; Gharaibeh et al., 2013; Hong et al., 2011; Nilakant and Yoneki, 2014; Zou et al., 2013; Banerjee et al., 2013; Gao et al., 2014; Munguia et al., 2012; Sariyuce and Kaya, 2013) divide the graph for load balance based on simple parameters or local information like the size of the graph, the size of the BFS frontiers, or simply by placing high-degree vertices in the CPU and low-degree vertices in the GPU, in order to achieve graph degree homogeneity and optimize cache utilization.

Table 3. Heterogeneous parallel graph processing strategies

Reference	Architectures	Algorithm(s)	Partitioning Criteria
Gharaibeh et al.(2012), Gharaibeh and Elizeu, (2013), and Gharaibeh et al., (2013)	CPU + GPU	BFS, PageRank	Node degree
Hong et al. (2011)	CPU + GPU	BFS	Frontier size
Nilakant and Yoneki, (2014)	CPU + APU	BFS, PageRank	Node degree
Zou et al. (2013)	CPU + GPU	BFS	Switching: size of frontier, partitioning of frontier: architecture memory bandwidth
Banerjee et al. (2013)	CPU + GPU	BFS, connected components, all pairs shortest paths	Predetermined threshold
Gao et al. (2014)	CPU + MIC	BFS	Frontier size
Munguia et al. (2012)	CPU + GPU	BFS	Frontier size
Sariyuce and Kaya (2013)	CPU + GPU	Betweenness centrality	Dataset size

However, these works do not fully exploit the information encoded in the global topology properties inherent to complex networks to produce partitioning schemes suitable for real-world complex graphs. For example, an important step to understand the global structure of a complex network is to discover how dense connections are forming from simple cliques to larger clusters. A widely used definition of node clusters is that of k-cores.

Recall that the k-core decomposition identifies internal cores and decomposes the networks layer by layer, revealing the structure of the different k-shells from the innermost to the outermost one (Dorogovtsev et al., 2006). *Can a graph heterogeneous computing platform be benefited from partitioning strategies that are aware of global graph topology properties, like the graph coreness?*

The authors claim that it is possible to adapt the multilevel approach for heterogeneous computing on complex networks under the premise that a "representative" coarse graph of a complex network would allow us to obtain unbalanced partitions on real-world scale-free graphs. For our purposes, a "representative" coarse graph is a smaller graph that preserves a set of global and scaling properties of the original graph.

The authors have previously shown (Garcia-Robledo et al., 2016) that the differentiation between core and non-core nodes through the k-core graph decomposition is useful for designing new graph coarsening algorithms that preserve important complex network properties like the average degree, the average path length, and the scale-free degree distribution.

If one has to combine vertices to obtain reduced and coarse versions of graphs, one would delete those nodes that are least central or contract edges whose contraction cause the minimum impact on the global graph topology. Good candidate edges for contraction would likely to be incident to the least important vertices, i.e. those that lie on the *peripheries* of a complex network.

In this way, the k-core decomposition of complex networks can be exploited as a criterion for the visitation of vertices and the contraction of edges in order to obtain reduced versions of a graph that preserve topological properties like the scale-freeness and the small-worldness of the original graph. The authors claim that k-core-based coarsening algorithms can be embedded into the coarsening stage of a multilevel partitioning approach with the goal of obtaining unbalanced graph partitions for load balancing between multicores and GPUs.

SUMMARY AND DISCUSSION

The use of heterogeneous computing for accelerating graph algorithms is an emerging research area. Most of the work on complex network partitioning is geared towards community detection. Most community detection algorithms are quadratic, which makes hard its application on million-node graphs.

There is a lack of works that approach the unbalanced graph partitioning problem on complex networks for heterogeneous computing. Existing unbalanced partitioning algorithms that minimize the number of crossing edges might not be adequate in practice since they focus on minimizing the communications rather than maximizing the suitability of partitions to the processors.

On the other hand, we believe that the idea of multilevel unbalanced graph partitioning can be extended to handle large complex networks for heterogeneous computing.

Current works on graph heterogeneous computing do not fully exploit the information encoded in the topology inherent to complex networks. In this regard, exploiting global topological properties of networks, like the k-core decomposition, is a key factor to find partitions that are suitable to heterogeneous processors. Finding partitions with different topologies can improve the performance of processors with different granularity.

By considering the previous commentaries, the authors pose the following research question: *is it possible to embed a* k *-core-based coarsening strategy into a multilevel partitioning strategy to produce graph partitions that fit different architectures in a graph heterogeneous computing setup?*

The next chapter will be devoted to answer this question.

REFERENCES

Abou-Rjeili, A., & Karypis, G. (2006). Multilevel Algorithms for Partitioning Power-Law Graphs. *Proceedings of the 20th IEEE International Parallel & Distributed Processing Symposium (IPDPS'06)*, 124–124.

Banerjee, D., Sharma, S., & Kothapalli, K. (2013). Work Efficient Parallel Algorithms for Large Graph Exploration. *Proceedings of the 20th Annual International Conference on High Performance Computing (HiPC'13)*, 433–442. doi:10.1109/HiPC.2013.6799125

Borgatti, S., Everett, M., & Shirey, P. (1990). LS Sets, Lambda Sets and Other Cohesive Subsets. *Social Networks*, *12*(4), 337–357. doi:10.1016/0378-8733(90)90014-Z

Brandes, U., Delling, D., Gaertler, M., Görke, R., Hoefer, M., Nikoloski, Z., and Wagner, D. (2007). *On Finding Graph Clusterings With Maximum Modularity*. Academic Press.

Brandes, U., & Fleischer, D. (2005). Centrality Measures Based on Current Flow. *Proceedings of the 22nd Symposium of Theoretical Aspects of Computer Science (STACS'05)*, 533–544.

Buluc, A., Meyerhenke, H., Safro, I., Sanders, P., & Schulz, C. (2013). *Recent Advances in Graph Partitioning*. arXiv:13113144 [csDS]

Chamberlain, B. (1998). *Graph Partitioning Algorithms for Distributing Workloads of Parallel Computations. Technical report*. University of Washington.

Chhugani, J., Satish, N., Kim, C., Sewall, J., & Dubey, P. (2012). Fast and Efficient Graph Traversal Algorithm for CPUs: Maximizing Single-Node Efficiency. *Proceedings of the 26th IEEE International Parallel and Distributed Processing Symposium (IPDPS'12)*, 378–389. doi:10.1109/IPDPS.2012.43

Donetti, L., & Munoz, M. (2004). Detecting Network Communities: A New Systematic and Efficient Algorithm. *Journal of Statistical Mechanics, 2004*(7028), P10012. doi:10.1088/1742-5468/2004/10/P10012

Dorogovtsev, S., Goltsev, A., & Mendes, J. (2006). K-Core Organization of Complex Networks. *Physical Review Letters, 96*(4), 040601. doi:10.1103/PhysRevLett.96.040601 PMID:16486798

Duch, J., & Arenas, A. (2005). Community Detection in Complex Networks Using Extremal Optimization. *Physical Review E: Statistical, Nonlinear, and Soft Matter Physics, 72*(2), 027104. doi:10.1103/PhysRevE.72.027104 PMID:16196754

Fortunato, S. (2010). Community Detection in Graphs. *Physics Reports, 486*(3), 75–174. doi:10.1016/j.physrep.2009.11.002

Fortunato, S., Latora, V., & Marchiori, M. (2004). Method to Find Community Structures Based on Information Centrality. *Physical Review E: Statistical, Nonlinear, and Soft Matter Physics, 70*(5), 056104. doi:10.1103/PhysRevE.70.056104 PMID:15600689

Gao, T., Lu, Y., Zhang, B., & Suo, G. (2014). Using the Intel Many Integrated Core to Accelerate Graph Traversal. *International Journal of High Performance Computing Applications, 28*(3), 255–266. doi:10.1177/1094342014524240

Garcia-Robledo, A., Diaz-Perez, A., & Morales-Luna, G. (2016). Characterization and Coarsening of Autonomous System Networks: Measuring and Simplifying the Internet. In Advanced Methods for Complex Network Analysis, (pp. 148–179). IGI Global.

Garey, M., Johnson, D., & Stockmeyer, L. (1976). Some Simplified NP-complete Graph Problems. *Theoretical Computer Science, 1*(3), 237–267. doi:10.1016/0304-3975(76)90059-1

Gharaibeh, A., Costa, L., Elizeu, S., & Ripeanu, M. (2013). On Graphs, GPUs, and Blind Dating: A Workload to Processor Matchmaking Quest. *Proceedings of the 27th IEEE International Symposium on Parallel & Distributed Processing (IPDPS'13)*, 851–862. doi:10.1109/IPDPS.2013.37

Gharaibeh, A., & Elizeu, S. (2013). *Efficient Large-Scale Graph Processing on Hybrid CPU and GPU Systems*. arXiv:13123018 [csDC]

Gharaibeh, A., Lauro, C., Elizeu, S., & Matei, R. (2012). A Yoke of Oxen and a Thousand Chickens for Heavy Lifting Graph Processing. *Proceedings of the 21st International Conference on Parallel Architectures and Compilation Techniques (PACT'12)*, 345–354. doi:10.1145/2370816.2370866

Girvan, M., & Newman, M. (2002). Community Structure in Social and Biological Networks. *Proceedings of the National Academy of Sciences of the United States of America*, *99*(12), 7821–7826. doi:10.1073/pnas.122653799 PMID:12060727

Guimera, R., & Amaral, L. (2005). Functional Cartography of Complex Metabolic Networks. *Nature*, *433*(7028), 895–900. doi:10.1038/nature03288 PMID:15729348

Hong, S., Oguntebi, T., & Olukotun, K. (2011). Efficient Parallel Graph Exploration on Multi-Core CPU and GPU. *Proceedings of the 2011 International Conference on Parallel Architectures and Compilation Techniques (PACT'11)*, 78–88. doi:10.1109/PACT.2011.14

Honghua-Yang, H., & Wong, D. (1996). Efficient Network Flow Based Min-Cut Balanced Partitioning. *IEEE Transactions on Computer-Aided Design of Integrated Circuits and Systems*, *15*(12), 1533–1540.

Hou, B., & Yao, Y. (2010). CommPar: A Community-Based Model Partitioning Approach for Large-Scale Networked Social Dynamics Simulation. *Proceedings Del 14th IEEE/ACM International Symposium on Distributed Simulation and Real Time Applications (DS-RT'2010)*, 7–13. doi:10.1109/DS-RT.2010.10

Karypis, G., & Kumar, V. (1998). METIS: A Software Package for Partitioning Unstructured Graphs, Partitioning Meshes, and Computing Fill-Reducing Orderings of Sparse Matrices. User manual. Academic Press.

Lang, K. (2004). *Finding Good Nearly Balanced Cuts in Power Law Graphs. Technical report. Yahoo!* Research.

Lang, K. (2005). *Fixing Two Weaknesses of the Spectral Method. Technical report. Yahoo!* Research.

Lumsdaine, A., Gregor, D., Hendrickson, B., & Berry, J. (2007). Challenges in Parallel Graph Processing. *Parallel Processing Letters*, *17*(1), 5–20. doi:10.1142/S0129626407002843

Madduri, K. (2008). *A High-Performance Framework for Analyzing Massive Complex Networks* (PhD thesis). Georgia Institute of Technology.

Munguia, L., Bader, D., & Ayguade, E. (2012). Task-Based Parallel Breadth-First Search in Heterogeneous Environments. *Proceedings of the 19th International Conference on High Performance Computing (HiPC'12)*, 1–10. doi:10.1109/HiPC.2012.6507474

Newman, M. (2005). A Measure of Betweenness Centrality Based on Random Walks. *Social Networks*, 27(1), 39–54. doi:10.1016/j.socnet.2004.11.009

Newman, M., & Girvan, M. (2004). Finding and Evaluating Community Structure in Networks. *Physical Review. E*, 69(2), 026113. doi:10.1103/PhysRevE.69.026113 PMID:14995526

Nilakant, K., & Yoneki, E. (2014). On the Efficacy of APUs for Heterogeneous Graph Computation. *Proceedings of the 4th Workshop on Systems for Future Multicore Architectures (SFMA'14)*, 2–7.

Pellegrini, F., & Roman, J. (1996). Scotch: A Software Package for Static Mapping by Dual Recursive Bipartitioning of Process and Architecture Graphs. *Proceedings of the 1996 International Conference and Exhibition on High-Performance Computing and Networking (HPCN'96)*, 493–498. doi:10.1007/3-540-61142-8_588

Radicchi, F., Castellano, C., Cecconi, F., Loreto, V., & Parisi, D. (2004). Defining and Identifying Communities in Networks. *Proceedings of the National Academy of Sciences of the United States of America*, 101(9), 2658–2663. doi:10.1073/pnas.0400054101 PMID:14981240

Reichardt, J., & Bornholdt, S. (2006). Statistical Mechanics of Community Detection. *Physical Review E: Statistical, Nonlinear, and Soft Matter Physics*, 74(1), 016110. doi:10.1103/PhysRevE.74.016110 PMID:16907154

Rosvall, M., & Bergstrom, C. (2008). Maps of Random Walks on Complex Networks Reveal Community Structure. *Proceedings of the National Academy of Sciences of the United States of America*, 105(4), 1118–1123. doi:10.1073/pnas.0706851105 PMID:18216267

Safro, I., Sanders, P., & Schulz, C. (2014). Advanced Coarsening Schemes for Graph Partitioning. *Journal of Experimental Algorithmics*, 19, 369–380.

Sanders, P., & Schulz, C. (2012). *High Quality Graph Partitioning. Technical report*. Karlsruhe Institute of Technology.

Sariyüce, A., & Kaya, K. (2013). Betweenness Centrality on GPUs and Heterogeneous Architectures. *Proceedings of the 6th Workshop on General Purpose Processor Using Graphics Processing Units (GPGPU-6)*, 76–85. doi:10.1145/2458523.2458531

Shen, Y., & Zeng, G. (2005). An Unbalanced Partitioning Scheme for Graph in Heterogeneous Computing. *Proceedings of the 2005 Grid and Cooperative Computing (GCC'05)*, 1167–1172. doi:10.1007/11590354_139

Walshaw, C., & Cross, M. (2007). *Jostle: Parallel Multilevel Graph-Partitioning Software-An Overview. Technical report*. University of Greenwich.

Zhang, B., Wu, J., Tang, Y., & Zhou, J. (2011). Betweenness-Based Algorithm for a Partition Scale-Free Graph. *Chinese Physics B*, *20*(11), 118903. doi:10.1088/1674-1056/20/11/118903

Zou, D., Dou, Y., Wang, Q., Xu, J., & Li, B. (2013). Direction-Optimizing Breadth-First Search on CPU-GPU Heterogeneous Platforms. *Proceedings of the 10th IEEE International Conference on High Performance Computing and Communications & IEEE International Conference on Embedded and Ubiquitous Computing (HPCC/EUC'13)*, 1064–1069. doi:10.1109/HPCC. and.EUC.2013.150

Chapter 5
Topology–Aware Load–Balance Schemes for Heterogeneous Graph Processing

ABSTRACT

Inspired by the insights presented in Chapters 2, 3, and 4, in this chapter the authors present the KCMAX (K-Core MAX) and the KCML (K-Core Multi-Level) frameworks: novel k-core-based graph partitioning approaches that produce unbalanced partitions of complex networks that are suitable for heterogeneous parallel processing. Then they use KCMAX and KCML to explore the configuration space for accelerating BFSs on large complex networks in the context of TOTEM, a BSP heterogeneous GPU + CPU HPC platform. They study the feasibility of the heterogeneous computing approach by systematically studying different graph partitioning strategies, including the KCMAX and KCML algorithms, while processing synthetic and real-world complex networks.

INTRODUCTION

A major strategy for graph heterogeneous computing processing is that of *heterogeneous partitioning* in which computation proceeds in parallel on two or more parallel architectures (such as CPUs and GPUs) at the same time (Nilakant and Yoneki, 2014). Thus, a fundamental problem in heterogeneous

DOI: 10.4018/978-1-5225-3799-1.ch005

partitioning computing is to decide how to partition and then distribute the graph among the available processors.

Most conventional graph partitioning algorithms produce equivalent partitions and focus to reduce communication costs by minimizing the edge cut. However, in heterogeneous computing, the computing power of different processors varies, so that the size of the tasks to be scheduled should not be the same. What kind of partitions should new graph partitioning techniques produce to fit the capabilities of different parallel architectures, reduce the computation time of partitions, and benefit from the heterogeneous computing approach?

According to Gharaibeh et al. (2013) and Gharaibeh and Elizeu (2013), a graph partitioning strategy for heterogeneous computing should have: (1) low space and time complexity, (2) the ability to handle scale-free graphs, (3) the ability to handle large graphs, and (4) focus on the reduction of computation time. Additionally, a heterogeneous partitioning approach must find a trade-off between the overhead of partitioning the input and synchronizing the processors, and the gain in overall computation throughput (Nilakant and Yoneki, 2014). Having fast (linear-time) algorithms for partitioning graphs is both useful and relevant.

Gharaibeh et al. (2013) and Gharaibeh and Elizeu (2013) also show that it is possible to render communication overhead negligible in kernels like BFS and PageRank, and it is suggested that the graph partitioner should focus on producing partitions that minimize computing time rather than communication time. How to produce graph partitions that fit the capabilities of different parallel architectures, reduce the computation time of partitions, and benefit from the heterogeneous computing approach?

In this chapter, the graph partitioning problem for heterogeneous computing is re-stated as subgraph search problems to fit graph partitions to parallel architectures in an efficient manner. The objective is to present the synergy between Network Science and HPC data by studying techniques for graph partitioning based on the coreness of complex networks for load distribution on heterogeneous computing platforms.

Specifically, unbalanced graph partitioning algorithms are proposed to bisect complex networks by:

1. Finding the densest subgraph through the recursive removal of the core of complex networks, as defined by the k-core decomposition.

2. Finding unbalanced partitions by calculating central subgraphs of coarse graphs produced by considering both the k-core decomposition of the original graphs and the centrality of coarse subgraphs.

To study the benefits of the proposed subgraph search approach, the proposed partition algorithms are integrated into a BSP-based heterogeneous computing platform. An experimental performance analysis is then conducted by traversing large real-world and synthetic complex networks on CPU + GPU.

RELATED WORK

As discussed in the previous chapter, there are works in literature that combine the capacities of heterogeneous processors for accelerating a variety of graph computing applications. Common processors combinations are CPU + GPU (Gharaibeh et al., 2012; Gharaibeh et al., 2013; Hong et al., 2011; Zou et al., 2013; Banerjee et al., 2013; Munguia et al., 2012), CPU + APU's (Nilakant and Yoneki, 2014), and CPU + MIC's (Gao et al., 2014). We describe these works in the following paragraphs.

Totem (Gharaibeh et al., 2012; Gharaibeh and Elizeu, 2013; Gharaibeh et al., 2013) is a graph computation framework that exploits single-node multicore+GPU heterogeneous systems. Totem follows the Bulk Synchronous Parallel computational model, where graph processing is divided in stages, each one consisting in the following steps: computation, communication, and synchronization. The BSP approach minimizes PCI-Express communication overhead by batching data transfers in the communication step. Graph partitioning is focused on minimizing computation time rather than communication by placing high-degree vertices in the CPU and low-degree vertices in the GPU.

Hong et al. (2011) propose a heterogeneous computing methodology for processing BFS. First, it is presented a hybrid method for GPU that combines a queue-based method (use of local next-level queues and batch insertion of nodes into a global queue), and a read-based method (next-level and current-level queues that are implemented together). The read-based method is used if the frontier has many nodes; otherwise the queue-based method is used. Additionally, it is proposed a queue-based CPU+GPU method, where the GPU is used only if there is an exponential growth in the size of the frontiers. The CPU is initially used, but once GPU execution is initiated, execution never returns to the CPU.

Zou et al., (2013) propose a heterogeneous computing strategy for BFS that combines CPU+GPU. It exploits a hybrid top-down/bottom-up BFS approach proposed by Beamer et al. (2012) and Beamer et al. (2013). In the conventional top-down BFS, each vertex looks for unvisited vertices in its neighborhood; whereas in the bottom-up BFS, each unvisited vertex tries to find any parent in its neighborhood (Beamer et al., 2012). The switching from CPU-only to CPU+GPU mode is driven by the frontier size. For each BFS level, the heterogeneous strategy maps the exploration of small scale vertex frontiers to the CPU using the top-down method, and it maps the exploration of large scale vertex frontier to the CPU+GPU using the bottom-up approach. Frontier workload is distributed among the CPU and GPU according to the memory bandwidth of each architecture.

Banerjee et al. (2013) introduce a graph pruning + CPU+GPU heterogeneous computing approach as a technique to reduce the size of the graph and the execution time of BFS and connected components. The result of the computation on the reduced graph is extended to the original graph. Both the CPU and the GPU work in a synchronous manner to perform the exploration of each BFS frontier. The GPU does a fine-grained partitioning of the graph adjacency list, whereas the CPU does a more coarse-grained execution on the remaining portion using the same algorithm.

Munguia et al. (2012) propose two CPU+GPU heterogeneous schemes for BFS based on the frontier size. The parallelization strategy is decoupled from the underlying hardware by introducing the notion of graph traversal tasks. The first scheme is switched-based. A workload limit is defined to decide when to transfer a task between the GPU and the CPU. For a given task, if the number of vertices to be traversed in the frontier is higher than the limit, the task will exploit the GPU; otherwise it will use the CPU. The second is a cooperative two-phase scheme. In the execution phase, both CPU and GPU work simultaneously on mutually independent task sets, creating two disjoint sets of visited/new frontier vertices. Then, in the communication phase the disjoint sets are communicated to the other architecture.

Sariyuce and Kaya (2013) investigate a heterogeneous CPU+GPU strategy for accelerating the betweenness centrality. The strategy simply treats the GPU as another CPU core, based on the empirical observation that the CPU and the GPU show the same performance when calculating the betweenness centrality. Load is distributed evenly among available CPU cores+GPU. Optimizations for the GPU implementation include: the virtualization of the vertices with high degree (to solve the imbalance problem on scale-free graphs), strided access to adjacency lists (for improved coalescing), removal of the vertices with degree 1 (for graph compression), and graph ordering (for maximizing the number of active threads in a warp and minimize thread divergence overhead).

Finally, there are other works that propose CPU+GPU heterogeneous approaches for solving other graph-related problems, such as a cooperative/partition-based list ranking (where the GPU uses CPU-generated random numbers) (Banerjee and Kothapalli, 2011), connected components (where each architecture finds connected components in their partitions and then the components are combined) (Banerjee and Kothapalli, 2011), and a switched-based graph maximum flow (He and Hong, 2010) where a switching mechanism performs the push operation on the CPU and the re-label operation on the GPU.

Gharaibeh et al. (2012) and Gharaibeh et al. (2013) stress that a graph partitioner should focus on producing partitions that minimize computing time rather than communication time. Taking into account that algorithms like BFS are memory bounded, it is important that partitions are cache-friendly. Cache-friendliness is achieved by Gharaibeh et al. (2012) and Gharaibeh et al. (2013) by placing high-degree vertices in CPU and low-degree vertices in the GPU. Similarly, Nilakant and Yoneki (2014) observe an increased performance when placing low-degree nodes on the GPU and large-degree nodes on the CPU for BFS. In addition, Nilakant and Yoneki (2014) also suggest that homogeneity of the node degrees placed on the GPU might help to minimize GPU's thread divergence.

However, besides the degree of nodes, current works on graph heterogeneous computing do not fully exploit the information encoded in the topology inherent to complex networks to produce novel partitioning schemes for scale-free graphs. How to consider the topological aspects of real-world graphs for the development of efficient graph partitioning algorithms with heterogeneous computing in mind?

THE MAXIMUM GRAPH PROCESSING RATE PROBLEM

The role of the GPU in a CPU + GPU platform is that of relieving the work of the CPU. *Which nodes and edges should be left in the CPU and which nodes and edges should be moved to the GPU?*

The performance of parallel architectures when processing graph problems in benchmarks like the Graph500 is measured in Traversed Edges Per Second (TEPS). TEPS is a measurement of the processing *rate* or *throughput*, stated in terms of both the number of visited edges and the overall time taken to traverse them.

Let $G = (V, E)$ be a graph. Let $TEPS(G)$ be the processing rate achieved when solving a problem (e.g. a BFS traversal) on G. A vertex $\mathcal{K}_\mathcal{H}$-partition is a collection of $\mathcal{K}$ vertex sets $V = \{\mathcal{P}_1, \mathcal{P}_2, ..., \mathcal{P}_\mathcal{K}\}$ such that $\bigcup_i \mathcal{P}_i = V$, $\mathcal{P}_i \cap \mathcal{P}_j = 0$ whenever $i \neq j$, and $TEPS(G)$ is maximized. The vertex $\mathcal{K}_\mathcal{H}$-partition determines a map $\mathcal{W} : V \rightarrow \mathcal{V}$ such that $\forall v \in V : v \in \mathcal{W}(v)$.

The problem of partitioning a graph in order to maximize the performance of a parallel computing platform can be stated as follows.

- **Problem:** The Maximum Graph Processing Rate Problem (MGPRP)
- **Instance:** A graph $G = (V, E)$ of n vertices, and a positive integer $\mathcal{K} \in \mathbb{Z}^+$.
- **Solution:** A vertex $\mathcal{K}_\mathcal{H}$-partition $\mathcal{V} = \{\mathcal{P}_1, \mathcal{P}_2, ..., \mathcal{P}_\mathcal{K}\}$ such that $TEPS(G)$ is maximized.

This work focuses on solving the problem for $\mathcal{K} = 2$ on a CPU + GPU heterogeneous graph computing platform, i.e. the problem of bisecting the set of vertices V to process a graph problem by combining a single CPU and a single GPU. Note that even for $\mathcal{K} = 2$ the search space is large, as there is an exponential number of possible bisections: 2^n.

Solving MGPRP in heterogeneous computing platforms is challenging, since an overall platform performance is not necessarily obtained by simply minimizing the processing time of all the available processors, as in homogeneous computing. Solving MGPRP might require finding a trade-off: reducing the partition processing time on one kind of processor at the expense of increasing the partition processing time on another kind of processor, in order to achieve an overall platform performance improvement.

As it will be shown, not every vertex bisection has the same impact on the performance of a CPU + GPU architecture. The mentioned facts and the size of real-world complex networks make desirable to exploit heuristics guided by topological aspects inherent to complex networks, like their coreness and the centrality of their vertices.

PARTITIONING BY FINDING THE MOST DENSE SUBGRAPH

Graph density is a key factor that affects the suitability of graph partitions to parallel architectures. As a graph becomes denser, its degree distribution tends to be more homogeneous, and the problem becomes more structured.

There is evidence that complex networks are integrated of: (1) a dense partition of well-connected vertices and (2) a comparatively larger, sparse and homogeneous partition of low-degree vertices (Carmi et al., 2007). Finding a bisection that splits the graph into two partitions with different topologies, namely a dense partition and a very sparse partition, is useful to leverage the combined computing power of CPUs and GPUs.

The Maximum Density Subgraph Problem

Let $d(G)$ be the density of a graph G. The search of the densest subgraph can be stated as follows:

- **Problem:** Maximum Density Subgraph Problem (MDSP) (Feige et al., 2001)
- **Instance:** A graph $G = (V, E)$.
- **Solution:** A vertex subset $\mathcal{P}_{dense} = \arg\max_{\mathcal{P} \subseteq V} d(G^{\mathcal{P}})$, where $G^{\mathcal{P}} = G \mid \mathcal{P}$ is the subgraph of G induced by the vertex set $\mathcal{P}$.

When the number of nodes in $\mathcal{P}_{dense}$ is restricted, MDSP is known to be NP-hard (Feige et al., 2001). However, MDSP with no subgraph size restrictions MDSP can be solved in polynomial time (Feige et al., 2001).

The underlying hypothesis in this section is as follows: it is possible to obtain good approximated solutions for MGPRP by producing approximated size-unrestricted solutions for MDSP, with the objective of producing unbalanced partitions (namely, a dense partition and a sparse partition) in an efficient manner, for graph load-balancing between a CPU and a GPU.

KCMax Greedy Unbalanced Bisection

How to locate the vertices that belong to the dense area of a complex network? Vertices at the highest k-cores are located in the network's densest area, the area that roughly maintains the clustering structure of the graph (Gleich and

Seshadhri, 2012). The k-core decomposition represents a useful yet easy to calculate heuristic for deciding which vertices belong to the dense partition and which belong to the sparse one.

The k-core decomposition identifies internal cores and decomposes the networks layer by layer, revealing the structure of the different k-shells from the out-most one to the most internal one. We describe our KCMax algorithm (Garcia-Robledo et al., 2015) that exploits the notion of k-core decomposition to greedily find good approximated solutions for the MDSP.

By repeatedly extracting the highest core of the network, defined as set of vertices having the highest k-shell index, the dense area of the network can be separated from the sparse one. This separation would produce a bisection of the graph that can be exploited for load distribution on CPU + GPU heterogeneous platforms.

Algorithm in Figure 1 lists the KCMax graph bisection algorithm. KCMax starts by calculating the k-shell decomposition to identify the nodes at the highest non-empty k-shell, k^{max}-shell. Then, it appends the vertices at k^{max}-shell to the list of nodes in the dense partition of the graph $\mathcal{P}_{dense}$. The nodes at k^{max}-shell are removed from G, and only the giant component of G is retained for the next iteration. The algorithm repeats this procedure until there are no remaining nodes in G left. The nodes that do not belong

Figure 1. The KCMax unbalanced partitioning heuristic

Input: $G = (V, E)$
Output: $\mathcal{P}_{dense}, \mathcal{P}_{sparse}$
  $\mathcal{P}_{dense} \leftarrow \emptyset$
  $\mathcal{P}_{sparse} \leftarrow \emptyset$
  $G' \leftarrow G$ // $G' = (V', E')$, where $V' = V, E' = E$
  while $|V'| > 0$ **do**
        $S \leftarrow \text{ShellDecomposition}(G)$
        $V_{k^{max}} \leftarrow \text{GetMaxShell}(S)$
        $\mathcal{P}_{dense} \leftarrow \mathcal{P}_{dense} \cup V_{k^{max}}$
        $G' \leftarrow \text{DeleteVertices}(G', V_{k^{max}})$
        $G' \leftarrow \text{GiantComponent}(G')$
  end while
  $\mathcal{P}_{sparse} \leftarrow V'/\mathcal{P}_{dense}$
  return $\mathcal{P}_{sparse}, \mathcal{P}_{dense}$

to $\mathcal{P}_{dense}$ at the end of the process are assigned to the sparse partition $\mathcal{P}_{sparse}$, and the partitions $\mathcal{P}_{dense}$ and $\mathcal{P}_{sparse}$ are returned.

Given the fact that the size of the highest k-shell of a graph is orders of magnitude smaller than the size of the original graph, only the giant component is kept after removing the $k^{\max}$-shell. This step has a two-fold effect. First, it assigns to the sparse partition $\mathcal{P}_{sparse}$ those small components that result from removing the core of the graph, helping the heuristic to focus on the component that is more likely to contain strongly connected nodes. Second, it helps the algorithm to reduce the size of the graph quicker, greatly reducing the number of iterations.

Let ι be the number of iterations of algorithm in Figure 1. In each iteration, a k-core decomposition, two vertex set removals, and a giant component calculation are performed. The k-core decomposition can be calculated in $O(m)$ time. On the other hand, the removal of a vertex set from G can be performed in $O(n + m)$ time. Likewise, the calculation of the giant component can be done in $O(n + m)$ time. Obtaining a subgraph induced by the giant component takes $O(n + m)$, as well. The number of iterations ι depends on the size of the $k^{\max}$ cores. Thus, the time complexity of the KCMax algorithm is bounded by $O(\iota(4m + 3n))$.

The KCMax algorithm can be further accelerated by considering a pre-processing step, that first appends to $\mathcal{P}_{sparse}$ the nodes at the first k-shells and remove $\mathcal{P}_{sparse}$ from G before starting the search for the dense area. This preprocessing step is motivated by the empirical observation that the nodes at the first k-shells are unlikely to belong to the dense partition of the graph as they are very likely to hold a low clustering degree.

PARTITIONING BY A MULTILEVEL APPROACH

The MSDP, introduced in the previous section, is actually equivalent to the problem of finding the induced subgraph with *maximum average degree* (Feige et al., 2001). The degree of vertices actually represents the most basic measure of vertex centrality. *Can the centrality of nodes be exploited for load balance in heterogeneous computing?* To address this research question, this section introduces a computational problem closely related to MSDP: the Maximum Centrality Subgraph Problem (MCSP).

The Maximum Centrality Subgraph Problem

A generalized definition of MCSP in terms of node centrality can be stated as follows:

- **Problem:** Most Central Subgraph Problem (MCSP)
- **Instance:** A graph $G = (V, E)$ and a centrality metric γ.

- **Solution:** A vertex subset $\mathcal{P}_{central} = \arg\max_{\mathcal{P} \subseteq V} \dfrac{\sum_{u \in \mathcal{P}} \Gamma_u}{|\mathcal{P}|}$, where Γ_u is the centrality of vertex u according to the centrality metric γ.

For large graphs, following the node-sorting strategy proposed by Gharaibeh et al. (2013), Gharaibeh and Elizeu (2013) and Nilakant and Yoneki (2014) for MCSP would seem reasonable. However, this would actually involve calculating a centrality metric γ for all nodes first, which can be unfeasible for quadratic-time centrality metrics, such as the betweenness centrality, or even for less expensive metrics when evaluated on large graphs.

Size-bounded graph problems can be tackled by means of *graph coarsening*. Unfortunately, solving MCSP in coarse graphs might not necessarily solve the problem for the original graph. When using coarsening algorithms that combine nodes with very different degrees, like the ones based on our CKE framework (Garcia-Robledo et al., 2016a). Coarse nodes might map to finer nodes with different centralities. This might result in scenarios where, for example, high-centrality coarse nodes map to finer nodes with highly mixed centralities in the finer graphs.

Still, CKE-like graph coarsening can be useful for efficiently obtaining unbalanced partitions while considering the concept of centrality. Even when the centrality of coarse nodes might not directly map to the centrality of the original nodes, it might provide a good-enough approximation useful for creating highly unbalanced partitions in a fraction of the time needed to calculate the centrality of the original nodes.

Bisecting a complex network into highly unbalanced partitions can be useful for identifying the small proportion of nodes and edges that have to be moved to the GPU in order to improve the performance of the CPU, and to ultimately improve the overall heterogeneous computing performance.

The underlying hypothesis in this section is as follows: it is possible to obtain good approximated solutions for MGPRP by considering the centrality of nodes of coarse graphs, with the objective of producing highly unbalanced partitions (namely, a large partition and a small partition) of the original graphs in an efficient manner, for graph load-balancing between a CPU and a GPU.

KCML Multilevel-Like Unbalanced Bisection

We now describe our KCML (K-Core Multi-Level) algorithm (Garcia-Robledo et al., 2016b) for complex network bisection. KCML is a multilevel-like heuristic that exploits the k-core decomposition of complex networks to obtain coarse graphs, with the objective of enabling the efficient calculation of centrality metrics to produce unbalanced partitions that suit different parallel hardware architectures.

A k-core-based graph coarsening strategy, like the CKE framework previously introduced in this work, can be embedded into a multilevel graph partitioning framework. However, unlike the CKE framework which contracts one edge at a time, the multilevel processing of large graphs needs the contraction of multiple edges to produce a low number of coarse graphs in less iterations (Abou-Rjeili and Karypis, 2006).

Our multilevel partitioning strategy which integrates a k-core-based graph coarsening strategy in the coarsening phase. The idea is to involve the use of a hierarchy of representative graphs across the whole multilevel process (algorithm in Figure 2):

1. **Coarsening Phase:** The original graph G is coarsened into a series of successively coarser graphs $G'_1, ..., G'_h$ by means of *maximal matchings*.

Figure 2. The KCML unbalanced partitioning algorithm

$$\textbf{Input: } G = (V, E), \gamma, \delta, n_{max}$$
$$\textbf{Output: } \mathcal{P}_{small}, \mathcal{P}_{large}$$
$$G', \mathcal{X} \leftarrow \text{CoarseGraph}(G, n_{max})$$
$$U \leftarrow \text{SortNodesByCentralityDecremental}(G', \gamma)$$
$$\mathcal{P}_{large} \leftarrow \emptyset$$
$$\mathcal{P}'_{central} \leftarrow \text{GetSlice}(U, \delta)$$
$$\textbf{for } u \in \mathcal{P}'_{central} \textbf{ do}$$
$$\qquad \mathcal{P}_{large} \leftarrow \mathcal{P}_{large} \cup \text{ProjectVertex}(u, \mathcal{X}, V)$$
$$\textbf{end for}$$
$$\mathcal{P}_{small} \leftarrow V / \mathcal{P}_{large}$$
$$\textbf{return } \mathcal{P}_{small}, \mathcal{P}_{large}$$

The coarsening phase consists on (1) matching the nodes at the lowest k-shell with their neighbors at the farther k-shell, (2) contracting the matched nodes, and (3) repeat the process until reaching a specific percentage of nodes in the coarse graph (algorithm in Figure 3).

2. **Partitioning Phase:** The nodes of the coarsest graph G'_{h-1} are sorted by its centrality in descending order (by using a centrality metric γ), and then partitioned into two balanced partitions.

3. **Uncoarsening and Refinement Phase:** The partitioning of G'_{h-1} is directly projected to G'_{h-2}; and the process is repeated and terminated at G, i.e. the uncoarsening stage consists only of assigning the same part number for a fine vertex as the one assigned to its associated coarse vertex (algorithm in Figure 4).

Figure 3. The KCML unbalanced partitioning algorithm (coarsening)

Input: $G = (V, E), n_{max}$
Output: $G', \mathcal{X}$ // G' is the coarse graph, $\mathcal{X}$ is the coarse-to-fine vertex mapping
$\quad S \leftarrow \text{ShellDecomposition}(G)$
$\quad G' \leftarrow G$ // $G' = (V', E')$, where $V' = V, E' = E$
$\quad \mathcal{X} \leftarrow \emptyset$
$\quad$ **while** $|V'| > n_{max}$ **do**
$\quad\quad \mathcal{M} \leftarrow \emptyset$
$\quad\quad matched \leftarrow \emptyset$
$\quad\quad V^{\min} \leftarrow \text{GetNodesAtShell}(G', S, minS)$
$\quad\quad$ **for** $u \in \{x | x \in V^{\min} \land x \notin matched\}$ **do**
$\quad\quad\quad N_u \leftarrow \{x | \{u, x\} \in E' \land x \notin matched\}$
$\quad\quad\quad$ **if** $N_u \neq \emptyset$ **then**
$\quad\quad\quad\quad v \leftarrow \text{SelectNeighbor}(u, G, S)$
$\quad\quad\quad\quad \mathcal{M} \leftarrow \mathcal{M} \cup \{\{u, v\}\}$
$\quad\quad\quad\quad matched \leftarrow matched \cup \{u\} \cup \{v\}$
$\quad\quad\quad$ **end if**
$\quad\quad$ **end for**
$\quad\quad$ **for** $u \in \{x | x \in V' \land x \notin matched\}$ **do**
$\quad\quad\quad \mathcal{M} \leftarrow \mathcal{M} \cup \{\{u, u\}\}$
$\quad\quad$ **end for**
$\quad\quad$ **for** $\{u, v\} \in \mathcal{M}$ **do**
$\quad\quad\quad G', w \leftarrow \text{ContractEdge}(G', u, v)$
$\quad\quad\quad \mathcal{X}_w \leftarrow \{u, v\}$
$\quad\quad\quad S_w \leftarrow \min S_u, S_v$
$\quad\quad$ **end for**
$\quad$ **end while**
$\quad$ **return** $G', \mathcal{X}$

Figure 4. The KCML unbalanced partitioning algorithm (uncoarsening)

Input: $w, \mathcal{X}, V$
Output: V_w // The set of vertices in the original V mapped to w in the coarse
   graph
   if $w \in V$ **then**
      return $\{w\}$
   else
      $\{u, v\} \leftarrow \mathcal{X}_w$
      return ProjectVertex(u) $\cup$ ProjectVertex(v)
   end if

Core-Based Maximal Matching Coarsening

The coarsening phase in KCML is based on the finding of a maximal matching and the contraction of the edges participating in the matching to get a coarser version of the graph. A *matching* $\mathcal{M}$ is a set of edges without common vertices. A *maximal matching* is a matching with the following property: if an edge not in the matching is added, it would not be a matching anymore.

The presence of hubs in complex networks negatively impacts the quality of partitions of multilevel algorithms. In particular, the matching process is inefficient when applied over high degree nodes, causing the memory requirements for the storage of the hierarchy of coarse graphs to increment (Abou-Rjeili and Karypis, 2006, Zhang et al., 2011). This evidences the need for new methods that integrate information about the topology of a scale-free graph (e.g. its degree distribution and its degree-degree correlation) to improve the quality of partitions of multilevel approaches. As stated by Abou-Rjeili and Karypis (2006): "coarsening methods need to be developed that do not exhibit the limitations of current matching-based approaches."

Recall that N_u denotes the nearest neighbors of vertex u. Consider the following function definitions:

- $S \leftarrow$ ShellDecomposition(G): given G, returns the k-shell decomposition sequence S, where S_u denotes the k-shell index of vertex u

- $\mathcal{S}_k \leftarrow$ GetNodesAtShell(G, S, k): given G and the k-shell decomposition sequence S, it returns $\mathcal{S}_k = \{u \mid u \in V \wedge S_u = k\}$, i.e. the nodes with shell index k.

- $u \leftarrow$ SelectNeighbor(v, G, S): given v, G and S, returns the neighbor $u \in N_v$ of v at the farther k-shell, so that $u \leftarrow \max \arg_{u \in N_v} \{\mid S_v - S_u \mid\}$.

- $G', S' \leftarrow \text{ContractEdge}(\{u, v\}, G, S)$: given G, returns a new simple graph G' with $|V| - 1$ vertices, where the edge $\{u, v\} \in E$ has been contracted. Given S, it also returns the updated S' set, with the k-shell index and the centrality of the new combined vertex v_{new}. Let w be the vertex $w = \max \arg_{w \in \{u,v\}} \{S_w\}$, i.e. the vertex with the largest k-shell index between u and v. v_{new} acquires the k-shell index of w, so that $S'_{v_{new}} = S_w$.

The coarsening phase in KCML consists on finding a maximal matching $\mathcal{M}$ by matching edges connecting vertices located at *distant* k-cores. Algorithm in Figure 3 shows the graph coarsening process of the KCML heuristic.

The algorithm starts by calculating the k-core decomposition and generating S by using ShellDecomposition(). Then, for each unmatched node u in the graph, it uses SelectNeighbor() to select the unmatched neighbor in $v \in N_u$ located at the most distant k-shell. Next, it adds the match $\{u, v\}$ to the matching set $\mathcal{M}$. The algorithm then matches each node u that was not matched in the previous stage with itself, adding the match $\{u, u\}$ to $\mathcal{M}$.

In the last stage, the algorithm uses ContractEdge() to contract the edges represented by the matchings in $\mathcal{M}$ to create a coarser graph G'. Each matching $\{u, v\}$ is replaced by a new vertex w in the coarse graph. $\mathcal{X}_w$ keeps track of the original vertices u, v in the finer graph that originated w.

This coarsening process is repeated until the coarse graph has less vertices than n_{max}. Algorithm in Figure 3 returns the coarse graph G' and a vertex mapping $\mathcal{X}$.

The proposed coarsening algorithm is inspired on both the implementation of the coarsening algorithms in the METIS package (Karypis and Kumar, 1998) and the CKE framework. Previously, we found that contracting edges joining vertices at distant k-shells is useful for getting *representative* coarse graphs that preserve complex network metrics like the average degree and the average path length. The motivation of selecting the vertices at the lowest k-shell for the matchings is that a large proportion of nodes are located in lower k-cores in complex networks. This increases the chances of getting a large number of matchings and reduces the graph faster.

ContractEdge() makes sure that the new vertex *inherits* the k-shell index and the centrality of one of the contracting vertices, so there is no need to calculate the decomposition and the centrality again. The inheritance of the k-shell index also guarantees that there will be always at least a non-empty k-shell.

The two most expensive operations in the KCML algorithm are the k-core decomposition, which takes $O(m)$, and the centrality metric on the coarse graph. Let h be the number of coarse levels needed to reach n_{max} nodes. Let where n_i and m_i be the number of nodes and links of G_i, the graph at the ith level. The coarsening process at the ith level takes $O(m_i + n_i)$, In this setting, the KCML algorithm runs in $O(m + \sum_{i=1}^{h}(m_i + n_i)) + O(\gamma)$ time, where $O(\gamma)$ is the time of the centrality metric γ on the coarsest graph. $O(\gamma)$ can be as little as $O(n_h)$ for metrics like the degree centrality. Unlike the KCMax heuristic, KCML involves only a single k-core decomposition calculation, and no connected components computation. Time for the centrality metric is considerably reduced for a sufficiently low n_{max}, as it is calculated once on the coarsest graph, not the original one.

Centrality-Based Balanced Graph Bisection

Algorithm in Figure 2 contains the main KCML heuristic, and integrates Algorithms in Figures 3 and 4. It first calculates a coarse version of G, and then divides the coarse graph based on the coarse node centralities. The partitioning of the coarse graph is then projected to the original graph.

Consider the following function definitions:

- $G', \mathcal{X} \leftarrow \text{CoarseGraph}(G, n_{max})$: Given a graph G and n_{max}, returns a coarse graph with at most $n_{max} - 1$ nodes (algorithm in Figure 3).
- $U \leftarrow \text{SortNodesByCentralityDescremental}(G, \gamma)$: Given G, $n = |V(G)|$ and a vertex centrality algorithm γ, returns the n-tuple $U = (u_1, u_2, ..., u_n)$, where u_1 is the vertex with highest centrality, u_2 is the vertex with second highest centrality, and u_n is the vertex with the lowest centrality.
- $U_\delta \leftarrow \text{GetSlice}(U, \delta)$: Given $\delta \in [0,1]$ and U, it returns $U_\delta = \{u_i \mid u_i \in U \wedge i \leq \lfloor \delta |U| \rfloor \}$, i.e. the set of the first $\lfloor \delta n \rfloor$ elements of U.

- $\mathcal{P} \leftarrow \text{ProjectVertex}(u, \mathcal{X}, V)$: Given a vertex $u \in V(G')$ in a coarse graph G' of a graph G, a vertex mapping $\mathcal{X}$ and the set vertices of the original graph V, it returns the vertices $\mathcal{P} \subseteq V$ mapped to the coarse vertex u (algorithm in Figure 4).

Main KCML algorithm in Figure 2 starts by finding a coarse version of G, G', by using CoarseGraph(). Then, it calculates the centrality Γ_u of the nodes in the coarse graph G' and gets $\mathcal{P}'_{central} \subseteq V'$ corresponding to the δ percentage of vertices with the highest centrality, by using GetSlice(). Then, for each of the coarse vertices in $\mathcal{P}'_{central}$, the algorithm adds to $\mathcal{P}_{large}$, the largest partition of the original graph, the projection of the coarse nodes in $V(G')$, according to the map set $\mathcal{X}$ calculated in the coarsening phase. Finally, the algorithm returns as the largest partition of G the set $\mathcal{P}_{large}$ and it returns the complement of $\mathcal{P}_{large}$ as the smallest partition.

The time for executing the centrality metric γ is reduced given that γ is calculated on the coarse and smaller graph G' and not on the original graph G. The size of G' can be tuned by manipulating n_{new}. The calculation of compute-intensive centrality metrics, like the betweenness or the closeness centralities can be accelerated with the proposed multilevel-like approach, even when the graphs are reduced to only a half or a third of the original graph size.

CORE-BASED BISECTION OF COMPLEX NETWORKS

To study the behavior of both KCMax and KCML, we partitioned the real-world and R-MAT (Chakrabarti et al., 2004) graphs listed in Table 1. In this work we used the undirected and simplified (no loops or parallel edges) versions of the giant component of the original graphs, which account for the majority of the original nodes and edges. Considering only the simplified and undirected giant components will allow us to perform single-source BFS traversals on connected graphs in a heterogeneous computing platform, producing more uniform performance measurements regardless of the sources selected to perform the traversals. The R-MAT model was used to generate some graph instances since it is the basis for the Graph500 graph generator that produces complex network-like synthetic networks.

Table 1. Experimented dataset of real-world and synthetic complex networks; n = number of nodes, m = number of edges

Graph	Type		n	m
as-skitter	Internet	Real-world	1,694,616	11,094,209
cit-Patents	Citation	Real-world	3,764,117	16,511,740
soc-LiveJournal1	Social	Real-world	4,843,953	42,845,684
rmat-s19f16	R-MAT	Synthetic	199,795	7,249,166
rmat-s20f16	R-MAT	Synthetic	388,237	14,845,842
rmat-s21f16	R-MAT	Synthetic	754,655	30,291,808
rmat-s22f16	R-MAT	Synthetic	1,465,467	61,606,418
rmat-s23f16	R-MAT	Synthetic	2,844,024	124,943,700

Table 2 presents the properties of the sparse and dense partitions obtained by running the KCMax algorithm on the large real-world and R-MAT networks listed in Table 1. Note that, although the density of the induced subgraphs of both the sparse and the dense partitions is low, the dense partition is up to two

Table 2. Properties of the sparse and dense partitions produced by the KCMax graph bisection algorithm on a variety of large real-world complex networks. In the table: n = nodes, $\sum k_i$ = sum of the degrees of the vertices in the partition, d = density of the subgraph induced by the partition, and c = number of components in the subgraph induced by the partition. The value $\sum k_i$ allows to calculate the proportion of edges in the partition, where the number of edges in the partition $\approx (\sum k_i) / 2$

Graph	Property	Sparse Partition	Dense Partition
as-skitter	n	1,565,489 (92.38%)	129,127 (7.62%)
	$\sum k_i$	11,041,869 (49.76%)	11,146,549 (50.24%)
	d (c)	2.17×10^{-6} (242,272)	3.2×10^{-4} (2)
soc-LiveJournal1	n	4,687,387 (96.77%)	156,566 (3.23%)
	$\sum k_i$	59,300,536 (69.20%)	26,390,832 (30.80%)
	d (c)	2.351×10^{-6} (182,963)	7.6×10^{-4} (12)

continued on following page

Table 2. Continued

Graph	Property	Sparse Partition	Dense Partition
cit-Patents	n	3,641,824 (96.75%)	122,293 (3.25%)
	$\sum k_i$	28,351,467 (85.85%)	4,672,013 (14.15%)
	$d(c)$	2.007×10^{-6} (18,396)	1.9×10^{-4} (12)
rmat-s19f16	n	187,182 (93.69%)	12,613 (6.31%)
	$\sum k_i$	4,194,109 (28.93%)	10,304,223 (71.07%)
	$d(c)$	2.85×10^{-5} (54,717)	4.4×10^{-2} (1)
rmat-s20f16	n	346,454 (89.24%)	41,783 (10.76%)
	$\sum k_i$	5,405,672 (18.21%)	24,286,012 (81.79%)
	$d(c)$	6.663×10^{-6} (146,591)	1.1×10^{-2} (1)
rmat-s21f16	n	694,969 (92.09%)	59,686 (7.91%)
	$\sum k_i$	12,738,505 (21.03%)	47,845,111 (78.97%)
	$d(c)$	4.608×10^{-6} (266,040)	1.04×10^{-2} (1)
rmat-s22f16	n	1,384,025 (94.44%)	81,442 (5.56%)
	$\sum k_i$	30,509,065 (24.76%)	92,703,771 (75.24%)
	$d(c)$	3.375×10^{-6} (470,963)	1.03×10^{-2} (1)
rmat-s23f16	n	2,735,042 (96.17%)	108,982 (3.83%)
	$\sum k_i$	71,988,375 (28.81%)	177,899,025 (71.19%)
	$d(c)$	2.436×10^{-6} (831,778)	1.04×10^{-2} (1)

orders of magnitude denser than the sparse one in real-world complex networks, and up to four times denser in R-MAT networks. Also, note that while the sparse partitions are composed of thousands of connected components, the dense partitions are composed of one, two or at most a dozen of connected components.

Also, note how in the experimented synthetic R-MAT graphs, and in real-world graphs like as-skitter and soc-LiveJournal1, a small proportion of the nodes are connected by a high proportion of edges in the dense partition. For example, in the as-skitter graph 7.62% of the nodes account for 50.24% of the edges, while in soc-LiveJournal1 the 3.23% of the nodes account for 30.8% of edges. Note that in the as-skitter, a *natural* balance was found between the sparse and the dense regions in the number of edges.

Table 3 presents the properties of the sparse and dense partitions obtained by running the KCML algorithm on the large real-world and R-MAT synthetic networks listed in Table 1. For each complex network, Table 3 shows the partitioning data when using different centrality metrics for bisecting the coarse graphs: eigenvector centrality (as-skitter); node degree (cit-Patents and rmat-s21f16); neighbor degree centrality (rmat-s19f16); and the k-shell index (soc-LiveJournal1, rmat-s20f16, rmat-s22f16 and rmat-s23f16).

Table 3. Properties of the sparse and dense partitions produced by the KCML graph bisection algorithm on a variety of large real-world complex networks. In the table: n = nodes, $\sum k_i$ = sum of the degrees of the vertices in the partition, d = density of the subgraph induced by the partition, and c = number of components in the subgraph induced by the partition. The value $\sum k_i$ allows to calculate the proportion of edges in the partition, where the number of edges in the partition $\approx (\sum k_i)\,/\,2$

Graph	Property	Smaller Partition	Larger Partition
as-skitter	n	243,430 (14.36%)	1,451,186 (85.64%)
	$\sum k_i$	609,823 (2.75%)	21,578,595 (97.25%)
	$d\ (c)$	2×10^{-6} (186,829)	1×10^{-5} (1)
soc-LiveJournal1	n	600,327 (12.39%)	4,243,626 (87.61%)
	$\sum k_i$	1,513,265 (1.77%)	84,178,103 (98.23%)
	$d\ (c)$	1×10^{-6} (457,441)	5×10^{-6} (1)
cit-Patents	n	554,934 (14.74%)	3,209,183 (85.26%)
	$\sum k_i$	1,374,457 (4.16%)	31,649,023 (95.84%)
	$d\ (c)$	$< 1 \times 10^{-6}$ (504,664)	3×10^{-6} (132)

continued on following page

Table 3. Continued

Graph	Property	Smaller Partition	Larger Partition
rmat-s19f16	n	70,148 (35.11%)	129,647 (64.89%)
	$\sum k_i$	2,101,338 (14.49%)	12,396,994 (85.51%)
	d (c)	6.3×10^{-5} (19,841)	6.31×10^{-4} (198)
rmat-s20f16	n	51,736 (13.33%)	336,501 (86.67%)
	$\sum k_i$	96,814 (0.33%)	29,594,870 (99.67%)
	d (c)	$< 1 \times 10^{-6}$ (51,513)	2.61×10^{-4} (1)
rmat-s21f16	n	102,686 (13.61%)	651,969 (86.39%)
	$\sum k_i$	183,823 (0.30%)	60,399,793 (99.70%)
	d (c)	$< 1 \times 10^{-6}$ (102,506)	1.42×10^{-4} (1)
rmat-s22f16	n	208,380 (14.22%)	1,257,087 (85.78%)
	$\sum k_i$	365,499 (0.30%)	122,847,337 (99.70%)
	d (c)	$< 1 \times 10^{-6}$ (207,621)	7.8×10^{-5} (1)
rmat-s23f16	n	415,246 (14.60%)	2428,778 (85.40%)
	$\sum k_i$	698,069 (0.28%)	249,189,331 (99.72%)
	d (c)	$< 1 \times 10^{-6}$ (413,741)	4.2×10^{-5} (1)

KCML tends to assign a large number of nodes (in addition to a large number of edges) to the large partitions. The large partitions showed a less number of components than the smaller partitions. In fact, the number of nodes in the small partitions was comparable to the number of components in these partitions, suggesting that the small partitions were mostly integrated of low-degree nodes that appear as isolated when considering the induced subgraphs.

Note that KCML partitions obtained with the node degree (cit-Patents and rmat-s21f16) had very different topology when compared to the corresponding

KCMax partitions, showing a lower density and a higher number of nodes. As stated before, central subgraphs in the coarse graphs are not necessarily the same than the central subgraphs of the original graphs.

Yet, offloading the identified larger partitions to the GPU and leaving selected nodes and edges in the CPU showed to be advantageous for enhancing the heterogeneous performance, as it will be further developed in the next section.

EXPERIMENTS ON HETEROGENEOUS COMPUTING PLATFORM

This section presents a study on the performance of the Totem CPU + GPU BSP graph computing platform when executing SS-BFS's by considering different graph partitioning strategies for load balancing, including KCMax and KCML, on both synthetic R-MAT and real-world complex networks.

Experimentation Setup

Experiments consisted in accelerating a recurrent kernel in complex network measurement, SS-BFS, on the Totem platform (Gharaibeh et al., 2013). Totem implements a heterogeneous version of the level-sync visitor SS-BFS algorithm reported by Hong et al. (2011), which is suitable for processing low-diameter graphs (Gharaibeh et al., 2013).

Experiments were executed on the Xiuhcoatl Hybrid Supercomputer, by combining an Intel Xeon Processor X5675 CPU and an NVIDIA Tesla C2050/2070 GPU. Totem was run on the various complex networks listed in Table 1. For each graph, 64 SS-BFS runs were performed starting from random vertices. CPU experiments were single-core, GPU experiments were single-GPU, and hybrid experiments combined 1 CPU core + 1 GPU.

In each SS-BFS run, the following graph bisection algorithms for distributing nodes between the CPU and the GPU were compared (Table 4): RANDOM bisection, TOTEM-HIGH bisection, TOTEM-LOW bisection, KCMAX bisection, inverse KCMAX bisection (KCMAX-INV), KCML bisection (KCML-γ), and inverse KCML bisection (KCML-γ-INV), where γ is the used centrality algorithm. RANDOM bisection divides the vertex set randomly into two balanced partitions.

Table 4. Experimented graph partitioning algorithms (Proc. = Processor)

Partitioning	CPU	GPU	Considered Topology Metrics
RANDOM	Random	Random	N/A
TOTEM-HIGH	High degree nodes	Low degree nodes	Degree
TOTEM-LOW	Low degree nodes	High degree nodes	Degree
KCMAX	Dense partition	Sparse partition	k-shells
KCMAX-INV	Sparse partition	Dense partition	k-shells
KCML-DEG	Smaller partition	Larger partition	k-shells, degree
KCML-DEG-INV	Larger partition	Smaller partition	k-shells, degree
KCML-NEI	Smaller partition	Larger partition	k-shells, neighbor degree
KCML-NEI-INV	Larger partition	Smaller partition	k-shells, neighbor degree
KCML-KSH	Smaller partition	Larger partition	k-shells
KCML-KSH-INV	Larger partition	Smaller partition	k-shells
KCML-EIG	Smaller partition	Larger partition	k-shells, eigenvector centrality
KCML-EIG-INV	Larger partition	Smaller partition	k-shells, eigenvector centrality

TOTEM-HIGH and TOTEM-LOW bisection algorithms, proposed by Gharaibeh et al. (2013), are based on the node degree. In TOTEM-HIGH, the high-degree vertices are assigned to the CPU until 50% of the edges and their corresponding vertices are placed on the host. The remaining vertices and their edges are placed on the GPU. For TOTEM-LOW, the low-degree vertices are assigned to the CPU until it holds 50% of the edges. 50% is the default value in the Totem benchmark application.

KCMAX algorithms assign the nodes corresponding to the dense partition to the CPU and the nodes of the sparse partition to the GPU, while the KCMAX-INV partitionings assign the partitions in the opposite order. KCML-γ algorithms assign the nodes corresponding to the smaller partition to the CPU and the nodes of the larger partition to the GPU, while the KCML-γ-INV partitionings assign the partitions in the opposite order.

For KCML-γ, different node centrality algorithms were experimented: node degree (KCML-DEG/KCML-DEG-INV), average neighbor degree (KCML-NEI/KCML-NEI-INV), k-shell index (KCML-KSH/KCML-KSH-

INV), and eigenvector centrality (KCML-EIG/KCML-EIG-INV). Value δ for KCML-γ and KCML-γ-INV algorithms was set to 0.5 (50%) to match the value used for the share of edges assigned to the CPU in TOTEM-HIGH/ TOTEM-LOW. Graphs were coarsened to 30% of nodes for the KCML partitionings.

Raw processing rates are measured in millions of TEPS (MTEPS) in Figure 5. The corresponding MTEPS for BFS is calculated by dividing the sum of the degrees of the visited vertices by the execution time. Figures 6 and 7 compare the performance of different partitionings to the performance of TOTEM-HIGH and the GPU alone, respectively.

In order to perform these comparisons, the MTEPS relative change percentages with respect to TOTEM-HIGH and the GPU alone were calculated. For values greater than the reference value, the relative change is a positive number and for values that are smaller, the relative change is negative.

Therefore, positive relative change percentages denote an enhancement in performance when compared to either TOTEM-HIGH or the GPU alone, whereas negative relative change percentages denote a relative detriment in performance.

Impact of the Bisections on Performance

Figure 5 shows the raw performance observed with the various partitioning algorithms. As noted by Gharaibeh et al. (2012) and Gharaibeh et al. (2013), and as confirmed in this work, the characteristics of the graph partitions have an important impact in the platform performance. Leaving the vertices with the highest degree on the CPU and placing the nodes with the lowest degree on the GPU proved to be the best approach for TOTEM partitionings.

However, placing the dense partitions generated by KCMAX on the CPU produced higher throughputs than TOTEM-HIGH on the three experimented real-world graph instances, while placing the sparser KCMAX-INV partitions on the CPU produced higher throughputs than TOTEM-HIGH on 4 out of 5 synthetic graphs. Furthermore, offloading the larger partitions generated by KCML to the GPU produced the highest throughputs for all experimented networks.

Can a heterogeneous computing platform be benefited by a partitioning strategy that exploits the structure (coreness and density) of the network? Yes. The KCML partitionings produced the best CPU + GPU hybrid platform performance for all real-world complex networks.

Figure 5. Performance (MTEPS) of different partitioning algorithms on complex and R-MAT networks

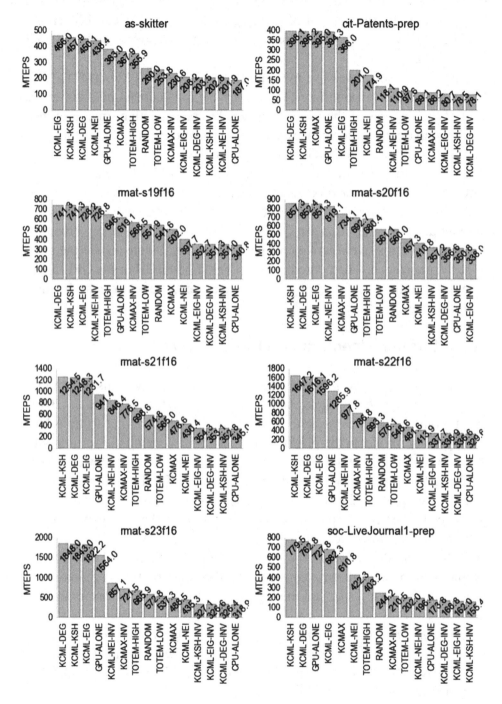

Figure 6 shows the MTEPS relative change percentage between the TOTEM-HIGH partitioning and the other partitioning algorithms.

On real-world complex networks, when compared to TOTEM-HIGH, KCMAX partitionings performance enhancement on the three graphs: around 3% on as-skitter, 96% on cit-Patents-prep, and 51% on soc-LiveJournal1-prep. On synthetic R-MAT networks, when compared to TOTEM-HIGH, KCMAX-INV partitionings produced a performance enhancement on 4 out of 5 graphs: around 7% on rmat-s20f16, 11% on rmat-s21f16, 13% on rmat-s22f16, and 8% on rmat-s23f16.

On real-world complex networks, when compared to TOTEM-HIGH, KCML partitionings produced a performance increase on all graphs: up to around 30% on as-skitter, 98% on cit-Patents, and 93% on soc-LiveJournal1-prep. On synthetic R-MAT networks, when compared to TOTEM-HIGH, KCML partitionings produced a performance enhancement on all graphs: up to around 14% on rmat-s19f16, 26% on rmat-s20f16, 79% on rmat-s21f16, 137% on rmat-s22f16, and 177% on rmat-s23f16.

The CPU represented the bottleneck for all graph instances. As partition algorithms offloaded more edges to the GPU, the CPU showed a remarkable increase of performance. However, partitionings that produced the best hybrid performance on both real-world and synthetic networks were those that not only offloaded the largest share of edges to the GPU, but also found the right set of nodes and edges to move to the GPU.

Homogeneous vs. Heterogeneous

Is it beneficial to partition the graph and process it in parallel on both the CPU and the GPU instead of processing it on a single hardware architecture only? Yes. Figure 7 shows the MTEPS relative change percentage between the GPU alone and the hybrid approach with different partitioning algorithms. Positive relative changes represent performance enhancements whereas negative relative changes represent the opposite.

When using the KCML partitionings, Figure 7 shows that the TOTEM partitioning approaches were unable to outperform the GPU alone in any graph instance. In contrast, KCMAX and the KCMAX-INV partitionings allowed the hybrid approach to outperform the GPU alone on the cit-Patents-prep (0.2%) and the rmat-s20f16 (6%) networks, respectively. Furthermore, the KCML partitionings enabled the hybrid approach to outperform the GPU

Figure 6. Relative change percentage between the performance (MTEPS) of TOTEM-HIGH and different partitioning algorithms on complex and R-MAT networks

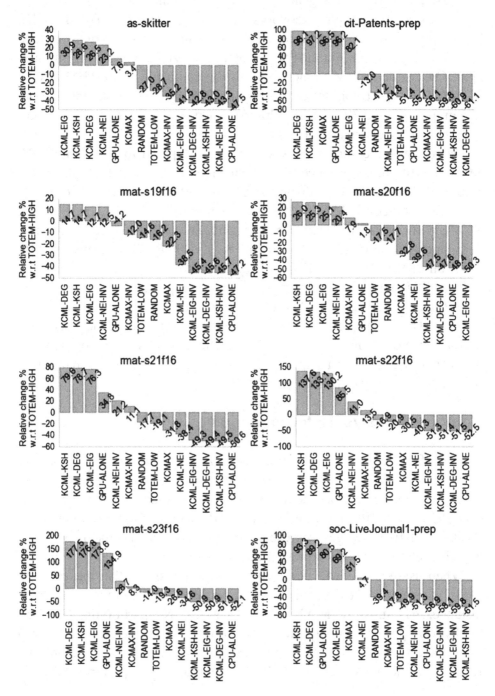

Figure 7. Relative change percentage between the performance (MTEPS) of the GPU alone and the hybrid approach with different partitioning algorithms on complex and R-MAT networks

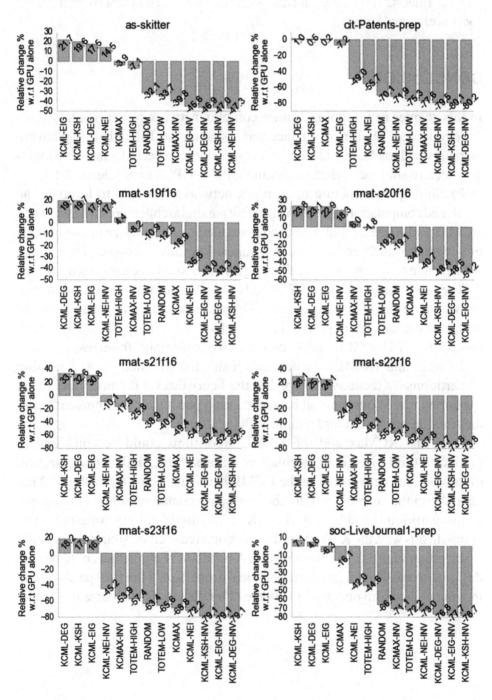

alone in all graphs with performance enhancements of up to around 21% on as-skitter, 1% on cit-Patents, 19% on rmat-s19f16, 23% on rmat-s20f16, 33% on rmat-s21f16, 28% on rmat-s22f16, 18% on rmat-23f16, and 7% on soc-LiveJournal1-prep.

CONCLUSION

In this chapter new topology-aware complex network bisection algorithms were proposed. Their performance was tested on the Totem hybrid platform on real-world loads. In addition, it was shown the expected gain over single-architecture solutions when exploiting CPU + GPUs to accelerate BFS.

Exploiting the structure of complex networks can help to leverage the combined computational power of different parallel architectures. The proposed KCMax and KCML graph bisection heuristics, that capitalize on the notions of subgraph search and k-core decomposition, increased the performance of the Totem platform when accelerating SS-BFS's on large complex networks.

The benefits of combining CPUs and GPUs depend on the specific complex network type and instance. An overall improvement over single architecture performance can be observed in general on large R-MAT graphs when combining CPU + GPU and k-core-based partitioning strategies.

KCMax and KCML can be easily extended to calculate any number of partitions by recursively applying the heuristics on the bisection, or by exploiting more conventional balanced graph partition algorithms for graph distribution on, for example, multi-GPU platforms.

Also, the KCMax and the KCML algorithms could be combined to produce a third bisection algorithm as follows. First, find a coarse version of the complex network, as in the KCML heuristic. Then, apply the KCMax heuristic in the coarse graph to obtain a dense coarse partition and a sparse coarse partition. Finally, project the KCMax bisection to the original set of nodes. In this way, the KCMax would work on a reduced version of the original graph rather than the original network. A refinement algorithm could be also designed to maximize specific topological properties of the final partitions by moving nodes from one partition to the other during the uncoarsening stage.

REFERENCES

Abou-Rjeili, A., & Karypis, G. (2006). Multilevel Algorithms for Partitioning Power-Law Graphs. *Proceedings of the 20th IEEE International Parallel & Distributed Processing Symposium (IPDPS'06)*, 124–124.

Banerjee, D., Sharma, S., & Kothapalli, K. (2013). Work Efficient Parallel Algorithms for Large Graph Exploration. *Proceedings of the 20th Annual International Conference on High Performance Computing (HiPC'13)*, 433–442. doi:10.1109/HiPC.2013.6799125

Banerjee, D. S., & Kothapalli, K. (2011). Hybrid Algorithms for List Ranking and Graph Connected Components. *Proceedings of the 18th International Conference on High Performance Computing (HiPC'11)*, 1-10. doi:10.1109/HiPC.2011.6152655

Beamer, S., Asanovic, K., & Patterson, D. (2012). Direction-Optimizing Breadth-First Search. *Proceedings of the 2012 International Conference on High Performance Computing, Networking, Storage and Analysis (SC'12)*, 1–10.

Beamer, S., Buluc, A., Asanovi, K., & Patterson, D. (2013). *Distributed Memory Breadth-First Search Revisited: Enabling Bottom-Up Search.* Academic Press.

Carmi, S., Havlin, S., Kirkpatrick, S., Shavitt, Y., & Shir, E. (2007). A Model of Internet Topology Using K-Shell Decomposition. *Proceedings of the National Academy of Sciences of the United States of America*, 104(27), 11150–11154. doi:10.1073/pnas.0701175104 PMID:17586683

Chakrabarti, D., Zhan, Y., & Faloutsos, C. (2004). R-Mat: A Recursive Model for Graph Mining. *Proceedings of the 2004 SIAM Annual Meeting*, 442–446. doi:10.1137/1.9781611972740.43

Feige, U., Peleg, D., & Kortsarz, G. (2001). The Dense K-Subgraph Problem. *Algorithmica*, 29(3), 410–421. doi:10.1007/s004530010050

Gao, T., Lu, Y., Zhang, B., & Suo, G. (2014). Using the Intel Many Integrated Core to Accelerate Graph Traversal. *International Journal of High Performance Computing Applications*, 28(3), 255–266. doi:10.1177/1094342014524240

Garcia-Robledo, A., Diaz-Perez, A., & Morales-Luna, G. (2015). Exploring the Feasibility of Heterogeneous Computing of Complex Networks for Big Data Analysis. In *Emerging Technologies for a Smarter World (CEWIT), 2015 12th International Conference & Expo On*, (pp. 1–6). IEEE. doi:10.1109/CEWIT.2015.7338160

Garcia-Robledo, A., Diaz-Perez, A., & Morales-Luna, G. (2016a). Characterization and Coarsening of Autonomous System Networks: Measuring and Simplifying the Internet. In Advanced Methods for Complex Network Analysis, (pp. 148–179). IGI Global.

Garcia-Robledo, A., Diaz-Perez, A., & Morales-Luna, G. (2016b). Partitioning of Complex Networks for Heterogeneous Computing: A Methodological Approach. In *Networking, Sensing, and Control (ICNSC), 2016 IEEE 13th International Conference On*, (pp. 1–6). IEEE. doi:10.1109/ICNSC.2016.7479015

Gharaibeh, A., Costa, L., Elizeu, S., & Ripeanu, M. (2013). On Graphs, GPUs, and Blind Dating: A Workload to Processor Matchmaking Quest. *Proceedings of the 27th IEEE International Symposium on Parallel & Distributed Processing (IPDPS'13)*, 851–862. doi:10.1109/IPDPS.2013.37

Gharaibeh, A., & Elizeu, S. (2013). *Efficient Large-Scale Graph Processing on Hybrid CPU and GPU Systems.* arXiv:13123018 [csDC]

Gharaibeh, A., Lauro, C., Elizeu, S., & Matei, R. (2012). A Yoke of Oxen and a Thousand Chickens for Heavy Lifting Graph Processing. *Proceedings of the 21st International Conference on Parallel Architectures and Compilation Techniques (PACT'12)*, 345–354. doi:10.1145/2370816.2370866

Gleich, D., & Seshadhri, C. (2012). Vertex Neighborhoods, Low Conductance Cuts, and Good Seeds for Local Community Methods Categories and Subject Descriptors. *Proceedings of the 18th ACM SIGKDD International Conference on Knowledge Discovery and Data Mining (KDD'12)*, 597–605. doi:10.1145/2339530.2339628

He, Z., & Hong, B. (2010). Dynamically Tuned Push-Relabel Algorithm for the Maximum Flow Problem on CPU-GPU-Hybrid Platforms. *2010 IEEE International Symposium on Parallel & Distributed Processing (IPDPS)*, 1–10.

Hong, S., Oguntebi, T., & Olukotun, K. (2011). Efficient Parallel Graph Exploration on Multi-Core CPU and GPU. *Proceedings of the 2011 International Conference on Parallel Architectures and Compilation Techniques (PACT'11)*, 78–88. doi:10.1109/PACT.2011.14

Karypis, G., & Kumar, V. (1998). METIS: A Software Package for Partitioning Unstructured Graphs, Partitioning Meshes, and Computing Fill-Reducing Orderings of Sparse Matrices. User manual. Academic Press.

Munguia, L., Bader, D., & Ayguade, E. (2012). Task-Based Parallel Breadth-First Search in Heterogeneous Environments. *Proceedings of the 19th International Conference on High Performance Computing (HiPC'12)*, 1–10. doi:10.1109/HiPC.2012.6507474

Nilakant, K., & Yoneki, E. (2014). On the Efficacy of APUs for Heterogeneous Graph Computation. *Proceedings of the 4th Workshop on Systems for Future Multicore Architectures (SFMA'14)*, 2–7.

Sariyüce, A., & Kaya, K. (2013). Betweenness Centrality on GPUs and Heterogeneous Architectures. *Proceedings of the 6th Workshop on General Purpose Processor Using Graphics Processing Units (GPGPU-6)*, 76–85. doi:10.1145/2458523.2458531

Zhang, B., Wu, J., Tang, Y., & Zhou, J. (2011). Betweenness-Based Algorithm for a Partition Scale-Free Graph. *Chinese Physics B*, *20*(11), 118903. doi:10.1088/1674-1056/20/11/118903

Zou, D., Dou, Y., Wang, Q., Xu, J., & Li, B. (2013). Direction-Optimizing Breadth-First Search on CPU-GPU Heterogeneous Platforms. *Proceedings of the 10th IEEE International Conference on High Performance Computing and Communications & IEEE International Conference on Embedded and Ubiquitous Computing (HPCC/EUC'13)*, 1064–1069. doi:10.1109/HPCC.and.EUC.2013.150

Chapter 6
Trends and Challenges in Large–Scale HPC Network Analysis

ABSTRACT

Many algorithms in graph analytics can be sped up by using the power of low-cost but massively parallel architectures, such as GPUs. On the other hand, the storage and analysis capabilities needed for large-scale graph analytics have motivated the development of a new wave of HPC technologies, including MapReduce-like BSP distributed analytics, No-SQL data storage and querying, and homogeneous and hybrid multi-core/GPU graph supercomputing. In this chapter, the authors review these trends and current challenges for HPC large-scale graph analysis.

INTRODUCTION

Many algorithms in Big Data analytics can be sped up using the power of low-cost but massively parallel architectures, such as GPUs. This kind of parallel commodities are playing a significant role in large-scale modeling (Hassibi and Dean, 2012). GPUs, for example, have already shown impressive speedups in other tasks, such as the visualization of networks (Sharma et al., 2011).

On the other hand, there are projects that bring graph algorithms to the realm of data analytics by implementing the bulk synchronous parallel (BSP) model for distributed network computation. Consider the example of Google

DOI: 10.4018/978-1-5225-3799-1.ch006

Pregel (Malewicz et al., 2010a), a massive network analysis API designed for distributed environment that, along with MapReduce, represented an important component of the Google technological infrastructure for the processing of massive amounts of data. Apache Giraph[1] is the open-source counterpart to Pregel that is currently used by Facebook for analyzing huge social graphs.

Another HPC initiative for network analytics are No-SQL graph databases, which address the challenge of "leveraging complex and dynamic relationships in highly connected data to generate insight and competitive advantage" (Robinson et al., 2013). Graph databases, like Neo4j[2], OrientDB[3], and InfiniteGraph[4], are able to store networks with up to billions of nodes, provide network-oriented query languages, a flexible data model, pattern matching queries, traversal-optimized storage, path retrieval, and in some cases distributed storage capabilities.

In summary, the storage and analysis capabilities needed for large-scale graph analytics have motivated the development of a new wave of HPC technologies and challenges. In this chapter we review these and other trends for HPC large-scale graph analysis and storage, as well as opportunities for research.

HOMOGENEOUS PARALLEL GRAPH PROCESSING

The first form of parallelism that the data analytics and complex network community exploits is homogeneous computing, i.e. parallel computing where all the processors are of the same-kind.

There is a list of publicly available libraries that exploit homogeneous parallel processing, i.e. the use of a single HPC parallel architecture (e.g. a multicore server or a HPC cluster) to power the processing of large networks modeled after real-world phenomena. The following subsections list works that exploit homogeneous parallel processing for efficient graph algorithm execution. A summary of the reviewed works is shown in Table 1.

Multicore Graph Computing

The following are libraries that exploit multicore architectures for HPC graph processing. Small-world Network Analysis and Partitioning (SNAP) (Madduri, 2008) is a software platform for the measurement of centrality metrics and the

Table 1. Homogeneous parallel graph processing libraries

Library	Architecture	Load Distribution
Parallel Boost Graph Library (PBGL)	Cluster HPC	Uses **ghost nodes** to locally represent the neighbors of nodes assigned to a specific processor.
MultiThreaded Graph Library (MTGL)	Cray MTA-2 y Cray XMT	Does not implement **any graph distribution strategy**. This task is performed by the execution environment of the Cray MTA.
Small-world Network Analysis and Partitioning (SNAP)	Cray XMT	Representation of graphs based on **optimized adjacency lists** that exploit the cache of processors.
SUPE-Net	Cluster HPC	Nodes are distributed by using a **community detection method** and a classic balanced partitioning technique.
Pregel	Cluster HPC	Assignation of nodes to partitions depends on the **node identifier** and on a simple **round-robin function.**
ParallelX Graph Library (PXGL)	Cluster HPC	Allows the definition of a **distribution policy** that maps named objects to physical memory spaces.
Combinatorial BLAS	Cluster HPC	Maps **blocks of the graph matrix** to a logic array of $\sqrt{p} \times \sqrt{p}$ processors.

detection of communities that exploits the small-world property of complex networks and the Cray XMT. SNAP implements a collection of fine-grained parallel kernel cores optimized for small-world networks like BFS, shortest paths, minimum spanning trees, and connected components. SNAP represents static graphs through adjacency lists optimized for exploiting the processor cache. For algorithms that work on dynamic and growing graphs, SNAP implements dynamic and resizable adjacency arrays that can be reordered in function of the vertex/edge identifiers.

The MultiThreaded Graph Library (MTGL) is a library for graphs processing inspired on the Boost Graph Library and originally designed for the Cray MTA-2 and the Cray XMT. MTGL follows the visitor design pattern to offer a variety of graph algorithms such as connected components, graph isomorphism, and *s-t* connectivity. The Cray MTA running environment is in charge of task partitioning and distribution, so MTGL doesn't provide any of these facilities. Recently, MTGL was implemented on the QThreads library to exploit conventional multicore CPUs.

Cluster Graph Computing

In general terms, there exist two models to program distributed memory systems: message-passing and distributed shared memory (DSM). On the one hand, the message-passing model implemented by the Message Passing Interface standard (MPI), assumes that each process has its own local memory, and establishes that processes are not allowed to directly access the memory from others processes. The only available mechanism to communicate data between processes is passing messages via send and receive primitives. On the other hand, DSM provides a global memory shared across processes, so each process is able to access data not only from its local memory but from the memory local to other processes. An example of a DSM model is the Active Global Address Space (AGAS).

The following are libraries that exploit the mentioned cluster models for HPC graph processing.

Parallel boost Graph Library (PBGL) is a library of graph algorithms that exploits MPI for distributed memory parallel architectures. PBGL represents graphs through distributed adjacency lists. In PBGL, property maps store and associated vertices and data. PBGL uses ghost vertices to locally represent remote adjacent vertices. Ghost vertices allow PBGL to locally traverse neighbor vertices and determine which vertices are remotely stored, in order to minimize communication costs. However, this strategy is not scalable to scale-free graphs, due to the high memory requirements of hubs.

ParallelX Graph Library (PXGL) (Stark, 2011) is a library of graph algorithms that exploits both shared memory and distributed memory parallel architectures. PXGL is written on the ParallelX platform, which in turn is based on the AGAS model that provides a virtual shared memory environment and a unified memory namespace. ParallelX named objects (e.g. threads and data) move between physical memory address spaces, keeping their object names and virtual references. Likewise, ParallelX provides a set of lightweight synchronization and threading primitives based on events. ParallelX allows the definition of load distribution policies for mapping objects and physical memory spaces, which can be specified in function of the application load requirements, the complexity of algorithms, and the underlying hardware architecture.

Combinatorial BLAS is a library for graph analysis written on MPI for distributed memory architectures. Combinatorial BLAS provides a set of linear algebra algorithms optimized for sparse matrices, such as sparse matrix-

matrix multiplications and SpMVs. Linear algebra algorithms are used as building blocks for algorithms like betweenness centrality and community detection. Combinatorial BLAS defines a logical square matrix of $\sqrt{p} \times \sqrt{p}$ processors to distribute matrices to 2D blocks. Additionally, sparse matrices can be compressed using the CSR and CSC formats.

Finally, SUPE-Net and CommPar are parallel simulation environments of social networks. They target HPC clusters and adopt a processor virtualization approach to choose the best load distribution strategy. The graph is partitioned by exploiting community detection and balanced graph partitioning techniques.

FRAMEWORKS FOR PROCESSING LARGE-SCALE GRAPHS

Complex networks are made of billions of entities, imposing the need to build frameworks for the processing of such huge graphs. In this section, a comprehensive review of most significant graph processing frameworks is done. For the sake of space, only a small set of significant cases is considered. An interested reader can look at the two excellent surveys available (Batarfi et al., 2015, McCune et al., 2015). After some brief review, comments about programming model, synchronization requirement and performance are done. Important efforts to evaluate performance in different systems can be review in two technical reports available (Guo et al., 2013, Doekemeijer and Varbanescu, 2014). While these works provide useful insights on the underlying framework data structures and implementations, the application and user perspectives are still lacking. Then, some space is devoted to comment, from an application perspective, about reported performance, current challenges and opportunities in synchronous versus asynchronous graph processing.

Projects like GBase, Hama and PEGASUS are efforts to bring Network Science to the realm of Big Data by adapting the industry-proven MapReduce model for large-scale distributed graph computation. Likewise, Bulk Synchronous Process and Asynchronous Parallel (AP) platforms, such as Google's Pregel (Malewicz et al., 2010b), Apache Spark's GraphX (Xin et al., 2013) and Dato's GraphLab (Low et al., 2012), are following a similar approach than MapReduce in a more graph-oriented fashion. Specifically, Pregel has inspired a new generation of graph processing projects, including GraphX, Giraph (Avery and Kunz, 2011) and Giraphx (Tasci and Demirbas, 2013) all of which use the BSP model. Moreover, non-distributed BSP frameworks, like Totem (Gharaibeh et al., 2013) and GraphChi (Kyrola et al., 2012), enable analysts to leverage the capabilities of single-node systems by combining different commodity hardware architectures like multicores and GPUs.

Distributed vs. Shared Memory Graph Processing Frameworks

Although many frameworks for large scale graphs are based on distributed systems, there still are some proposals based on a single machine approach which imply a shared memory programming model. The target platform is one of the major distinctions between graph processing frameworks: to choose between distributed or shared memory is a major concern for the user to create an application for large-scale graph processing.

A distributed system consists of multiple processing units where each unit has its own private memory. Data is partitioned and distributed among the separate nodes and explicit communication (message-passing) is required to synchronize computation. Scaling out refers to adding more processing units to the system to solve larger problems. On the other hand, shared-memory allows for efficient inter-process communication, as multiple tasks have access to the same memory. A shared memory platform does not imply a single processing unit. The challenges in graph processing, poor data locality and irregular memory accesses, make shared memory architectures well suited for graph processing. However, shared memory architectures usually support a limited amount of physical memory which limits scalability to solve larger problems. Nevertheless, communication is efficient, cost is lower, and debugging is simpler than in distributed systems. In addition, the user does not have to deal with managing a cluster, and the framework does not have to deal with problems inherent to distributed computing like fault tolerance.

MapReduce-Based Graph Processing Frameworks

General-purpose distributed data processing frameworks such as MapReduce are well suited form analyzing unstructured and tabular data. In principle, the MapReduce framework provides a simple but powerful programming model that enables developers to easily build scalable parallel algorithms to process massive amounts of data on clusters of commodity computers. MapReduce was inspired by the functional programming paradigm, the *map* and reduce *tasks* work with immutable *key/value* pairs of data. The output from the *map* tasks will be the input for the *reduce* tasks (grouped by key). Programs are written in a serial fashion and will be automatically parallelized. Tasks are independent so simply rescheduling failed tasks allows for failure recovery (Dean and Ghemawat, 2008).

Although the basic MapReduce model can be used to process large-scale graphs, pure MapReduce-based frameworks are not efficient for directly implementing iterative graph algorithms which often require multiple stages of complex joins. In general, graph processing algorithms are iterative and need to traverse the graph in some way. The general-purpose mechanisms defined in such MapReduce-based distributed frameworks are not designed to leverage the common patterns and structure in iterative graph algorithms. Graph algorithms can be written as a sequence of MapReduce invocations that requires passing the entire state of the graph from one stage to the next. Due to the graph structure, it is observed a huge network traffic leading to inefficient performance due to the additional communication and associated serialization overhead in addition to the need of the coordination steps in a MapReduce sequence. Because of that, some approaches have been proposed to overcome limitations found on graph algorithms implemented on pure MapReduce frameworks.

The *Surfer* system, one of the first attempts to create a large-scale graph processing engine, is based upon to basic primitives for programmers: MapReduce and propagation (Chen et al., 2010). MapReduce is used to process key-value pairs in parallel, and propagation is used to transfer information along edges. Two functions are required: transfer and combine. Transfer is responsible to transport information from a vertex to its neighbors, and combine is used to aggregate the received information at each vertex. An important aspect found in Surfer is the partition strategy which divides the large graph into many partitions of similar sizes. Each computer node in the distributed system holds several graph partitions and manages propagation doing as many local operations as it can before exchanging messages with other nodes in the system.

PEGASUS is a large-scale graph mining library that has been implemented on the top of the Hadoop framework, a quite common MapReduce implementation (Kang et al., 2011a). PEGASUS has built-in functions to perform typical graph mining tasks such as computing the diameter of a graph, performing a graph traversal, and finding the connected components. PEGASUS uses the matrix-vector algebraic approach to perform most of its operations. The library has been utilized to discover patterns on near-cliques and triangles in large-scale graphs by MapReduce-based applications.

GBASE is also a MapReduce-based framework focused in partitioning the graph into blocks and storing each block using a method called block compression (Kang et al., 2011b). GBASE distributes vertex according to the partition locality, which is vertex belonging to same partition are placed near each other. All non-empty blocks are compressed and stored together with some metadata. GBASE supports queries like neighborhood, induced subgraph, k-core and crossed-edges. GBASE organize partitions by using grid storage and it tries to minimize disk accesses and answer queries by applying a MapReduce-based algorithm.

BSP Graph Processing Frameworks

A commonly-used more elaborated model is the Directed Acyclic Graph (DAG), in which, an application is represented as a DAG, vertices represents tasks and edges represent flow of data. For MapReduce, the DAG is simple with two vertices (*map* and *reduce*) and one edge joining them. DAGs cannot express iterative applications, because of the acyclic property. This can be worked around by adding an iterate task that executes a DAG until a convergence condition is met. Applying such programming model for massively processing large amounts of data can lead to the Bulk Synchronous Parallel (BSP) computing model. Formerly proposed by Leslie Valiant (Valiant, L. 1990), the BSP model was created to simplify the design of software for parallel systems. At the most basic level, BSP is a two-step process performed iteratively and synchronously: (1) perform task computing on local data and (2) communicate the results, repeating the two step as many iterations needed. In BSP, each compute/communication iteration is called a superstep, with synchronization of the parallel tasks occurring at the superstep barriers.

Billion-node graphs that exceed the memory capacity of commodity machines are not well supported by MapReduce-based frameworks. A new type of frameworks challenges the user to *"think like a vertex"* (TLAV) and implements graph analysis programs from the perspective of a vertex rather than a graph, providing a natural way to express and compute many iterative graph algorithms. As a result TLAV approaches improves vertex locality and exhibits some approximation of linear scalability.

Pregel system (Malewicz et al., 2010a), introduced by Google and implemented in C/C++, is the first BSP implementation that provides an

API specifically tailored for graph algorithms following the TLAV model. Graph algorithms are developed in terms of what each vertex has to compute based on local vertex data, as well as data from incident edges and adjacent vertices. The Pregel frameworks splits computation into BSP-style supersteps in which each vertex executes the user-defined vertex function and then send results to neighbors along graph edges. The user focuses on specifying the computation on the graph vertices and the communication between among them without concerning about the underlying organization or resource allocation of the graph data. Pregel works on a distributed system where graph vertices are allocated in the different machines achieving that all associated neighbors are assigned to the same node. Graph processing algorithms are then represented as supersteps where each step defines each active vertex has to compute and edges represent communication channels to transmit results from one vertex to another. Since Pregel is a BSP-based framework, supersteps always end with a synchronization barrier, which guarantees that messages sent in a given superstep are received at the beginning of the next superstep. Vertices may change states between active and inactive, depending on the overall state of execution. Pregel terminates when all vertices halt and no more messages are exchanged.

GraphX is a distributed graph engine built on top of Spark, which is a MapReduce-like general data-parallel engine currently released as an Apache project (Xin et al., 2013). Spark's programming model consists of:

1. An in-memory data abstraction called Resilient Distributed Datasets (RDD), and
2. A set of deterministic parallel operation on RDDs that can be invoked using data primitives such as map, filter, join, and group by.

A Spark's program is a directed acyclic graph (DAG) of Spark's primitives, which are applied in a set of initial or transformed RDDs (Zaharia et al. 2010). GraphX extends Spark's RDD abstraction to introduce Resilient Distributed Graph (RDG) which associates records with vertices and edges in a graph and provides a collection of expressive computational graph primitives. GraphX introduced the concept of graph-parallel framework to process big graphs in a large-scale distributed system. GraphX introduced new operations to simplify graph construction, transformation, and analysis. The GraphX RDG leverages advances in distributed graph representation and exploits the graph structure to minimize communication and storage overhead. Most graph-parallel systems partition the graph by constructing an edge-cut which uniquely assigns vertices to machines while allowing edges to span across machines. The communication and storage overhead of an edge-cut is directly proportional to the number of edges that are cut. In order to reduce communication overhead and ensure balanced computation it is need to minimize both the number of cut edges as well as the number of vertices assigned to the most loaded machine. However, for most large-scale real-world graphs, constructing an optimal edge-cut can be prohibitively expensive. GraphX relies on a flexible vertex-cut partitioning to encode graphs as horizontally partitioned collections. A vertex-cut partitioning promotes to evenly assign edges to machines leaving vertices to span multiple machines. A vertex-data table is used to represent each vertex partition; an edge table is used to represent each edge partition replication those vertices having an edge crossing from one partition to another. Finally, a vertex map indexes all copies for each vertex.

Apache Giraph is an open source project which uses Java to implement ideas and implementation of Pregel specification is made on the top of the Hadoop framework infrastructure (Avery and Kunz, 2011). Giraph was initially developed by Yahoo and later Facebook used it to build its Graph Search Services. Giraph uses the Pregel's programming model which is vertex-centric programming abstraction adapting the BSP model. Giraph runs synchronous graph processing jobs as Map-only jobs and uses Hadoop Distributed File System (HDFS) for storing graph data. Giraph also takes advantage of Apache Zookeeper for periodic checkpoints, failure recovery and to coordinate superstep execution. Giraph is executed in-memory which can speed-up job execution. However, Giraph can fail processing a workload requiring more than physical available memory.

Single-Machine Graph Processing Frameworks

An important issue of TLAV graph processing frameworks is how data is shared between vertex programs. The two typical models to do that in distributed systems are message-passing and shared memory. In the message-passing systems, data is exchanged between processes through messages, whereas in shared-memory systems data for one process is directly and immediately accessible to another process. Shared-memory exposes vertex data as shared variables that can be directly read or modified by other vertex programs. Shared –memory avoids the additional memory overhead generated by messages and does not require intermediate worker processes. Shared-memory is often implemented by TLAV frameworks developed for a single-machine since some challenges to a shared-memory implementation arise in the distributed setting such as consistency access to remote vertices. In addition, race conditions may arise when adjacent vertex resides in a remote machine. Memory consistency can be guaranteed serializing accesses by following a mutual exclusion protocol.

GiraphX is a synchronous shared-memory implementation following the Giraph model (Tasci and Demirbas, 2013). Serialization of shared vertex access is provided through locking of border vertices, without local cached copies. GiraphX showed a reduced overhead compared to message-passing in Giraph, achieving 35% faster convergence when computing PageRank in a large Web graph.

GraphLab is an open-source large scale graph processing projects implemented in C++, formerly started at CMU and currently supported by GraphLab Inc. GraphLab is a shared-memory abstraction using Gather, Apply, and Scatter (GAS) processing model similar to, but also fundamentally different from, BSP model employed in Pregel (Low et al., 2012). In the GAS model, a vertex collects information about its neighborhood in the *Gather* phase; performs the computations in the *Apply* phase; and in the *Scatter* phase updates its adjacent vertices and edges.

GraphLab initial proposal was a single-machine system there is also a distributed implementation. The GraphLab abstraction consists of the three main parts: the *data graph*, the *update* function and the *sync* operation. The *data graph* represents a user's program state that both stores mutable user-defined data and encodes computational dependencies. The *update function* is a stateless procedure that modifies the data within the scope of a vertex and schedules the future execution of update functions on other vertices. The *sync operation* concurrently writes global aggregates which were read by update functions.

In GraphLab vertices can directly pull their neighbor's data through Gather phase, without the need to explicitly receive messages from them. In Pregel, neighbor vertices push data to a vertex via messages. GraphLab can work in two execution modes: synchronous or asynchronous. Like BSP, the synchronous mode uses the notion of superstep barriers, while the asynchronous more does not require such global synchronization. GraphLab automatically enforces serialization by preventing adjacent vertex program from running concurrently. The vertices in a neighborhood use locks which are sequentially grabbed by a fine-grained locking protocol. Border vertices are provided locally cached ghost copies of remote neighbors. Consistency between ghosts and the original vertex is maintained by the locking mechanism.

The flow of information in GraphLab vertex programs works in pull mode, that is, from neighboring vertices inward to the active vertex requiring neighbor's data. Asynchronous shared memory frameworks, like GraphLab, may execute faster because of prioritized execution and low communication overhead, but at the expense of added complexity for scheduling and maintaining consistency. When the number of machines and partitions increase, more time and resources become a challenge for the locking protocol's scalability.

GraphChi is a centralized system, implemented in C++ that can process massive graphs from secondary storage in a single machine (Kyrola et al., 2012). It is a Parallel Sliding Window (PSW) mechanism to process very large graphs from disk moving a fraction of the graph to memory and requiring a small number of sequential disk accesses. PSW exhibits good performance in both SSD and traditional hard drives. GraphChi partitions the input graph into subgraphs where edges are sorted by the source id. A sequential stream is used to load the edges in memory. Using CSR and CSC representations, GraphChi avoids finding efficient graph cuts which is a costly operation. PSW implements the asynchronous model of computation in which an update function can use the most recent values of edges and vertices without the need of global barrier synchronization. GraphChi also supports dynamic selective scheduling allowing update functions doing graph modifications to enlist vertices to be updated.

PSW partitions vertices into disjoint sets, associating with each interval a subset containing all the interval's incoming edges, sorted by source index. Intervals are selected to form balanced subsets and the number of intervals is chosen so any interval can fit completely in memory. A sliding window is maintained over every interval, so when vertices from one subset are updated from incoming edges, the results can be sequentially written to the outgoing edges found in sorted order in the window of the subset. GraphChi can efficiently solve graph analytics problems with a conventional desktop computer that were previously only accessible to large-scale cluster computing. GraphChi relatively outperforms other distributed systems, per-node basis.

Heterogeneous Graph Processing Frameworks

Heterogeneous systems can be used at different levels: processing units, storage devices, communication channels, for example. An important class of heterogeneous systems is the one using both CPU and graphical processing units (GPUs) to accelerate the processing of large graphs. Host processing units are optimized to fast sequential processing while GPUs bring massive hardware multithreading able to mask memory access latency. Such an hybrid systems have the potential to cope with the heterogeneous structure of real graphs and enable high performance graph processing. The most representative hybrid framework combining GPU and CPU processing units is Totem (Gharaibeh et al., 2013). Totem is also a BSP-based framework in which each processing element (the CPU and the GPU) executes computations asynchronously on its local memory during the computation phase. In the communication phase, the processing elements exchange messages that are necessary to update their status before the next computation starts. The main challenge in Totem is to partition the graph in such a way that resulting partitions must be mapped to processing elements according their different architectural characteristics. Totem showed how to partition a graph, and processing tasks, to efficiently use both the traditional CPU cores and the GPUs. Totem divides a graph in at least two partition kinds using the degree distribution of the input graph to place high degree vertices in one partition class and the other ones are put together into the other class. Totem showed that efficiently mapping both partitions to different architectures depends basically on graph's size. Very large graphs not fitting into GPU memory can be distributed placing the high-degree vertices in CPU cores and the low-degree vertices into GPUs. For graph instances knowing that high-degree partition fits into GPU memory, processing the low-degree vertex partition into CPU can improve performance. Totem's important contribution was that, in the case of scale-free graphs, using simple aggregation techniques, the communication overhead between the two kind of architectural systems, can be significantly reduced to the point that it becomes negligible relative to the processing time. In contrast, partitioning algorithms that aim to reduce communication by computing minimal cuts have high computational or space complexity and may be themselves harder than graph processing required. Chapter 4 contains a fully comprehensive discussion about the graph partition problem and new partitioning strategies based on hybrid computations were shown in Chapter 5.

Graph Processing Framework Discussion

A taxonomy of the reviewed graph-processing frameworks can be observed in Table 2. Different dimensions can be used to classify discussed frameworks.

Table 2. Frameworks for processing large-scale graphs

Framework	Year	Architecture Implementation	Base System	Computational Model	Communication Model
Surfer	2010	Distributed Memory	MapReduce	Graph-centric	Message passing
PEGASUS	2009	Distributed Memory	MapReduce	Matrix-centric	Dataflow
GBase	2011	Distributed Memory	MapReduce	Matrix-centric	Dataflow
Pregel	2010	Distributed Memory	BSP-based	Vertex-centric	Message passing
GraphX	2013	Distributed Memory	BSP-based	Graph-centric	Dataflow
Giraph	2012	Distributed Memory	BSP-based	Vertex-centric	Dataflow
GiraphX	2013	Distributed Memory	BSP-based	Vertex-centric	Shared Memory
GraphLab	2010	Single machine/ Distributed memory	GAS model	Vertex-centric	Shared Memory
GraphChi	2012	Single Machine	Sequential Model	Vertex-centric, PSW	Shared Memory
Totem	2012	Hybrid CPU+GPU	BSP-based	Graph-centric	Hybrid CPU+GPU

For the sake of simplicity, four dimensions are selected in this chapter. A detailed review of different platform's properties is presented in (Doekemeijer et al., 2014). The target platform is one of the major distinctions between frameworks, most of them are distributed memory systems, but there are some shared-memory systems used as a single-machine or centralized systems. A special case is Totem which is a single-machine hybrid system having multicore CPUs and GPUs. The first distributed frameworks, like Surfer, PEGASUS and GBase, were based on MapReduce, the general-purpose distributed data processing. The next generation of distributed graph-processing frameworks, Pregel, GraphX, Giraph and GiraphX are based on the BSP model of computation with a synchronous execution mode.

The hybrid framework, Totem, is also based in the BSP model. GraphLab is based in the Gather, Apply, Scatter model which is similar to the BSP model but with some differences that allow having a synchronous or asynchronous execution mode. A different framework is GaphChi which is a single-machine implementation framework relying on a Parallel Sliding Window mechanism for processing very large graphs from disk. Pegasus and GBase follow a computation model focused in matrix representations of graphs paying attention on the matrix computations and storage. Most of the frameworks employ a vertex-centric computational model, in which user-defined programs center on a vertex rather than a graph. Such an approach improves locality, demonstrates linear scalability, and provides a natural way to express and compute many iterative graph algorithms. In contrast, Surfer, GraphX and Totem use a graph-centric approach in which rather than limiting computation scope to a single vertex, these systems perform computations on graph partitions. Finally, graph-processing frameworks can be classified also according their memory model to share information. GiraphX, GraphLab and GraphChi are based on a global shared-address memory space. Surfer and Pregel are elaborations of a pure message-passing model in which state is local and messages flow through the system to update external entities. The Totem's hybrid model is a combination of both shared-memory and message-passing model. Shared-memory is used to access vertex data in the same partition and message-passing is necessary to access state of vertices in different partitions. The dataflow model is a message-passing model emphasizing that flow of information goes from a vertex to its neighbors. In distributed memory frameworks, the dataflow communication model is also to indicate that state (data) flows through the system towards the next phase of computation.

Challenges and Opportunities About Graph Processing Frameworks

We have discussed ten different frameworks which are representative of the diversity of available systems. However, there is a growing number of large scale graph processing systems. In (Doekemeijer et al., 2014) 83 different frameworks were reviewed. Because of that, users now face the challenge of selecting of selecting an appropriate platform for their specific application and requirements. The obvious strategy is to select the graph-processing framework offering the best performance for a specific application but it is required to have a common perspective to evaluate. In (Guo et al., 2013) three different dimensions of diversity were studied to evaluate performance in graph-processing platforms: dataset, algorithm, and platform diversity.

Starting by platform diversity, it is the result of the wide spectrum of systems which are influenced by the wide diversity of infrastructure (compute and storage systems). According to Table 2 and to those systems reviewed in

Doeckemeijer et al. (2014) we can select single-machine, distributed systems, or hybrid systems. Perhaps the first criterion to follow is selecting the platform according to the graph size instances. Single machines and hybrid systems are primary limited by memory capacity. If graph instances are able to fit in memory, they can be entirely processed by a single machine or a hybrid system. An interesting proposal is GraphChi framework which can process large instances partially loaded into main memory. Regarding performances, it is well known that shared memory offers betters results than distributed systems but they are limited by memory capacity. Distributed systems are primarily designed to process very large graph instances.

To evaluate performance it is necessary to execute some representative algorithms in selected graph instances. Algorithm diversity is an outcome of the different goals of processing graphs, for example, shortest paths, PageRank, subgraph matching, and centrality or betweenness metrics. In one hand, there exists a large variety of graph processing algorithms which can be categorized into several groups by functionality and consumption of resources. Representative classes of algorithms used in practice are: statistics, traversals, connected components, and evolution. On the other hand, low-level implementations of such algorithms allow for very specific architectural optimizations, but are subject to substantial implementation effort. As a result, parallelizing graph algorithms with efficient performance is a very challenging task. The computation cost is typically driven by the structure of node-edge relations of the underlying graph. Finding a low-cost graph partitioning strategy that can maximize locality of processing and achieve good load balancing is a very challenging task. In addition, communication overhead in very large graph instances can dominate execution times in distributed systems having a significant impact on the degree of parallelism.

Datasets is the third diversity dimension needed to be considered. Dataset diversity is the result of the wide set of application domains for graph data. Instances can be real phenomena or it can by synthetically generated. Benchmarks can be selected with a variety of values for the number of nodes and edges, and with different structure. In general, designing a good benchmark is challenging task due to the many aspects that should be considered which can influence the adoption and the usage scenarios of the benchmark. Unfortunately, there is clear lack of standard benchmarks that can be employed in graph-processing evaluation.

Finally, an important aspect to reason about performance behavior is to identify the systems parameters to be monitor and the metrics that can be used to characterize framework performance. The general performance aspects can be raw processing power, resource usage, scalability and processing overheads. Those performance aspects can be observed by monitoring traditional system parameters like lifetime of each processing job, the CPU and network load, the OS memory consumption, and the disk I/O, to name some parameters. Those observed parameters should be translated to relevant performance metrics such as vertices per second, edges per second, horizontal and vertical scalability, computation and communication time, and time overhead. The reader can be interested in the methodology proposed in (Guo et al., 2013) to evaluate and compare graph-processing frameworks.

NO-SQL LARGE-SCALE GRAPH STORAGE

Relational databases can be used to store graph data. If an edgelist graph representation is used, a table with two columns is enough for that purpose. In such a data model, registers would represent individual graph edges whereas columns would represent the source and the target nodes. Edge and node labels and attributes can be stored in separated tables joined together by foreign keys (Liu, 2014). However, the costs of complex join operations needed to add, manage and update the structure of the graph have a negative overall impact on the database performance (Prasanth and Arul, 2014).

According to Angles (2012) a graph database is a database where data is modeled after graphs or hypergraphs, and where the operations over the database are expressed in terms of graph-based operations. Graph databases are particularly useful to store and query labeled data graphs where vertices and edges have proprieties and each edge have a label describing the relationship between pair of vertices (Ammar, 2016).

In contrast to RDBMs, in graph databases there is a single data structure: the graph itself. There are neither tables nor join operations involved. Graph database systems follow index free adjacency, in which every node maintains direct reference to the adjacent nodes. This means that the graph can be traversed without the need for a global index. Under this data organization, query time is no longer tied to the total size of the graph and is instead directly proportional to the length of the graph searched (Kaliyar, 2015).

As RDBMs, graph database systems provide CRUD (Create, Read, Update, and Delete) methods. A search or query in a graph database is called "traversal". These queries are designed to start at a specific node and discover its connections to other nodes while considering the queried relationships (Vyawahare and Karde, 2015).

Vyawahare and Karde (2015) list three types of graph databases: true graph databases, triple stores and RDBSs that provide graphical capabilities. A true graph database supports index free adjacency whereas a triple store (also known as RDF database) does not. Also, true graph databases are specially designed to support graphs where properties may be assigned to vertices and/or links.

The main advantages of the power of graph databases are presented by Vyawahare and Karde (2015) as follows:

- **Performance:** The graph database performance should be higher than that of RDBMs and other No-SQL stores when dealing with connected data by providing direct access to relationships facilitating the joining of multiple data sources.
- **Flexibility:** Graph databases allows dynamic schema: they allow the addition of new links, vertices and subgraphs to an existing graph without "disturbing" existing queries and application functionality.
- **Agility:** Based on their flexibility, graph databases prevent us to have to model our domain in exhaustive detail ahead of time.

Examples of Graph Databases

Examples of modern graph databases include AllegroGraph, HypergraphDB, InfiniteGraph, and Neo4j. As we will further develop, most of them provide the expected components of full-featured database system: a user interface or API, languages for data definition, manipulation and querying, a query optimizer, a database engine (middleware), a storage engine, a transaction engine, as well as management features, such as tuning, backup and recovery (Angles, 2012).

Neo4j[5] is an open source disk-based transactional graph database. In Neo4j both nodes and relationship can contain properties. It scales to billions of nodes and relationships in a network (Kaliyar, 2015).

Sparksee[6] (formerly known as DEX) is graph database written in C++. A Sparksee graph is a labeled directed attributed multigraph where nodes and edges in a graph can hold data and where there may be multiple edges between the same nodes even if they are from the same edge type. Its implementation is based on bitmaps to ensure a good performance in the management of very large graphs (Angles, 2012). Sparksee offers partial ACID transaction support because atomicity and isolation cannot be always guaranteed (Kaliyar, 2015).

InfiniteGraph[7] is a distributed graph database with a lock server that handles lock requests from database applications. It provides graph-wise indexes on multiple key fields (Kaliyar, 2015). Its focus of attention is to provide business, social and government with intelligence through graph analysis (Angles, 2012).

HyperGraphDB[8] is a database that implements the hypergraph data model where the notion of edge is extended to connect more than two nodes. This model allows a natural representation of higher-order relations, and is particularly useful for modeling data of areas like knowledge representation, artificial intelligence and bio-informatics (Angles, 2012). AllegroGraph[9] is a graph database designed with Semantic Web standards (RDF, SPARQL and OWL) in mind that also provides special features for GeoTemporal Reasoning and Social Network Analysis (Angles, 2012).

Blueprints[10] defines a series of fundamental methods for property (directed, edge-labeled, attributed, multi-graph) graphs, such as the addition and removal of vertices, retrieval of a vertex by identifier, retrieval of vertices by attribute value, etc. Its objective is to provide a middleware that abstracts the implementation details of graph databases and to make it possible to switch from a graph database to another. One disadvantage of this approach is that database features that are not considered in the middleware are not always accessible to the developer (Jouili and Vansteenberghe, 2013).

Titan[11] is a scalable graph database by the creators of Blueprints that is optimized for storing and querying graphs containing hundreds of billions of vertices and edges distributed across a multi-machine cluster. Titan is a transactional database that claims to support thousands of concurrent users executing complex graph traversals in real time.

OrientDB[12] is an open source graph database with a hybrid model: Document Database and Object Orientation. Specifically, it is a document-based database, but the relationships are managed as in graph databases with direct connections between records. It can work in schema-less mode, schema-full or a mix of both. It also provides advanced features like SQL queries, and access to local/remote/in-memory databases (Liu, 2014).

Jouili and Vansteenberghe (2013) compare four graph databases: Neo4j, DEX (Sparksee), Titan and OrientDB on different types of workloads. They concluded that for read-write workloads Neo4j, Titan and OrientDB's performances degrade notoriously. However, they also found that, in general, Neo4j outperforms all the other databases under traversal workloads. As for read-only intensive workloads, they found that Neo4j, DEX, Titan and OrientDB achieve similar performances.

On the other hand, Mpinda et al. (2015) found that when comparing Neo4j and OrientDB without indexing techniques, Neo4j shows better retrieval performance. However, when using indexing techniques, Neo4j's retrieval has less performance than OrientDB.

Even when some of the described disk-based centralized (single-machine) graph databases provide the means for implementing or performing graph operations such as graph traversals or shortest-paths, these primitives are generally considerably slower when compared to implementations on top of main-memory BSP-based distributed graph processing platforms like Apache Giraph (Thompson, 2013).

Graph Query Languages

Some of the mentioned graph databases offer the possibility of performing direct queries to the graph through specialized graph query languages. These query languages can be categorized into two types: declarative pattern matching language and traversal scripting language (Wang et al., 2015).

SPARQL[13] is the high-level declarative standardized query language for RDF by W3C based on graph patterns. SPARQL consists of two parts: a query language and a protocol. The query language consists of triple patterns, conjunctions, disjunctions, and optional patterns. The idea is to match the triples in the SPARQL query with the existing RDF triples. The SPARQL protocol was designed to transmit the queries and the results between the client and the SPARQL engine through HTTP (Wang et al., 2015). Blueprints API support a navigational and procedural interface data model similar to RDF (Thompson, 2013).

Gremlin[14] is a graph traversal language expressed in the Groovy Java dialect. Gremlin is a functional language whereby traversal operators are chained together to form path-like expressions. Gremlin allows the definition of exact traverse patterns, simplifying the task of designing graph data mining on top of a supported graph database (Wang et al., 2015).

Cypher[15] is the declarative graph query of Neo4j based on the Property Graph model. As a declarative language, it focuses on the clarity of expressing what to retrieve from a graph in such a way that, when the physical data structure is changed, the user doesn't need to update the queries. As such, Cypher borrows keywords from SQL, as well as pattern matching expressions from SPARQL (Wang et al., 2015). It also allows updating the graph database.

An open research topic is to design a language that can blend together the strengths from both declarative and traversal graph languages. As a young field, it is also yet to explore how to design a non-traversal/non-declarative language that can query graphs in an expressive, intuitive and efficient manner (Wang et al., 2015).

Graph Partitioning for Distributed Graph Databases

Distributed graph databases distribute large graphs across different sites when it is infeasible to query and store them on a single site, and are characterized by real-time querying that traverse edges to fetch neighbor's information.

Because of the large size of graphs, most databases use random partitioning (Buerli and Obispo, 2012). To construct partitions, more advanced graph partition techniques try to find a good compromise between reducing server communication cost, which is defined in most cases by the number of edge-cuts, and reducing server-processing loads. The aim is to improve query response time while minimizing the data storage cost. Other approaches are based on the community structure to group the graph nodes and reducing the edge-cut load. For example, Wang et al. (2014) propose a multi-level label propagation method for graph partitioning, previously used for iterative community detection in social networks.

Another option is to consider the read requests to a vertex, in such a way that the proposed graph partitioning algorithm assign vertices to sites based on how much this assignment will improve query response time. To approximate query times and simulate query workloads, the number of edge-cuts between partitions can be utilized. The approach presented by Zheng et al. (2016) goes one step further and take care of the volume of transferred data, the network heterogeneity and the shared resource contention in multicore systems to model workload.

Opportunities and Challenges About Large-Scale Graph Storage Databases

According to Thompson (2013) some of the central research challenges for graph databases include:

- **Schema Agnostic Query:** There are challenges in how to represent the results of schema-agnostic queries and provide people with guidance on how to take advantage of initial results. Progress on this research line would enable:
  - People to ask natural language questions and
  - Machines to identify possibly interesting patterns in the data.
- **Queries Against the Open Web:** Another challenge is that of allowing a regular user to issue queries on the open Web to obtain sub-graphs for entities and concepts of interest, much in the same way as regular users can now query the Web using general-purpose engines like Google.
- **Finding Interesting Patterns or Predictions in Graph Data (Graph Data Mining):** As discussed previously, one of recent developments in graph data mining is the BSP-based vertex programming abstraction. However, research challenges exist in:
  - Efficient scaling of graph data mining to large clusters and many-core hardware,
  - Graph APIs that simplify the implementation of data mining algorithms while allowing to efficiently parallelize the work,
  - Integrating rich graph models: typed links, link weights, attribute values, etc.

In addition to this, research on efficient graph partitioning schemes is relevant and needed in order to (1) obtain novel algorithms that scale well to large graphs and (2) to exploit the opportunities for parallelization on new multi/many-core hardware to accelerate the stage of load distribution.

CONCLUSION

In this chapter we discussed the new wave of current HPC technologies and challenges in the context of large-scale graph processing and storage. On the one hand, parallelizing graph algorithms with efficient performance is a very challenging task, since computation is driven by the structure of the underlying graph. On the other hand, finding a low-cost graph partitioning strategy that can maximize locality of processing and achieve good load balancing is even harder.

There is a growing number of large scale graph processing systems, but users now face the challenge of selecting an appropriate platform for their specific requirements. In this regard, a set of seven selected parallel computing graph processing frameworks was studied. Additionally, a taxonomy of ten selected single-machine, distributed and hybrid graph-processing frameworks that follow a MapReduce-like approach was presented, and four dimensions were used to classify the discussed frameworks.

In graph databases there is a single data structure: the graph itself. In this chapter we also described six state-of-the-art graph database systems. Most of them provide the expected components of full-featured database system, like a user interface or API, a database engine and management features. Some of the reviewed graph databases even offer the possibility of performing direct queries to the graph through specialized graph query languages, which fall in two categories: declarative pattern matching and traversal scripting. An open research topic is to design a language that can bring together the best from both worlds.

In addition to this, research on efficient graph partitioning schemes is also relevant for graph storage: novel algorithms that scale well and exploit parallelism can help to unleash the benefits of distributed graph processing and storage systems.

REFERENCES

Ammar, A. B. (2016). *Query optimization techniques in graph databases.* arXiv preprint arXiv:1609.01893

Angles, R. (2012). A comparison of current graph database models. In *Data Engineering Workshops (ICDEW), 2012 IEEE 28th International Conference on*, (pp. 171–177). IEEE. doi:10.1109/ICDEW.2012.31

Avery, C., & Kunz, C. (2011). Giraph: Large-scale Graph Processing Infrastructure on Hadoop. *Proceedings of the 2011 Hadoop Summit.*

Batarfi, O., Shawi, R., Fayoumi, A., Nouri, R., Beheshti, S., Barnawi, A., & Sakr, S. (2015). Large Scale Graph Processing Systems: Survey and an Experimental Evaluation. *Cluster Computing*, *18*(3), 1189–1213. doi:10.1007/s10586-015-0472-6

Buerli, M., & Obispo, C. (2012). *The current state of graph databases.* Department of Computer Science, Cal Poly San Luis Obispo.

Chen, R., Weng, X., He, B., & Yang, M. (2010). Large graph processing in the cloud. In *Proceedings of the SIGMOD*, (pp. 1123–1126). ACM.

Dean, J., & Ghemawat, S. (2008). MapReduce: Simplified data processing on large clusters. *Communications of the ACM, 51*(1), 107–113. doi:10.1145/1327452.1327492

Doekemeijer, N., & Varbanescu, A. (2014). *A Survey of Parallel Graph Processing Frameworks. Technical report.* Delft University of Technology.

Gharaibeh, A., Costa, L., & Ripeanu, M. (2013). Totem: Accelerating Graph Processing on Hybrid CPU + GPU Systems. *Proceedings of the 2013 GPU Technology Conference.*

Guo, Y., Biczak, M., & Verbanescu, A. (2013). *How Well do Graph-Processing Platforms Perform? An Empirical Performance Evaluation and Analysis: Extended Report. Technical report.* Delft University of Technology.

Hassibi, K., & Dean, J. (2012). *High Performance Data Mining and Big Data Analytics.* Wiley.

Jouili, S., & Vansteenberghe, V. (2013). An empirical comparison of graph databases. In *Social Computing (SocialCom), 2013 International Conference on*, (pp. 708–715). IEEE. doi:10.1109/SocialCom.2013.106

Kaliyar, K. R. (2015). Graph databases: A survey. In *Computing, Communication & Automation (ICCCA), 2015 International Conference on*, (pp. 785–790). IEEE. doi:10.1109/CCAA.2015.7148480

Kang, U., Tong, H., Sun, J., Lin, C.-Y., & Faloutsos, C. (2011b). GBASE: a scalable and general graph management system. *Proceedings of the international conference on Knowledge Discovery and Data Mining*, 1091–1099. doi:10.1145/2020408.2020580

Kang, U., Tsourakakis, C. E., & Faloutsos, C. (2011a). PEGASUS: Mining peta-scale graphs. *Knowledge and Information Systems, 27*(2), 303–325. doi:10.1007/s10115-010-0305-0

Kyrola, A., Blelloch, G., & Guestrin, C. (2012). Graphchi: Large-scale graph computation on just a PC. *Proceedings of the 2012 USENIX Symposium on Operating Systems Design and Implementation*, 31–46.

Liu, Y. (2014). *A Survey Of Persistent Graph Databases* (PhD thesis). Kent State University.

Low, Y., Bickson, D., Gonzalez, J., Guestrin, C., Kyrola, A., & Hellerstein, J. (2012). Distributed Graphlab: A Framework for Machine Learning and Data Mining in the Cloud. *Proceedings of the VLDB Endowment International Conference on Very Large Data Bases*, 5(8), 716–727. doi:10.14778/2212351.2212354

Lumsdaine, A., Gregor, D., Hendrickson, B., & Berry, J. (2007). Challenges in Parallel Graph Processing. *Parallel Processing Letters*, 17(1), 5–20. doi:10.1142/S0129626407002843

Madduri, K. (2008). *A High-Performance Framework for Analyzing Massive Complex Networks* (PhD thesis). Georgia Institute of Technology.

Malewicz, G., Austern, M., Bik, A., Dehnert, J., Horn, I., Leiser, N., & Czajkowski, G. (2010a). Pregel: A System for Large-Scale Graph Processing. *Proceedings of the 16th International Conference on Management of Data (COMAD'10)*, 135–146. doi:10.1145/1807167.1807184

Malewicz, G., Austern, M., Bik, A., Dehnert, J., Horn, I., Leiser, N., & Czajkowski, G. (2010b). Pregel: A System for Large-scale Graph Processing. *Proceedings of the 2010 ACM SIGMOD International Conference on Management of Data*, 135–146. doi:10.1145/1807167.1807184

McCune, R., Weninger, T., & Madey, G. (2015). Thinking like a Vertex: A Survey of Vertex-centric Frameworks for Large-scale Distributed Graph Processing. *ACM Computing Surveys*, 48(2), 1–39. doi:10.1145/2818185

Mpinda, S. A. T., Ferreira, L. C., Ribeiro, M. X., & Santos, M. T. P. (2015). *Evaluation of graph databases performance through indexing techniques*. Academic Press.

Prasanth, N., & Arul, K. (2014). Converting employee relational database into graph database. *Middle East Journal of Scientific Research*, 22(11), 1618–1621.

Robinson, I., Webber, J., & Eifrem, E. (2013). *Graph Databases*. O'Reilly Media.

Sharma, P., Khurana, U., Shneiderman, B., Scharrenbroich, M., & Locke, J. (2011). Speeding Up Network Layout and Centrality Measures for Social Computing Goals. *Proceedings of the 2011 International Conference on Social Computing, Behavioral-Cultural Modeling and Prediction*, 244–251. doi:10.1007/978-3-642-19656-0_35

Stark, D. (2011). *Advanced Semantics for Accelerated Graph Processing* (PhD thesis). Louisiana State University.

Tasci, S., & Demirbas, M. (2013). Giraphx: Parallel yet Serializable Large-scale Graph Processing. Proceedings of Euro-Par 2013 Parallel Processing, 458–469.

Thompson, B. (2013). *Literature survey of graph databases. Technical Report*. SYSTAP.

Valiant, L. G. (1990). A bridging model for parallel computation. *Communications of the ACM*, *33*(8), 103–111. doi:10.1145/79173.79181

Vyawahare, H., & Karde, P. (2015). An overview on graph database model. *International Journal of Innovative Research in Computer and Communication Engineering*, *3*(8).

Wang, L., Xiao, Y., Shao, B., & Wang, H. (2014). How to partition a billion-node graph. In *Data Engineering (ICDE), 2014 IEEE 30th International Conference on*, (pp. 568–579). IEEE. doi:10.1109/ICDE.2014.6816682

Wang, S.-T., Jin, J., Rivett, P., & Kitazawa, A. (2015). Technical survey graph databases and applications. *International Journal of Semantic Computing*, *9*(04), 523–545. doi:10.1142/S1793351X15500129

Xin, R., Gonzalez, J., Franklin, M., & Stoica, I. (2013). Graphx: A Resilient Distributed Graph System on Spark. *Proceedings of the 2013 International Workshop on Graph Data Management Experiences and Systems*. doi:10.1145/2484425.2484427

Zaharia, M., Chowdhury, M., Franklin, M. J., Shenker, S., & Stoica, I. (2010). Spark: cluster computing with working sets. *Proceedings of the HotCloud*.

Zheng, A., Labrinidis, A., Pisciuneri, P. H., Chrysanthis, P. K., & Givi, P. (2016). Paragon: Parallel architecture-aware graph partition refinement algorithm. EDBT, 365–376.

ENDNOTES

1   giraph.apache.org/
2   https://neo4j.com
3   orientdb.com
4   www.objectivity.com/products/infinitegraph/
5   https://neo4j.com
6   www.sparsity-technologies.com/
7   www.objectivity.com/products/infinitegraph/
8   hypergraphdb.org/
9   franz.com/agraph/allegrograph/
10 blueprints.tinkerpop.com/
11 titan.thinkaurelius.com/
12 orientdb.com/orientdb/
13 https://www.w3.org/TR/rdf-sparql-query/
14 gremlin.tinkerpop.com/
15 https://neo4j.com/developer/cypher-query-language/

Chapter 7
A Case Study on Citation Network Analysis

ABSTRACT

In this chapter, the authors present a case study of Network Analysis in the field of bibliometrics, focused on the identification of central academic articles based on complex network metrics that can be implemented with algorithms covered throughout this book. The authors analyze a scientific citation network and systematically obtain the most central papers considering different perspectives of the selected document collection. Later, they discuss the potential benefits that the parallel kernels and the topology-aware partitioning algorithms can offer in the context of the presented study case. Finally, the authors summarize this book's main contributions and offer some concluding remarks.

INTRODUCTION

As stressed throughout this book, complex networks are a powerful tool for representing multi-relational big data, and for modeling complicated data structures and their interactions. Due to their potential to represent the topology of numerous large-scale systems present in nature and technology, complex networks represent an essential framework for describing the behavior of complex phenomena. The applications of complex network analysis are diverse and given the increasing availability of raw data in different disciplines

DOI: 10.4018/978-1-5225-3799-1.ch007

it is now possible to exploit Network Science applications to steer research in fields ranging from social sciences, engineering, statistical physics, graph theory, and bibliometrics.

One of such applications is *network centrality analysis*. The applications of centrality analysis are various: to identify influential people in social networks, key infrastructure nodes in energy or urban networks, backbone autonomous systems in the topology of the Internet, key proteins in protein-protein interaction networks, etc. Centrality metrics quantify the importance of vertices. As discussed in Chapter 2, different centrality metrics consider different local or global aspects of the topology of a network to define the importance of the vertices: number of neighbors of a node, shortest distance between pairs of nodes, proportion of shortest paths passing through a node, the importance of neighboring nodes, etc.

In this book, we have studied algorithms that represent the building blocks of a variety of centrality complex network metrics. Particularly, the AS-BFS algorithm presented in Chapter 3 is the core kernel for centrality and global metrics such as the betweenness centrality, the stressness centrality, the diameter, the average path length, and the coreness centrality. We call such metrics AS-BFS aggregable metrics (Garcia-Robledo et al., 2017), since their calculation can be decomposed into partial measurements starting from different nodes that can be aggregated in the final stage to obtain the final metric values.

On the other hand, algorithms like the k-core decomposition presented in Chapter 2, allow us to obtain not only coarsening and unbalanced partitioning algorithms (Chapters 2 and 5), but also network fingerprints (Alvarez-Hamelin et al., 2005) to visually study the presence of complexity (or lack thereof) in a network, to determine, for example, if a centrality analysis will yield any useful result. k-core fingerprints also allow us to visually find similarity patterns among different large-scale networks, a remarkably difficult task if employing conventional graph visualization and force-directed network layout algorithms, from both the computational and the cognitive (visual) perspectives.

This chapter presents a case study that makes use of global, k-core and centrality metrics that can be calculated by implementing some of the core algorithmic kernels presented in this book. Specifically, we describe an application of network centrality analysis in the field of bibliometrics, focused on the identification of central academic articles based on the consensus of different complex network centrality metrics. Later, we discuss how this study case could be benefited from the parallel algorithms covered in Chapter

3 and from the partitioning algorithms reported in Chapter 5. Finally, in the last section we summarize our main contributions and offer some concluding remarks on the material presented throughout this book.

STUDY CASE: IDENTIFYING INFLUENTIAL PAPERS IN A CITATION NETWORK

Large collections of academic documents are now available through repositories such as Google Scholar and arXiv. From the data available in this kind of collections it is possible to construct diverse models to abstract different types of phenomena in the academic ecosystem. Examples of such models are *citation networks*. The objective of the analysis of a citation network is to discover and study the existing relationships among a set of scientific articles. Such relationships have the potential of revealing the evolution of a research field and the identification of influential articles that contributed to the development of a knowledge field. However, the more information available to build the network, the greater the difficulty in extracting useful information from such a collection of data.

In the field of bibliometrics, the centrality analysis of citation networks provides the necessary tools to evaluate the impact of papers in a research field, as well as to identify the sub-fields in which the papers have made major contributions, based on the characterization of the importance of the citation network nodes.

In the literature there are works that present different case studies with particular citation networks, from small networks consisting of up to 200 articles (Yang et al., 2007; Mahmood et al., 2013), to larger networks with thousands of articles (Fujita, 2012; Lu et al., 2006). These studies aim to obtain general information about the analysis of the appointments.

It is possible to find works that use intermediation measures for various purposes. Bollen et al. (2009) perform a Principal Component Analysis of 39 scientific impact metrics, including number of citations, impact factor, closeness centrality, H-index, PageRank, and centrality of intermediation. They conclude that the first principal component separates usage metrics and citation metrics, while the second main component separates metrics that express popularity and metrics that express prestige. Leydesdorff and Rafols (2011) investigate centrality metrics such as betweenness, Shannon's entropy, the Gini coefficient, and the Rao-Stirling index. It is found that the betweenness centrality, calculated from a cosine-normalized matrix, qualifies as a good index of inter-disciplinarity.

Kas et al. (2012) study the evolution of the field of high energy physics; and citation, publication and co-publication networks are investigated. They find that articles with high betweenness centrality tend to unite different sub-areas of research, and this is corroborated in clusters of citations observed in the network. Diallo et al. (2016) examine the extent to which different centrality metrics can be used to identify a set of key publications within a specialized journal. For this purpose, a set of data from the Public Library of Science (PLOS) is represented through a co-citation network and three centrality metrics are calculated: closeness centrality, betweenness and eigenvectors. They conclude that the centrality of eigenvectors represents an effective criterion to identify key publications and that there is a correlation between the metric and the degree of citations of the articles of the same journal.

However, to the best of our knowledge, the problem of finding a consensus among different centrality metrics to characterize the key publications from different topological perspectives of a given citation network has not been sufficiently explored in the literature. The next section describes a methodology for the study case of finding a consensus when different centrality metrics are used to obtain a single ranking of important publications in a citation network.

Citation Network Analysis Methodology

For this study case, we selected the arXiv HEP-TH (high-energy physics theory) citation graph (Leskovec et al., 2005), denoted as $G = (V, E)$, that covers all the citations within a dataset of $n = 27,770$ papers (V) with $m = 352,807$ edges (E). If a paper i cites paper j, the graph contains the directed edge $(i, j) \in E$. The data cover papers in the 124-months period from January 1993 to April 2003, and it represents the complete history of its HEP-TH section as of 2003 (Leskovec, 2005). The dataset is publicly available and was compiled by arXiv for the KDD Cup'03 competition.

There is a wide variety of centrality metrics in literature, ranging from degree-based (e.g. in-degree, out-degree), distance-based metrics (e.g. stress, betweenness, closeness), to eigen-based metrics (e.g. eigenvector centrality and PageRank). Unfortunately, there is no a "universal" centrality metric, and it is necessary to implement a methodology to reconcile the rankings produced by different metrics that contemplate different properties of the same network.

We now describe how degree, distance, and eigenvector-based centrality metrics can be used as criteria to determine central works based on the topology of a citation network (Yanez-Sierra et al., 2016):

1. **Citation Network Topology Analysis:** A statistical analysis is performed based on available metrics in the area of network sciences in order to evaluate the relevance of the vertices. The selected metrics can be local, global or centrality depending on the scope of the problem and the phenomenon to be analyzed.
2. **Node Centrality Analysis:** Given an initial group of centrality metrics, the centralities of all nodes in the network are calculated w.r.t. each centrality metric.
3. **Centrality Correlation Analysis:** A pair-wise correlation study is carried out between the centrality metrics by using the measurements obtained in Stage 2 and the Kendall tau-b coefficient, in order to group those centrality metrics that provide information related to the same phenomenon.
4. **Centrality Consensus Analysis:** A consensus among the selected metrics is made, in order to obtain a final ordering of the most relevant vertices (papers) of the collection.
5. **Similarity Analysis of Most Relevant Documents:** An analysis of the similarities among the l papers related to highly-related centrality metrics is carried out by using word frequency statistical methods like tag clouds.

Citation Network Topology Analysis

The purpose of the topology analysis is to determine whether the network has a trivial structure (e.g. random or regular) or a complex structure.

We found many connected components (20,086), which suggest a wide diversity of topics with different degree of influence in the field. On the other hand, the citation network presents the phenomenon of "six degrees of separation", given that most of the pairs of publications in the network appear to be connected by a short path compared to their high number of nodes, as the graph diameter suggests (37). Also, despite its low density (4.57×10^{-4}), the network presents a significant number of triangles or cycles of size three, which is reflected in a cluster coefficient of 0.33. This is significantly higher than the clustering expected in a random network ($1 / n$).

Figure 1 contains a visualization of the k-core decomposition of the arXiv's HEP-TH graph. In Figure 1 each ring of nodes corresponds to nodes labeled with different k-shell indexes. Random networks (e.g. Erdös-Rényi graphs) are usually composed of just a few rings. In contrast, the large quantity of rings of the HEP-TH network decomposition clearly departs from the expected pattern in a random network, providing additional evidence of the existence of a degree of complexity in the modeled citation phenomenon.

Overall, the topology analysis of arXiv's HEP-TH citation network suggests that the network cannot be explained by random graphs, since it presents interesting properties in its topology that encode non-trivial aspects about the complex ecosystem of academic contributions in arXiv's HEP-TH section. This conclusion justifies the use of centrality metrics that exploit local and global network patterns to identify key articles.

Figure 1. Visual depiction of the k-core decomposition of the arXiv HEP-TH graph. Internal light-colored node rings correspond to nodes with lower k-shell index, while outer darker-colored rings correspond to nodes with higher k-shell index. Node sizes are proportional to their degree.

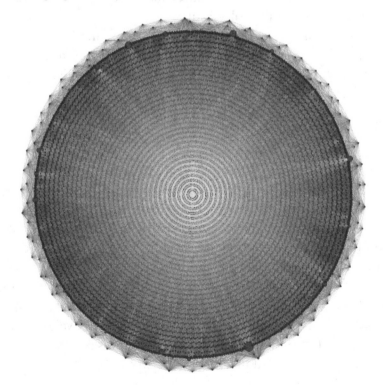

Node Centrality Analysis

As mentioned before, centrality metrics quantify the importance of each node individually. An example is the betweenness centrality, defined as the proportion of shorter paths passing through a given node. Another example is the closeness centrality, which is proportional to the length of the shortest paths between a node and the rest of the vertices.

The following set of centrality metrics was measured on the HEP-TH network to identify the most relevant articles from different perspectives of the topology of the network:

1. *In-Degree Centrality* (**IND**): It is the most intuitive centrality measure: the number of citations for each node, according to Google Scholar.
2. *Betweenness Centrality* (**BET**): It represents an index of the variety of disciplines that are connected thanks to the theme of an article.
3. *Closeness Centrality* (**CLO**): Articles with high centrality of closeness could have greater influence in a greater proportion of articles given their proximity in the hierarchy of citations.
4. *PageRank Centrality* (**PAG**): It gives greater weight not only to those publications that are highly cited, but also to those that are recursively cited by publications that in turn are highly cited.
5. *Hub-Score Centrality* (**HUB**): Calculates Kleinberg's hub score for the vertices of the graph, which estimates the value of links of a paper to other pages.

These criteria of vertex centrality were intentionally selected to consider three different aspects of the publications in the citation network: (1) the magnitude of the number citations (in-degree centrality and hub-score centrality); (2) distances between publications, to evaluate the existence of articles that act as bridges between different areas of knowledge (intermediation and closeness); and (3) measures that not only consider the number of citations of publications, but also the relevance of the documents that cite them (PageRank).

Centrality Metrics Correlation Analysis

To obtain an overall ranking from the individually calculated centrality metrics, it is necessary first to find those metrics that model the same trend or phenomenon within the network. In other words, we need to identify groups of centrality metrics that hold a high correlation when measured on a network of interest. The motivation of this step is: trying to conciliate rankings of metrics with low correlation could result in a biased ranking that obey the trends of only a subset of the metrics. The consensus should be made only among closely-related metrics to obtain a consistent ranking.

The Kendall's correlation coefficient, also known as the Kendall's tau-b coefficient (Sen, 1968), is a widely used non-parametric test that measures the ordinal association between two groups of measurements. The correlation between two Kendall variables will be high when the observations have a ranking value (relative position among the variables of observation) identical or similar.

By grouping metrics that exceed a Kendall correlation threshold[1], we get as many subsets of nodes as groups of highly correlated centrality metrics. Each subset is then studied separately. The different subsets of key nodes potentially represent different perspectives of the data in the network, usually not predictable to analyze.

By considering the measurements obtained during the centrality analysis of the arXiv's HEP-TH citation network, we obtained Kendall tau-b pairwise correlations for all centrality metrics pairs. Figure 2 shows the resulting heatmap. A hierarchical clustering algorithm applied on the correlation matrix allowed us to permute rows and columns to identify two groups of metrics with the highest correlation along the main diagonal:

1. **CLO-HUB Group:** It includes the closeness and the hub-score, with a Kendall tau-b correlation of 0.76.
2. **PAG-IND Group:** Groups to the PageRank and the in-degree centrality, with a Kendall tau-b correlation of 0.71.
3. **BET Group:** This group is integrated by a single centrality metric, the betweenness centrality, with Kendall tau-b correlations to other metrics ranging from 0.37 to 0.53.

Unexpectedly, the betweenness centrality is weakly correlated to the rest of the metrics on the HEP-TH network, including the closeness centrality, which is also based on the shortest-paths between papers. This suggests that it is the most discordant metric and as such should be considered separately in order to obtain reliable metrics consensus in the next stage of the methodology.

Figure 2. Heatmap of the correlation matrix for the experimented centrality complex network metrics. Highly-correlated metrics are presented in darker colors along the main diagonal.

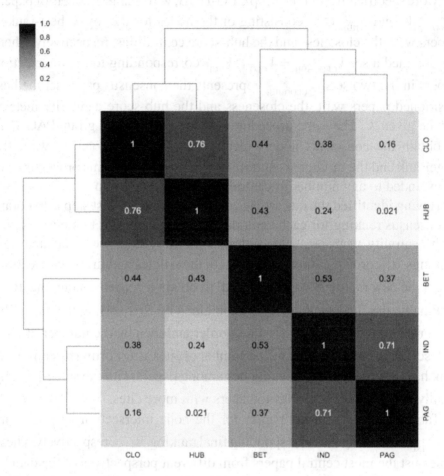

Consensus of Centrality Metrics

Each centrality metric induces a ranking of the citation network nodes in V when we order the nodes in descending order of their centrality. However, these rankings might be different for different centrality metrics, even for highly-correlated centrality metrics. Therefore, a mechanism of consensus among these rankings is needed to obtain a final ranking. To obtain such a consensus, for each highly-correlated centrality metric group (CLO-HUB and PAG-IND) we carried out the following steps. For each centrality metric in the group, we obtained a set of the top-k best-ranked papers[2]. Then, we calculated the intersection among these sets.

More specifically, for the group CLO-HUB, we obtained the sets of papers $V_{CLO} \subset V$ and $V_{HUB} \subset V$ consisting of the nodes for the top-k best-ranked papers w.r.t. the closeness and the hub-score centralities, respectively. Then, we obtained a set $V_{CLO \cap HUB} = V_{CLO} \cap V_{HUB}$ corresponding to the intersection papers in the two sets. $V_{CLO \cap HUB}$ represents the consensus paper set the best positioned papers w.r.t. the closeness and the hub-score centrality metrics for the given k. The same procedure was followed for the group PAG-IND to obtain the consensus node paper set $V_{PAG \cap IND} = V_{PAG} \cap V_{IND}$ w.r.t. the PageRank and the in-degree centralities. Please note that this procedure can be extended to any number of centrality metrics in a group > 2.

Having identified the key articles of the network, the last step is to obtain a consensus ranking for each centrality metric group. For this purpose, for each centrality metric π in a centrality metric group, we calculated new rankings R'_{π} corresponding to the order of the articles within the intersection. Then, the new rankings were averaged[3] to obtain a consensus ranking R'_{avg}.

Finally, the final ranking R_{final} is obtained by first sorting the papers by consensus ranking R'_{avg} in ascending order and then by the number of cites in descending order. Sorting by the number of cites after sorting by consensus rank has the objective of breaking ties among papers with the same R'_{avg}, by locally assigning higher ranks to papers with more cites.

Tables 1 and 2 lists the papers for the node intersection $V_{CLO \cap HUB}$ and $V_{PAG \cap IND}$ ordered by the corresponding final ranking R_{final}, respectively. These tables list the most central papers from different perspectives of the data.

Similarity Analysis of the Highest-Ranked Papers

The last stage of the study case is to find similarities among the most influential papers of each centrality metric group. Such a document similarity analysis can be carried out by an SME (subject-matter expert), or can be performed automatically through linguistic and statistical techniques borrowed from fields like Text Analytics.

Arguably, one of the most simple but surprisingly effective statistical techniques is based on a word frequency analysis and the visualization of the results by means of *tag clouds*. A tag cloud is a visual representation of

Table 1. Papers in $V_{CLO\cap HUB}$, i.e. the set of most influential papers w.r.t. the closeness and the hub-score centrality metrics, sorted by the final rank R_{final}

R_{final}	arXiv ID	R_{CLO}	R_{HUB}	R'_{CLO}	R'_{HUB}	R'_{avg}	Cites
1	9905111	2	1	1	1	1	807
2	0110055	11	2	2	2	2	5
3	0007170	14	3	3	3	3	78
4	9806199	21	7	5	6	5.5	88
5	0101126	26	4	7	4	5.5	60
6	0210157	23	5	6	5	5.5	4
7	9710046	27	9	8	7	7.5	72
8	9802051	28	10	9	8	8.5	87
9	9802067	17	32	4	16	10	164
10	0003136	31	15	11	10	10.5	179
11	9903268	35	13	13	9	11	0
12	9809039	33	19	12	11	11.5	85
13	0111284	30	31	10	15	12.5	1
14	9908199	37	21	15	12	13.5	0
15	0007195	43	25	17	13	15	10
16	9812196	38	26	16	14	15	7
17	9806123	36	33	14	17	15.5	1

free-form text data. It is typically used to discover key tags, i.e. prominent single words in a text corpus. The importance of each determines the font size or color in the visualization. This makes cloud tags useful for quickly identify and compare "prominent" terms.

For each centrality metric group, we identified the most prominent terms by concatenating the abstract paragraphs of all the papers and the obtaining a tag cloud. In this way, for example, to identify the most prominent terms for the papers in the CLO-HUB group, we concatenated the abstracts of the papers in $V_{CLO\cap HUB}$ and then obtained the corresponding tag cloud. We followed the same procedure for the group PAG-IND and for the top-20 best-ranked papers according to the betweenness centrality (BET group).

Figure 3 (top) shows the tag cloud for the most influential papers in $V_{CLO\cap HUB}$, i.e. w.r.t. the closeness and the hub-score centralities. The tag cloud suggest as prominent terms: Brane, String, Theory, and Duality. Branes are

Table 2. Papers in $V_{PAG \cap IND}$, i.e. the set of most influential papers w.r.t. the PageRank and the in-degree (number of cites) centrality metrics, sorted by the final rank R_{final}

R_{final}	arXiv ID	R_{PAG}	R_{IND}	R'_{PAG}	R'_{IND}	R'_{avg}	Cites
1	9711200	7	1	4	1	2.5	2,414
2	9407087	2	4	1	4	2.5	1,299
3	9510017	5	6	3	6	4.5	1,155
4	9503124	4	8	2	8	5	1,114
5	9802150	16	2	9	2	5.5	1,775
6	9610043	12	5	7	5	6	1,199
7	9802109	19	3	11	3	7	1,641
8	9408099	9	10	6	10	8	1,006
9	9410167	8	15	5	13	9	748
10	9510135	14	14	8	12	10	775
11	9906064	26	9	14	9	11.5	1,032
12	9510209	25	12.5	13	11	12	788
13	9908142	41	7	19	7	13	1,144
14	9401139	17	27	10	16	13	421
15	9412184	33	25	17	15	16	426
16	9504090	20	40	12	21	16.5	337
17	9601029	42	17	20	14	17	651
18	9501068	27	31	15	19	17	385
19	9411149	37	28	18	17	17.5	411
20	9301042	29	37	16	20	18	344
21	9602052	48	29	21	18	19.5	406

multidimensional objects whose characterization may lead to new insights into string theory itself (Bagger & Lambert, 2009). Branes are related to several theories in particle physics like string theory, super-string theory and M-theory.

Figure 3 (middle) shows the tag cloud for the most influential papers in $V_{PAG \cap IND}$, i.e. w.r.t. to the PageRank and the in-degree centralities. The tag cloud suggests the following prominent terms: String, Theory, Duality and Dimensions. String theory is a framework that tries to describe how strings, one-dimensional objects that replace physics particles, travel and interact

Figure 3. Tag cloud for the abstracts of the most influential papers w.r.t.: (top) the closeness and the hub-score centrality metrics; (middle) the PageRank and the in-degree centrality metrics; and (bottom) the betweenness centrality

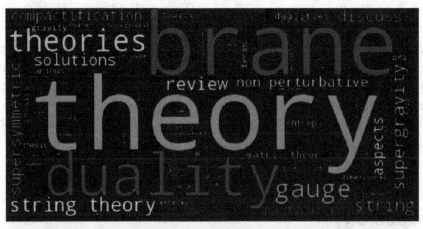

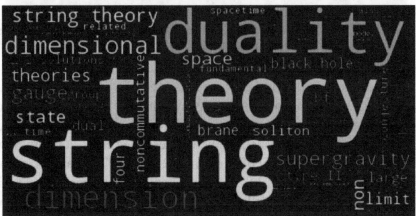

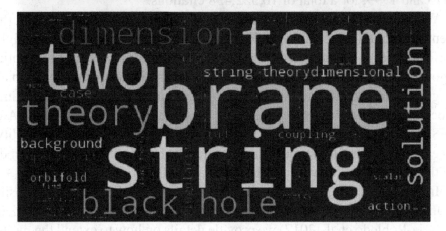

with each other. String duality, on the other hand, helps to relate different string theories.

Finally, Figure 3 (bottom) shows the tag cloud for the most influential papers w.r.t. the betweenness centrality. The tag cloud suggests that, unlike groups CLO-HUB and PAG-IND, the betweenness centrality brought up papers from a wider variety of sub-disciplines of theoretical high-energy physics, being prominent terms in the tag cloud: Brane, String, and Theory.

It is important to remark that the use of a network topology to obtain paper rankings allowed us to discover influential works in different branches of high-energy physics, which are not necessarily related to the papers with the highest number of cites. This could not be possible if we considered the number cites as the only valid criterion.

DISCUSSION

The usefulness of the study case can be emphasized by analyzing larger collections of documents. However, the calculation of AS-BFS metrics such as the betweenness centrality and the network diameter needs as many full BFS traversals as the total number of vertices (AS-BFS). This makes this kind of calculations unfeasible on commodity systems for large-scale real-world citation networks with millions of vertices and links. An example of such a citation network is the U.S. patent network (Leskovec et al., 2005) built with data from the National Bureau of Economic Research. The data set spans 37 years and includes all the 3,923,922 utility patents granted during that period. The citation network models all citations made by patents granted between 1975 and 1999, for a total of 16,522,438 citations.

We have estimated that obtaining the betweenness centrality of the mentioned citation network would take approximately 6 months on a high-performance AMD Opteron processor when exploiting an efficient sequential algorithm. We have also estimated that the graph diameter and average path length would take around 2.6 months of computing time each on the same processor (Garcia-Robledo et al., 2017). One solution is to approximate AS-BFS measurements, but this is not always possible. The betweenness centrality, for example, is hard to estimate, and the quality of the approximation depends on the selected source vertices (Bader et al., 2007).

In Chapter 3, we studied parallel kernels for AS-BFS that can be easily adapted to accelerate these algorithms on multi-core CPUs or GPU. In (Garcia-Robledo et al., 2017) we provide details on how to extend the multi-core AS-BFS parallel algorithm presented in Chapter 3 to implement the betweenness, the diameter, and the average path length on multi-core clusters.

On the other hand, we believe that the methodology presented throughout this book to get proper unbalanced partitioning algorithms for graph heterogeneous computing can be adapted to accelerate the calculations of expensive distance-based metrics like the betweenness and the graph diameter used in the study case, being all of these metrics instances of BFS-based calculations.

The predominant architecture in the TOP500 supercomputing index is the HPC cluster: a collection of complete and independent commercially-available systems connected through high-speed specialized networks. As of June 2017, all of the top four supercomputers used NVIDIA's latest P100 GPUs (Top Green 500, 2017). By combining (1) the insights and AS-BFS CPU/GPU parallel kernels reviewed in Chapter 3, (2) the unbalanced graph partitioning algorithms in Chapter 5, as well as (3) cluster BFS-aggregable algorithms (Garcia-Robledo et al., 2017), it is possible to extend the TOTEM platform or to develop new heterogeneous computing software platforms to accelerate BFS-based complex network algorithms on multi-core/GPU hybrid clusters and supercomputers.

We also believe that the methodology presented throughout this work can be adapted to accelerate other Graph500 benchmarks such as PageRank, as characterization, coarsening, and efficient partitioning of complex networks for graph parallel processing become more relevant as the scale of the networks increases. Thus, interesting research lines includes the adaptation of the complex network coarsening and partitioning algorithms developed in this work to accelerate other key Graph500 computations on hybrid cluster platforms.

REFERENCES

Alvarez-Hamelin, J. I., Dall'Asta, L., Barrat, A., & Vespignani, A. (2005). *K-core decomposition: A tool for the visualization of large scale networks.* arXiv preprint cs/0504107

Bader, D. A., Kintali, S., Madduri, K., & Mihail, M. (2007). Approximating betweenness centrality. In *Proceedings of the International Workshop on Algorithms and Models for the Web-Graph (WAW'07)*, (pp. 124–137). Springer. doi:10.1007/978-3-540-77004-6_10

Bagger, J., & Lambert, N. (2009, January 12). *Synopsis: String theory on the brane*. Retrieved September 21, 2017, from https://physics.aps.org/synopsis-for/10.1103/PhysRevD.79.025002

Barrat, A., Barthelemy, M., & Vespignani, A. (2008). *Dynamical Processes on Complex Networks*. Cambridge University Press. doi:10.1017/CBO9780511791383

Bollen, J., Van de Sompel, H., Hagberg, A., & Chute, R. (2009). A principal component analysis of 39 scientific impact measures. *PLoS One*, *4*(6), e6022. doi:10.1371/journal.pone.0006022 PMID:19562078

Caldarelli, G. (2007). *Scale-free Networks: Complex Webs in Nature and Technology*. Oxford University Press. doi:10.1093/acprof:oso/9780199211517.001.0001

Cherifi, H., Gonçalves, B., Menezes, R., & Sinatra, R. (2016). Complex Networks VII: *Proceedings of the 7th Workshop on Complex Networks CompleNet 2016* (Vol. 644). Springer.

Dehmer, M., & Basak, S. C. (2012). *Statistical and machine learning approaches for network analysis* (Vol. 707). John Wiley & Sons. doi:10.1002/9781118346990

Diallo, S. Y., Lynch, C. J., Gore, R., & Padilla, J. J. (2016). Identifying key papers within a journal via network centrality measures. *Scientometrics*, *107*(3), 1005–1020. doi:10.1007/s11192-016-1891-8

Dorogovtsev, S. N. (2010). *Lectures on Complex Networks* (Vol. 24). Oxford, UK: Oxford University Press. doi:10.1093/acprof:oso/9780199548927.001.0001

Fujita, K. (2012). Finding linkage between sustainability science and technologies based on citation network analysis. *Proceedings of the 5th IEEE International Conference on Service-Oriented Computing and Applications (SOCA'12)*, 1–6. doi:10.1109/SOCA.2012.6449422

Garcia-Robledo, A., Diaz-Perez, A., & Morales-Luna, G. (2017). Accelerating All-Sources BFS Metrics on Multi-core Clusters for Large-Scale Complex Network Analysis. In C. Barrios Hernández, I. Gitler, & J. Klapp (Eds.), *High Performance Computing. CARLA 2016. Communications in Computer and Information Science* (Vol. 697). Springer. doi:10.1007/978-3-319-57972-6_5

Kas, M., Carley, K. M., & Carley, L. R. (2012). Trends in science networks: Understanding structures and statistics of scientific networks. *Social Network Analysis and Mining, 2*(2), 169–187. doi:10.1007/s13278-011-0044-6

Kepner, J., & Gilbert, J. (2011). *Graph Algorithms in the Language of Linear Algebra*. Society for Industrial and Applied Mathematics. doi:10.1137/1.9780898719918

Leskovec, J. (2005). *High-energy physics theory citation network*. Retrieved from https://snap.stanford.edu/data/cit-HepTh.html

Leskovec, J., Kleinberg, J., & Faloutsos, C. (2005). Graphs over time: densification laws, shrinking diameters and possible explanations. *Proceedings of the 11th ACM SIGKDD International Conference on Knowledge Discovery in Data Mining*, 177–187. doi:10.1145/1081870.1081893

Leydesdorff, L., & Rafols, I. (2011). Indicators of the interdisciplinarity of journals: Diversity, centrality, and citations. *Journal of Informetrics, 5*(1), 87–100. doi:10.1016/j.joi.2010.09.002

Lu, W., Janssen, J., Milios, E., Japkowicz, N., & Zhang, Y. (2006). Node similarity in the citation graph. *Knowledge and Information Systems, 11*(1), 105–129. doi:10.1007/s10115-006-0023-9

Mahmood, Q., Qadir, M. A., & Afzal, M. T. (2013). Document similarity detection using semantic social network analysis on rdf citation graph. *Proceedings of the 9th International Conference on Emerging Technologies (ICET'13)*, 1–6. doi:10.1109/ICET.2013.6743548

Meghanathan, N. (Ed.). (2016). *Advanced Methods for Complex Network Analysis*. IGI Global. doi:10.4018/978-1-4666-9964-9

Newman, M. (2010). *Networks: An Introduction*. Oxford University Press. doi:10.1093/acprof:oso/9780199206650.001.0001

Newman, M., Barabasi, A. L., & Watts, D. J. (2011). *The Structure and Dynamics of Networks*. Princeton University Press.

Sen, P. K. (1968). Estimates of the regression coefficient based on kendall's tau. *Journal of the American Statistical Association, 63*(324), 1379–1389. doi:10.1080/01621459.1968.10480934

Top Green 500. (2017). Retrieved from https://www.top500.org/green500/lists/2017/06/

Yanez-Sierra, J., Garcia-Robledo, A., Diaz-Perez, A., & Garcia-Bernon, G. (2016). Una metodología para obtener el consenso de métricas en el análisis de redes de citación. In J.-A. Olvera-Lopez, I. Olmos-Pineada, & C. Zepeda-Cortes (Eds.), *Técnicas Computacionales y TIC* (pp. 37–51). Benemérita Universidad Autónoma de Puebla.

Yang, C., Wu, S.-H., & Lee, J. (2007). A study of collaborative product commerce by co-citation analysis and social network analysis. *Proceedings of the 2007 IEEE International Conference on Industrial Engineering and Engineering Management (IE&IM'07)*, 209–213. doi:10.1109/IEEM.2007.4419181

ENDNOTES

[1]   In this study we considered a correlation threshold of 0.7.

[2]   In this study we considered a value of $k = 50$.

[3]   Note that if centrality metrics have different priorities, a weighted average can be used here.

Conclusion

In this book, we have presented topology-aware algorithms for complex networks with applications in graph heterogeneous computing.

First, a graph coarsening approach, the CKE framework, was presented to exploit the k-core decomposition to reduce complex networks while preserving non-redundant metrics, as well as scaling metrics. The developed coarsening approach enabled the reduction and eventually the partitioning of complex networks for heterogeneous computing purposes. Later, it was empirically demonstrated how the diameter, the degree distribution, and the density of graphs influences the performance of multi-cores and GPU's when performing AS-BFS traversals. The presented study revealed that CPU's and GPU's are suitable for complementary kinds of graphs and BFS approaches. We also characterized how the diameter and the density affect the performance of each parallel architecture, observing that CPU's and GPU's are impacted by these properties in different ways when running visitation BFS's.

Next, the following topology-aware graph unbalanced partitioning algorithms were presented: KCMax and KCML. KCMax and KCML are based on the notion of sub-graph search. The presented algorithms make use of: (1) a centrifuge-like dense-area identification strategy and (2) k-core-based graph reductions in the coarsening stage of a multilevel-like algorithm. The load balance produced by KCMax and KCML helped to increase the performance of a BSP CPU + GPU heterogeneous platform when performing graph traversals on both real-world and R-MAT complex networks.

We showed that it is beneficial to exploit the structure of complex networks, like their coreness and centrality, for graph partitioning. The proposed graph bisection heuristics that capitalize on the notion of core-decomposition-based graph coarsening and centrality of nodes, increased the performance of the heterogeneous computing platform when accelerating BFS's on large complex networks. We also showed that it is beneficial to use a hybrid system to accelerate large-scale graph processing. However, performance profit depends on the specific complex network instance. Nonetheless, an overall improvement over the use of the GPU alone was observed on large-scale Internet, citation and synthetic networks when exploiting the proposed topology-aware partitioning algorithms.

We ended this book with a case study on a methodology for analyzing a citation network from the field of high-energy physics theory. The case study covered the application of various metrics covered in this book, a study on the correlations among different centrality metrics of interest, and the generation of consensus rankings of the most central papers from different perspectives of the studied network.

We believe that the methodology presented throughout this work can be adapted to accelerate other Graph500 benchmarks such as PageRank, as characterization, coarsening and efficient partitioning and analysis of complex networks for graph parallel processing become more relevant as the scale of the networks increases. Research lines include the adaptation of the complex network coarsening and partitioning algorithms developed in this work to accelerate other key Graph500 computations on hybrid cluster platforms.

The predominant architecture in the TOP500 supercomputing index is the HPC cluster: a collection of complete and independent commercially-available systems connected through high-speed specialized networks. As of June 2017, all of the top four supercomputers used NVIDIA's latest P100 GPU's (June 2017, 2017). By combining (1) the insights and AS-BFS CPU/GPU parallel kernels reviewed in Chapter 3, (2) the unbalanced graph partitioning algorithms in Chapter 5, as well as (3) cluster BFS-aggregable algorithms (Garcia-Robledo et al., 2017), it is possible to extend the TOTEM platform or to develop new heterogeneous computing software platforms to accelerate BFS-based complex network algorithms on multi-core/GPU hybrid clusters and supercomputers.

RECOMMENDED READINGS

Network Science is a relatively young field that has been mostly addressed from a theoretical physics-statistics perspective. Works that approach the new array of problems in Network Science from a Computer Science and Data Analytics point of view are scarce.

The following is a list of recommended introductory publications from well-known authors in the field that the reader might find useful for getting started in Network Science and complex network analysis:

- "Networks: An Introduction" by Newman (2010).
- "The Structure and Dynamics of Networks" by Newman, Barabasi, and Watts (2011).
- "Lectures on Complex Networks" by Dorogovtsev (2010).
- "Dynamical Processes on Complex Networks" by Barrat, Barthélemy, and Vespignani (2008).
- "Scale-free networks: Complex Webs in Nature and Technology" by Caldarelli (2007).

Most recent books reporting computation research in Network Science are actually proceedings of conferences, like the Workshop on Complex Networks CompleNet (Cherifi et al., 2016), or works that gather contributions from different disciplines, like those by Dehmer et al. (2012) and Meghanathan (2016). These works are recommended since they feature the latest research on algorithms and analysis in various areas and application domains.

Regarding parallel graph processing books, a recommended reading is that of Kepner and Gilbert (2011), who exploit the duality between graphs and sparse adjacency matrix representations.

REFERENCES

Barrat, A., Barthelemy, M., & Vespignani, A. (2008). *Dynamical Processes on Complex Networks*. Cambridge University Press. doi:10.1017/CBO9780511791383

Caldarelli, G. (2007). *Scale-free Networks: Complex Webs in Nature and Technology*. Oxford University Press. doi:10.1093/acprof:oso/9780199211517.001.0001

Cherifi, H., Gonçalves, B., Menezes, R., & Sinatra, R. (2016). Complex Networks VII: *Proceedings of the 7th Workshop on Complex Networks CompleNet 2016* (Vol. 644). Springer.

Dehmer, M., & Basak, S. C. (2012). *Statistical and machine learning approaches for network analysis* (Vol. 707). John Wiley & Sons. doi:10.1002/9781118346990

Dorogovtsev, S. N. (2010). *Lectures on Complex Networks* (Vol. 24). Oxford, UK: Oxford University Press. doi:10.1093/acprof:oso/9780199548927.001.0001

Garcia-Robledo, A., Diaz-Perez, A., & Morales-Luna, G. (2017). Accelerating All-Sources BFS Metrics on Multi-core Clusters for Large-Scale Complex Network Analysis. In C. Barrios Hernández, I. Gitler, & J. Klapp (Eds.), *High Performance Computing. CARLA 2016. Communications in Computer and Information Science* (Vol. 697). Springer. doi:10.1007/978-3-319-57972-6_5

Kepner, J., & Gilbert, J. (2011). *Graph Algorithms in the Language of Linear Algebra*. Society for Industrial and Applied Mathematics. doi:10.1137/1.9780898719918

Meghanathan, N. (Ed.). (2016). *Advanced Methods for Complex Network Analysis*. IGI Global. doi:10.4018/978-1-4666-9964-9

Newman, M. (2010). *Networks: An Introduction*. Oxford University Press. doi:10.1093/acprof:oso/9780199206650.001.0001

Newman, M., Barabasi, A. L., & Watts, D. J. (2011). *The Structure and Dynamics of Networks*. Princeton University Press.

The Green 500. (2017, June). Retrieved from https://www.top500.org/green500/lists/2017/06/

Related Readings

To continue IGI Global's long-standing tradition of advancing innovation through emerging research, please find below a compiled list of recommended IGI Global book chapters and journal articles in the areas of heterogeneous computing, complex network analysis, and high performance computing. These related readings will provide additional information and guidance to further enrich your knowledge and assist you with your own research.

Acharjya, D. P., & Mary, A. G. (2014). Privacy Preservation in Information System. In B. Tripathy & D. Acharjya (Eds.), *Advances in Secure Computing, Internet Services, and Applications* (pp. 49–72). Hershey, PA: IGI Global. doi:10.4018/978-1-4666-4940-8.ch003

Adhikari, M., Das, A., & Mukherjee, A. (2016). Utility Computing and Its Utilization. In G. Deka, G. Siddesh, K. Srinivasa, & L. Patnaik (Eds.), *Emerging Research Surrounding Power Consumption and Performance Issues in Utility Computing* (pp. 1–21). Hershey, PA: IGI Global. doi:10.4018/978-1-4666-8853-7.ch001

Adhikari, M., & Kar, S. (2016). Advanced Topics GPU Programming and CUDA Architecture. In G. Deka, G. Siddesh, K. Srinivasa, & L. Patnaik (Eds.), *Emerging Research Surrounding Power Consumption and Performance Issues in Utility Computing* (pp. 175–203). Hershey, PA: IGI Global. doi:10.4018/978-1-4666-8853-7.ch008

Adhikari, M., & Roy, D. (2016). Green Computing. In G. Deka, G. Siddesh, K. Srinivasa, & L. Patnaik (Eds.), *Emerging Research Surrounding Power Consumption and Performance Issues in Utility Computing* (pp. 84–108). Hershey, PA: IGI Global. doi:10.4018/978-1-4666-8853-7.ch005

Ahmad, K., Kumar, G., Wahid, A., & Kirmani, M. M. (2016). Software Performance Estimate using Fuzzy Based Backpropagation Learning. In G. Deka, G. Siddesh, K. Srinivasa, & L. Patnaik (Eds.), *Emerging Research Surrounding Power Consumption and Performance Issues in Utility Computing* (pp. 320–344). Hershey, PA: IGI Global. doi:10.4018/978-1-4666-8853-7. ch016

Ahmed, M. S., Houser, J., Hoque, M. A., Raju, R., & Pfeiffer, P. (2017). Reducing Inter-Process Communication Overhead in Parallel Sparse Matrix-Matrix Multiplication. *International Journal of Grid and High Performance Computing*, 9(3), 46–59. doi:10.4018/IJGHPC.2017070104

Akram, V. K., & Dagdeviren, O. (2016). On k-Connectivity Problems in Distributed Systems. In N. Meghanathan (Ed.), *Advanced Methods for Complex Network Analysis* (pp. 30–57). Hershey, PA: IGI Global. doi:10.4018/978-1-4666-9964-9.ch002

Alfredson, J., & Ohlander, U. (2015). Intelligent Fighter Pilot Support for Distributed Unmanned and Manned Decision Making. In K. Sarma, M. Sarma, & M. Sarma (Eds.), *Intelligent Applications for Heterogeneous System Modeling and Design* (pp. 1–22). Hershey, PA: IGI Global. doi:10.4018/978-1-4666-8493-5.ch001

Alling, A., Powers, N. R., & Soyata, T. (2016). Face Recognition: A Tutorial on Computational Aspects. In G. Deka, G. Siddesh, K. Srinivasa, & L. Patnaik (Eds.), *Emerging Research Surrounding Power Consumption and Performance Issues in Utility Computing* (pp. 405–425). Hershey, PA: IGI Global. doi:10.4018/978-1-4666-8853-7.ch020

Alsarhan, A., Abdallah, E. E., & Aljammal, A. H. (2017). Competitive Processors Allocation in 2D Mesh Connected Multicomputer Networks: A Dynamic Game Approach. *International Journal of Grid and High Performance Computing*, 9(2), 53–69. doi:10.4018/IJGHPC.2017040104

Amitab, K., Kandar, D., & Maji, A. K. (2016). Speckle Noise Filtering Using Back-Propagation Multi-Layer Perceptron Network in Synthetic Aperture Radar Image. In P. Mallick (Ed.), *Research Advances in the Integration of Big Data and Smart Computing* (pp. 280–301). Hershey, PA: IGI Global. doi:10.4018/978-1-4666-8737-0.ch016

Aslanpour, M. S., & Dashti, S. E. (2017). Proactive Auto-Scaling Algorithm (PASA) for Cloud Application. *International Journal of Grid and High Performance Computing*, *9*(3), 1–16. doi:10.4018/IJGHPC.2017070101

Balluff, S., Bendfeld, J., & Krauter, S. (2017). Meteorological Data Forecast using RNN. *International Journal of Grid and High Performance Computing*, *9*(1), 61–74. doi:10.4018/IJGHPC.2017010106

Baragi, S., & Iyer, N. C. (2016). Face Recognition using Fast Fourier Transform. In P. Mallick (Ed.), *Research Advances in the Integration of Big Data and Smart Computing* (pp. 302–322). Hershey, PA: IGI Global. doi:10.4018/978-1-4666-8737-0.ch017

Benson, I., Kaplan, A., Flynn, J., & Katz, S. (2017). Fault-Tolerant and Deterministic Flight-Software System For a High Performance CubeSat. *International Journal of Grid and High Performance Computing*, *9*(1), 92–104. doi:10.4018/IJGHPC.2017010108

Bhadoria, R. S. (2016). Performance of Enterprise Architecture in Utility Computing. In G. Deka, G. Siddesh, K. Srinivasa, & L. Patnaik (Eds.), *Emerging Research Surrounding Power Consumption and Performance Issues in Utility Computing* (pp. 44–68). Hershey, PA: IGI Global. doi:10.4018/978-1-4666-8853-7.ch003

Bhadoria, R. S., & Patil, C. (2016). Adaptive Mobile Architecture with Utility Computing. In G. Deka, G. Siddesh, K. Srinivasa, & L. Patnaik (Eds.), *Emerging Research Surrounding Power Consumption and Performance Issues in Utility Computing* (pp. 386–404). Hershey, PA: IGI Global. doi:10.4018/978-1-4666-8853-7.ch019

Bhargavi, K., & Babu, B. S. (2016). GPU Computation and Platforms. In G. Deka, G. Siddesh, K. Srinivasa, & L. Patnaik (Eds.), *Emerging Research Surrounding Power Consumption and Performance Issues in Utility Computing* (pp. 136–174). Hershey, PA: IGI Global. doi:10.4018/978-1-4666-8853-7.ch007

Bhat, C. G., & Kopparapu, S. K. (2017). Creating Sound Glyph Database for Video Subtitling. In M. S., & V. V. (Eds.), Multi-Core Computer Vision and Image Processing for Intelligent Applications (pp. 136-154). Hershey, PA: IGI Global. doi:10.4018/978-1-5225-0889-2.ch005

Bhoi, A. K., Sherpa, K. S., & Khandelwal, B. (2016). Baseline Drift Removal of ECG Signal: Comparative Analysis of Filtering Techniques. In P. Mallick (Ed.), *Research Advances in the Integration of Big Data and Smart Computing* (pp. 134–152). Hershey, PA: IGI Global. doi:10.4018/978-1-4666-8737-0.ch008

Bhura, M., Deshpande, P. H., & Chandrasekaran, K. (2016). CUDA or OpenCL: Which is Better? A Detailed Performance Analysis. In P. Mallick (Ed.), *Research Advances in the Integration of Big Data and Smart Computing* (pp. 267–279). Hershey, PA: IGI Global. doi:10.4018/978-1-4666-8737-0.ch015

Bisoy, S. K., & Pattnaik, P. K. (2016). Transmission Control Protocol for Mobile Ad Hoc Network. In P. Mallick (Ed.), *Research Advances in the Integration of Big Data and Smart Computing* (pp. 22–49). Hershey, PA: IGI Global. doi:10.4018/978-1-4666-8737-0.ch002

Borovikov, E., Vajda, S., Lingappa, G., & Bonifant, M. C. (2017). Parallel Computing in Face Image Retrieval: Practical Approach to the Real-World Image Search. In M. S., & V. V. (Eds.), Multi-Core Computer Vision and Image Processing for Intelligent Applications (pp. 155-189). Hershey, PA: IGI Global. doi:10.4018/978-1-5225-0889-2.ch006

Casillas, L., Daradoumis, T., & Caballe, S. (2016). A Network Analysis Method for Tailoring Academic Programs. In N. Meghanathan (Ed.), *Advanced Methods for Complex Network Analysis* (pp. 396–417). Hershey, PA: IGI Global. doi:10.4018/978-1-4666-9964-9.ch017

Chauhan, R., & Kaur, H. (2014). Predictive Analytics and Data Mining: A Framework for Optimizing Decisions with R Tool. In B. Tripathy & D. Acharjya (Eds.), *Advances in Secure Computing, Internet Services, and Applications* (pp. 73–88). Hershey, PA: IGI Global. doi:10.4018/978-1-4666-4940-8.ch004

Chen, G., Wang, E., Sun, X., & Lu, Y. (2016). An Intelligent Approval System for City Construction based on Cloud Computing and Big Data. *International Journal of Grid and High Performance Computing, 8*(3), 57–69. doi:10.4018/IJGHPC.2016070104

Chen, Z., Yang, S., Shang, Y., Liu, Y., Wang, F., Wang, L., & Fu, J. (2016). Fragment Re-Allocation Strategy Based on Hypergraph for NoSQL Database Systems. *International Journal of Grid and High Performance Computing, 8*(3), 1–23. doi:10.4018/IJGHPC.2016070101

Choudhury, A., Talukdar, A. K., & Sarma, K. K. (2015). A Review on Vision-Based Hand Gesture Recognition and Applications. In K. Sarma, M. Sarma, & M. Sarma (Eds.), *Intelligent Applications for Heterogeneous System Modeling and Design* (pp. 256–281). Hershey, PA: IGI Global. doi:10.4018/978-1-4666-8493-5.ch011

Coti, C. (2016). Fault Tolerance Techniques for Distributed, Parallel Applications. In Q. Hassan (Ed.), *Innovative Research and Applications in Next-Generation High Performance Computing* (pp. 221–252). Hershey, PA: IGI Global. doi:10.4018/978-1-5225-0287-6.ch009

Crespo, M. L., Cicuttin, A., Gazzano, J. D., & Rincon Calle, F. (2016). Reconfigurable Virtual Instrumentation Based on FPGA for Science and High-Education. In J. Gazzano, M. Crespo, A. Cicuttin, & F. Calle (Eds.), *Field-Programmable Gate Array (FPGA) Technologies for High Performance Instrumentation* (pp. 99–123). Hershey, PA: IGI Global. doi:10.4018/978-1-5225-0299-9.ch005

Daniel, D. K., & Bhandari, V. (2014). Neural Network Model to Estimate and Predict Cell Mass Concentration in Lipase Fermentation. In B. Tripathy & D. Acharjya (Eds.), *Advances in Secure Computing, Internet Services, and Applications* (pp. 303–316). Hershey, PA: IGI Global. doi:10.4018/978-1-4666-4940-8.ch015

Das, B., Sarma, M. P., & Sarma, K. K. (2015). Different Aspects of Interleaving Techniques in Wireless Communication. In K. Sarma, M. Sarma, & M. Sarma (Eds.), *Intelligent Applications for Heterogeneous System Modeling and Design* (pp. 335–374). Hershey, PA: IGI Global. doi:10.4018/978-1-4666-8493-5.ch015

Das, P. K. (2016). Comparative Study on XEN, KVM, VSphere, and Hyper-V. In G. Deka, G. Siddesh, K. Srinivasa, & L. Patnaik (Eds.), *Emerging Research Surrounding Power Consumption and Performance Issues in Utility Computing* (pp. 233–261). Hershey, PA: IGI Global. doi:10.4018/978-1-4666-8853-7.ch011

Das, P. K., & Deka, G. C. (2016). History and Evolution of GPU Architecture. In G. Deka, G. Siddesh, K. Srinivasa, & L. Patnaik (Eds.), *Emerging Research Surrounding Power Consumption and Performance Issues in Utility Computing* (pp. 109–135). Hershey, PA: IGI Global. doi:10.4018/978-1-4666-8853-7.ch006

Das, R., & Pradhan, M. K. (2014). Artificial Neural Network Modeling for Electrical Discharge Machining Parameters. In B. Tripathy & D. Acharjya (Eds.), *Advances in Secure Computing, Internet Services, and Applications* (pp. 281–302). Hershey, PA: IGI Global. doi:10.4018/978-1-4666-4940-8.ch014

Das, S., & Kalita, H. K. (2016). Advanced Dimensionality Reduction Method for Big Data. In P. Mallick (Ed.), *Research Advances in the Integration of Big Data and Smart Computing* (pp. 198–210). Hershey, PA: IGI Global. doi:10.4018/978-1-4666-8737-0.ch011

Das, S., & Kalita, H. K. (2016). Efficient Classification Rule Mining for Breast Cancer Detection. In P. Mallick (Ed.), *Research Advances in the Integration of Big Data and Smart Computing* (pp. 50–63). Hershey, PA: IGI Global. doi:10.4018/978-1-4666-8737-0.ch003

De Micco, L., & Larrondo, H. A. (2016). Methodology for FPGA Implementation of a Chaos-Based AWGN Generator. In J. Gazzano, M. Crespo, A. Cicuttin, & F. Calle (Eds.), *Field-Programmable Gate Array (FPGA) Technologies for High Performance Instrumentation* (pp. 43–58). Hershey, PA: IGI Global. doi:10.4018/978-1-5225-0299-9.ch003

de Souza, E. D., & Lima, E. J. II. (2017). Autonomic Computing in a Biomimetic Algorithm for Robots Dedicated to Rehabilitation of Ankle. *International Journal of Grid and High Performance Computing, 9*(1), 48–60. doi:10.4018/IJGHPC.2017010105

Deepika, R., Prasad, M. R., Chetana, S., & Manjunath, T. C. (2016). Adoption of Dual Iris and Periocular Recognition for Human Identification. In P. Mallick (Ed.), *Research Advances in the Integration of Big Data and Smart Computing* (pp. 250–266). Hershey, PA: IGI Global. doi:10.4018/978-1-4666-8737-0.ch014

Dey, P., & Roy, S. (2016). Social Network Analysis. In N. Meghanathan (Ed.), *Advanced Methods for Complex Network Analysis* (pp. 237–265). Hershey, PA: IGI Global. doi:10.4018/978-1-4666-9964-9.ch010

Don Clark, A. (2016). A Theoretic Representation of the Effects of Targeted Failures in HPC Systems. In Q. Hassan (Ed.), *Innovative Research and Applications in Next-Generation High Performance Computing* (pp. 253–276). Hershey, PA: IGI Global. doi:10.4018/978-1-5225-0287-6.ch010

Dutta, P., & Ojha, V. K. (2014). Conjugate Gradient Trained Neural Network for Intelligent Sensing of Manhole Gases to Avoid Human Fatality. In B. Tripathy & D. Acharjya (Eds.), *Advances in Secure Computing, Internet Services, and Applications* (pp. 257–280). Hershey, PA: IGI Global. doi:10.4018/978-1-4666-4940-8.ch013

Elkhodr, M., Shahrestani, S., & Cheung, H. (2016). Internet of Things Applications: Current and Future Development. In Q. Hassan (Ed.), *Innovative Research and Applications in Next-Generation High Performance Computing* (pp. 397–427). Hershey, PA: IGI Global. doi:10.4018/978-1-5225-0287-6.ch016

Elkhodr, M., Shahrestani, S., & Cheung, H. (2016). Wireless Enabling Technologies for the Internet of Things. In Q. Hassan (Ed.), *Innovative Research and Applications in Next-Generation High Performance Computing* (pp. 368–396). Hershey, PA: IGI Global. doi:10.4018/978-1-5225-0287-6.ch015

Elmisery, A. M., & Sertovic, M. (2017). Privacy Enhanced Cloud-Based Recommendation Service for Implicit Discovery of Relevant Support Groups in Healthcare Social Networks. *International Journal of Grid and High Performance Computing*, *9*(1), 75–91. doi:10.4018/IJGHPC.2017010107

Fazio, P., Tropea, M., Marano, S., & Curia, V. (2016). A Hybrid Complex Network Model for Wireless Sensor Networks and Performance Evaluation. In N. Meghanathan (Ed.), *Advanced Methods for Complex Network Analysis* (pp. 379–395). Hershey, PA: IGI Global. doi:10.4018/978-1-4666-9964-9.ch016

Fei, X., Li, K., Yang, W., & Li, K. (2016). CPU-GPU Computing: Overview, Optimization, and Applications. In Q. Hassan (Ed.), *Innovative Research and Applications in Next-Generation High Performance Computing* (pp. 159–193). Hershey, PA: IGI Global. doi:10.4018/978-1-5225-0287-6.ch007

Funes, M. A., Hadad, M. N., Donato, P. G., & Carrica, D. O. (2016). Optimization of Advanced Signal Processing Architectures for Detection of Signals Immersed in Noise. In J. Gazzano, M. Crespo, A. Cicuttin, & F. Calle (Eds.), *Field-Programmable Gate Array (FPGA) Technologies for High Performance Instrumentation* (pp. 171–212). Hershey, PA: IGI Global. doi:10.4018/978-1-5225-0299-9.ch008

Garcia-Robledo, A., Diaz-Perez, A., & Morales-Luna, G. (2016). Characterization and Coarsening of Autonomous System Networks: Measuring and Simplifying the Internet. In N. Meghanathan (Ed.), *Advanced Methods for Complex Network Analysis* (pp. 148–179). Hershey, PA: IGI Global. doi:10.4018/978-1-4666-9964-9.ch006

Garg, A., Biswas, A., & Biswas, B. (2016). Evolutionary Computation Techniques for Community Detection in Social Network Analysis. In N. Meghanathan (Ed.), *Advanced Methods for Complex Network Analysis* (pp. 266–284). Hershey, PA: IGI Global. doi:10.4018/978-1-4666-9964-9.ch011

Garg, P., & Gupta, A. (2016). Restoration Technique to Optimize Recovery Time for Efficient OSPF Network. In P. Mallick (Ed.), *Research Advances in the Integration of Big Data and Smart Computing* (pp. 64–88). Hershey, PA: IGI Global. doi:10.4018/978-1-4666-8737-0.ch004

Gazzano, J. D., Calle, F. R., Caba, J., de la Fuente, D., & Romero, J. B. (2016). Dynamic Reconfiguration for Internal Monitoring Services. In J. Gazzano, M. Crespo, A. Cicuttin, & F. Calle (Eds.), *Field-Programmable Gate Array (FPGA) Technologies for High Performance Instrumentation* (pp. 124–136). Hershey, PA: IGI Global. doi:10.4018/978-1-5225-0299-9.ch006

Geethanjali, P. (2014). Pattern Recognition and Robotics. In B. Tripathy & D. Acharjya (Eds.), *Advances in Secure Computing, Internet Services, and Applications* (pp. 35–48). Hershey, PA: IGI Global. doi:10.4018/978-1-4666-4940-8.ch002

Ghai, D., & Jain, N. (2016). Signal Processing: Iteration Bound and Loop Bound. In P. Mallick (Ed.), *Research Advances in the Integration of Big Data and Smart Computing* (pp. 153–177). Hershey, PA: IGI Global. doi:10.4018/978-1-4666-8737-0.ch009

Ghaiwat, S. N., & Arora, P. (2016). Cotton Leaf Disease Detection by Feature Extraction. In P. Mallick (Ed.), *Research Advances in the Integration of Big Data and Smart Computing* (pp. 89–104). Hershey, PA: IGI Global. doi:10.4018/978-1-4666-8737-0.ch005

Ghorpade-Aher, J., Pagare, R., Thengade, A., Ghorpade, S., & Kadam, M. (2016). Big Data: The Data Deluge. In P. Mallick (Ed.), *Research Advances in the Integration of Big Data and Smart Computing* (pp. 1–21). Hershey, PA: IGI Global. doi:10.4018/978-1-4666-8737-0.ch001

Gil-Costa, V., Molina, R. S., Petrino, R., Paez, C. F., Printista, A. M., & Gazzano, J. D. (2016). Hardware Acceleration of CBIR System with FPGA-Based Platform. In J. Gazzano, M. Crespo, A. Cicuttin, & F. Calle (Eds.), *Field-Programmable Gate Array (FPGA) Technologies for High Performance Instrumentation* (pp. 138–170). Hershey, PA: IGI Global. doi:10.4018/978-1-5225-0299-9.ch007

Goswami, S., Mehjabin, S., & Kashyap, P. A. (2015). Driverless Metro Train with Automatic Crowd Control System. In K. Sarma, M. Sarma, & M. Sarma (Eds.), *Intelligent Applications for Heterogeneous System Modeling and Design* (pp. 76–95). Hershey, PA: IGI Global. doi:10.4018/978-1-4666-8493-5.ch004

Guan, Q., DeBardeleben, N., Blanchard, S., Fu, S., Davis, C. H. IV, & Jones, W. M. (2016). Analyzing the Robustness of HPC Applications Using a Fine-Grained Soft Error Fault Injection Tool. In Q. Hassan (Ed.), *Innovative Research and Applications in Next-Generation High Performance Computing* (pp. 277–305). Hershey, PA: IGI Global. doi:10.4018/978-1-5225-0287-6.ch011

Guerrero, J. I., Monedero, Í., Biscarri, F., Biscarri, J., Millán, R., & León, C. (2014). Detection of Non-Technical Losses: The Project MIDAS. In B. Tripathy & D. Acharjya (Eds.), *Advances in Secure Computing, Internet Services, and Applications* (pp. 140–164). Hershey, PA: IGI Global. doi:10.4018/978-1-4666-4940-8.ch008

Habbal, A., Abdullah, S. A., Mkpojiogu, E. O., Hassan, S., & Benamar, N. (2017). Assessing Experimental Private Cloud Using Web of System Performance Model. *International Journal of Grid and High Performance Computing*, 9(2), 21–35. doi:10.4018/IJGHPC.2017040102

Habib, I., Islam, A., Chetia, S., & Saikia, S. J. (2015). A New Coding Scheme for Data Security in RF based Wireless Communication. In K. Sarma, M. Sarma, & M. Sarma (Eds.), *Intelligent Applications for Heterogeneous System Modeling and Design* (pp. 301–319). Hershey, PA: IGI Global. doi:10.4018/978-1-4666-8493-5.ch013

Hamilton, H., & Alasti, H. (2017). Controlled Intelligent Agents' Security Model for Multi-Tenant Cloud Computing Infrastructures. *International Journal of Grid and High Performance Computing*, 9(1), 1–13. doi:10.4018/IJGHPC.2017010101

Ileri, C. U., Ural, C. A., Dagdeviren, O., & Kavalci, V. (2016). On Vertex Cover Problems in Distributed Systems. In N. Meghanathan (Ed.), *Advanced Methods for Complex Network Analysis* (pp. 1–29). Hershey, PA: IGI Global. doi:10.4018/978-1-4666-9964-9.ch001

Ingale, A. G. (2014). Prediction of Structural and Functional Aspects of Protein: In-Silico Approach. In B. Tripathy & D. Acharjya (Eds.), *Advances in Secure Computing, Internet Services, and Applications* (pp. 317–333). Hershey, PA: IGI Global. doi:10.4018/978-1-4666-4940-8.ch016

Jadon, K. S., Mudgal, P., & Bhadoria, R. S. (2016). Optimization and Management of Resource in Utility Computing. In G. Deka, G. Siddesh, K. Srinivasa, & L. Patnaik (Eds.), *Emerging Research Surrounding Power Consumption and Performance Issues in Utility Computing* (pp. 22–43). Hershey, PA: IGI Global. doi:10.4018/978-1-4666-8853-7.ch002

K. G. S., G. M., S., Hiriyannaiah, S., Morappanavar, A., & Banerjee, A. (2016). A Novel Approach of Symmetric Key Cryptography using Genetic Algorithm Implemented on GPGPU. In G. Deka, G. Siddesh, K. Srinivasa, & L. Patnaik (Eds.), Emerging Research Surrounding Power Consumption and Performance Issues in Utility Computing (pp. 283-303). Hershey, PA: IGI Global. doi:10.4018/978-1-4666-8853-7.ch014

Kannan, R. (2014). Graphical Evaluation and Review Technique (GERT): The Panorama in the Computation and Visualization of Network-Based Project Management. In B. Tripathy & D. Acharjya (Eds.), *Advances in Secure Computing, Internet Services, and Applications* (pp. 165–179). Hershey, PA: IGI Global. doi:10.4018/978-1-4666-4940-8.ch009

Kasemsap, K. (2014). The Role of Knowledge Management on Job Satisfaction: A Systematic Framework. In B. Tripathy & D. Acharjya (Eds.), *Advances in Secure Computing, Internet Services, and Applications* (pp. 104–127). Hershey, PA: IGI Global. doi:10.4018/978-1-4666-4940-8.ch006

Khadtare, M. S. (2016). GPU Based Image Quality Assessment using Structural Similarity (SSIM) Index. In G. Deka, G. Siddesh, K. Srinivasa, & L. Patnaik (Eds.), *Emerging Research Surrounding Power Consumption and Performance Issues in Utility Computing* (pp. 276–282). Hershey, PA: IGI Global. doi:10.4018/978-1-4666-8853-7.ch013

Khan, A. U., & Khan, A. N. (2016). High Performance Computing on Mobile Devices. In Q. Hassan (Ed.), *Innovative Research and Applications in Next-Generation High Performance Computing* (pp. 334–348). Hershey, PA: IGI Global. doi:10.4018/978-1-5225-0287-6.ch013

Khan, M. S. (2016). A Study of Computer Virus Propagation on Scale Free Networks Using Differential Equations. In N. Meghanathan (Ed.), *Advanced Methods for Complex Network Analysis* (pp. 196–214). Hershey, PA: IGI Global. doi:10.4018/978-1-4666-9964-9.ch008

Khan, R. H. (2015). Utilizing UML, cTLA, and SRN: An Application to Distributed System Performance Modeling. In K. Sarma, M. Sarma, & M. Sarma (Eds.), *Intelligent Applications for Heterogeneous System Modeling and Design* (pp. 23–50). Hershey, PA: IGI Global. doi:10.4018/978-1-4666-8493-5.ch002

Konwar, P., & Bordoloi, H. (2015). An EOG Signal based Framework to Control a Wheel Chair. In K. Sarma, M. Sarma, & M. Sarma (Eds.), *Intelligent Applications for Heterogeneous System Modeling and Design* (pp. 51–75). Hershey, PA: IGI Global. doi:10.4018/978-1-4666-8493-5.ch003

Koppad, S. H., & Shwetha, T. M. (2016). Indic Language: Kannada to Braille Conversion Tool Using Client Server Architecture Model. In P. Mallick (Ed.), *Research Advances in the Integration of Big Data and Smart Computing* (pp. 120–133). Hershey, PA: IGI Global. doi:10.4018/978-1-4666-8737-0.ch007

Kumar, P. S., Pradhan, S. K., & Panda, S. (2016). The Pedagogy of English Teaching-Learning at Primary Level in Rural Government Schools: A Data Mining View. In P. Mallick (Ed.), *Research Advances in the Integration of Big Data and Smart Computing* (pp. 105–119). Hershey, PA: IGI Global. doi:10.4018/978-1-4666-8737-0.ch006

Kumar, S., Ranjan, P., Ramaswami, R., & Tripathy, M. R. (2017). Resource Efficient Clustering and Next Hop Knowledge Based Routing in Multiple Heterogeneous Wireless Sensor Networks. *International Journal of Grid and High Performance Computing, 9*(2), 1–20. doi:10.4018/IJGHPC.2017040101

Kunfang, S., & Lu, H. (2016). Efficient Querying Distributed Big-XML Data using MapReduce. *International Journal of Grid and High Performance Computing, 8*(3), 70–79. doi:10.4018/IJGHPC.2016070105

Li, Y., Zhai, J., & Li, K. (2016). Communication Analysis and Performance Prediction of Parallel Applications on Large-Scale Machines. In Q. Hassan (Ed.), *Innovative Research and Applications in Next-Generation High Performance Computing* (pp. 80–105). Hershey, PA: IGI Global. doi:10.4018/978-1-5225-0287-6.ch005

Lin, L., Li, S., Li, B., Zhan, J., & Zhao, Y. (2016). TVGuarder: A Trace-Enable Virtualization Protection Framework against Insider Threats for IaaS Environments. *International Journal of Grid and High Performance Computing*, *8*(4), 1–20. doi:10.4018/IJGHPC.2016100101

López, M. B. (2017). Mobile Platform Challenges in Interactive Computer Vision. In M. S., & V. V. (Eds.), Multi-Core Computer Vision and Image Processing for Intelligent Applications (pp. 47-73). Hershey, PA: IGI Global. doi:10.4018/978-1-5225-0889-2.ch002

Maarouf, A., El Qacimy, B., Marzouk, A., & Haqiq, A. (2017). Defining and Evaluating A Novel Penalty Model for Managing Violations in the Cloud Computing. *International Journal of Grid and High Performance Computing*, *9*(2), 36–52. doi:10.4018/IJGHPC.2017040103

Mahmoud, I. I. (2016). Implementation of Reactor Control Rod Position Sensing/Display Using a VLSI Chip. In J. Gazzano, M. Crespo, A. Cicuttin, & F. Calle (Eds.), *Field-Programmable Gate Array (FPGA) Technologies for High Performance Instrumentation* (pp. 1–16). Hershey, PA: IGI Global. doi:10.4018/978-1-5225-0299-9.ch001

Mahmoud, I. I., & El Tokhy, M. S. (2016). Development of Algorithms and Their Hardware Implementation for Gamma Radiation Spectrometry. In J. Gazzano, M. Crespo, A. Cicuttin, & F. Calle (Eds.), *Field-Programmable Gate Array (FPGA) Technologies for High Performance Instrumentation* (pp. 17–41). Hershey, PA: IGI Global. doi:10.4018/978-1-5225-0299-9.ch002

Mahmoud, I. I., Salama, M., & El Hamid, A. A. (2016). Hardware Implementation of a Genetic Algorithm for Motion Path Planning. In J. Gazzano, M. Crespo, A. Cicuttin, & F. Calle (Eds.), *Field-Programmable Gate Array (FPGA) Technologies for High Performance Instrumentation* (pp. 250–275). Hershey, PA: IGI Global. doi:10.4018/978-1-5225-0299-9.ch010

Maji, A. K., Rymbai, B., & Kandar, D. (2016). A Study on Different Facial Features Extraction Technique. In P. Mallick (Ed.), *Research Advances in the Integration of Big Data and Smart Computing* (pp. 224–249). Hershey, PA: IGI Global. doi:10.4018/978-1-4666-8737-0.ch013

Mallick, P. K., Mohanty, M. N., & Kumar, S. S. (2016). White Patch Detection in Brain MRI Image Using Evolutionary Clustering Algorithm. In P. Mallick (Ed.), *Research Advances in the Integration of Big Data and Smart Computing* (pp. 323–339). Hershey, PA: IGI Global. doi:10.4018/978-1-4666-8737-0.ch018

Mandal, B., Sarma, M. P., & Sarma, K. K. (2015). Design of a Power Aware Systolic Array based Support Vector Machine Classifier. In K. Sarma, M. Sarma, & M. Sarma (Eds.), *Intelligent Applications for Heterogeneous System Modeling and Design* (pp. 96–138). Hershey, PA: IGI Global. doi:10.4018/978-1-4666-8493-5.ch005

Manjaiah, D. H., & Payaswini, P. (2014). Design Issues of 4G-Network Mobility Management. In B. Tripathy & D. Acharjya (Eds.), *Advances in Secure Computing, Internet Services, and Applications* (pp. 210–238). Hershey, PA: IGI Global. doi:10.4018/978-1-4666-4940-8.ch011

Martinez-Gonzalez, R. F., Vazquez-Medina, R., Diaz-Mendez, J. A., & Lopez-Hernandez, J. (2016). FPGA Implementations for Chaotic Maps Using Fixed-Point and Floating-Point Representations. In J. Gazzano, M. Crespo, A. Cicuttin, & F. Calle (Eds.), *Field-Programmable Gate Array (FPGA) Technologies for High Performance Instrumentation* (pp. 59–97). Hershey, PA: IGI Global. doi:10.4018/978-1-5225-0299-9.ch004

Meddah, I. H., & Belkadi, K. (2017). Parallel Distributed Patterns Mining Using Hadoop MapReduce Framework. *International Journal of Grid and High Performance Computing*, 9(2), 70–85. doi:10.4018/IJGHPC.2017040105

Medhi, J. P. (2015). An Approach for Automatic Detection and Grading of Macular Edema. In K. Sarma, M. Sarma, & M. Sarma (Eds.), *Intelligent Applications for Heterogeneous System Modeling and Design* (pp. 204–231). Hershey, PA: IGI Global. doi:10.4018/978-1-4666-8493-5.ch009

Mishra, B. K., & Sahoo, A. K. (2016). Application of Big Data in Economic Policy. In P. Mallick (Ed.), *Research Advances in the Integration of Big Data and Smart Computing* (pp. 178–197). Hershey, PA: IGI Global. doi:10.4018/978-1-4666-8737-0.ch010

Mohan Khilar, P. (2014). Genetic Algorithms: Application to Fault Diagnosis in Distributed Embedded Systems. In B. Tripathy & D. Acharjya (Eds.), *Advances in Secure Computing, Internet Services, and Applications* (pp. 239–255). Hershey, PA: IGI Global. doi:10.4018/978-1-4666-4940-8.ch012

Mohanty, R. P., Turuk, A. K., & Sahoo, B. (2016). Designing of High Performance Multicore Processor with Improved Cache Configuration and Interconnect. In G. Deka, G. Siddesh, K. Srinivasa, & L. Patnaik (Eds.), *Emerging Research Surrounding Power Consumption and Performance Issues in Utility Computing* (pp. 204–219). Hershey, PA: IGI Global. doi:10.4018/978-1-4666-8853-7.ch009

Mohanty, S., Patra, P. K., & Mohapatra, S. (2016). Dynamic Task Assignment with Load Balancing in Cloud Platform. In G. Deka, G. Siddesh, K. Srinivasa, & L. Patnaik (Eds.), *Emerging Research Surrounding Power Consumption and Performance Issues in Utility Computing* (pp. 363–385). Hershey, PA: IGI Global. doi:10.4018/978-1-4666-8853-7.ch018

Mukherjee, A., Chatterjee, A., Das, D., & Naskar, M. K. (2016). Design of Structural Controllability for Complex Network Architecture. In N. Meghanathan (Ed.), *Advanced Methods for Complex Network Analysis* (pp. 98–124). Hershey, PA: IGI Global. doi:10.4018/978-1-4666-9964-9.ch004

Mukherjee, M. Kamarujjaman, & Maitra, M. (2016). Application of Biomedical Image Processing in Blood Cell Counting using Hough Transform. In N. Meghanathan (Ed.), Advanced Methods for Complex Network Analysis (pp. 359-378). Hershey, PA: IGI Global. doi:10.4018/978-1-4666-9964-9.ch015

Naseera, S. (2016). Dynamic Job Scheduling Strategy for Unreliable Nodes in a Volunteer Desktop Grid. *International Journal of Grid and High Performance Computing*, *8*(4), 21–33. doi:10.4018/IJGHPC.2016100102

Netake, A., & Katti, P. K. (2016). HTLS Conductors: A Novel Aspect for Energy Conservation in Transmission System. In P. Mallick (Ed.), *Research Advances in the Integration of Big Data and Smart Computing* (pp. 211–223). Hershey, PA: IGI Global. doi:10.4018/978-1-4666-8737-0.ch012

Nirmala, S. R., & Sarma, P. (2015). A Computer Based System for ECG Arrhythmia Classification. In K. Sarma, M. Sarma, & M. Sarma (Eds.), *Intelligent Applications for Heterogeneous System Modeling and Design* (pp. 160–185). Hershey, PA: IGI Global. doi:10.4018/978-1-4666-8493-5.ch007

Nirmala, S. R., & Sharma, P. (2015). Computer Assisted Methods for Retinal Image Classification. In K. Sarma, M. Sarma, & M. Sarma (Eds.), *Intelligent Applications for Heterogeneous System Modeling and Design* (pp. 232–255). Hershey, PA: IGI Global. doi:10.4018/978-1-4666-8493-5.ch010

Omar, M., Ahmad, K., & Rizvi, M. (2016). Content Based Image Retrieval System. In G. Deka, G. Siddesh, K. Srinivasa, & L. Patnaik (Eds.), *Emerging Research Surrounding Power Consumption and Performance Issues in Utility Computing* (pp. 345–362). Hershey, PA: IGI Global. doi:10.4018/978-1-4666-8853-7.ch017

Panda, M., & Patra, M. R. (2014). Characterizing Intelligent Intrusion Detection and Prevention Systems Using Data Mining. In B. Tripathy & D. Acharjya (Eds.), *Advances in Secure Computing, Internet Services, and Applications* (pp. 89–102). Hershey, PA: IGI Global. doi:10.4018/978-1-4666-4940-8.ch005

Pang, X., Wan, B., Li, H., & Lin, W. (2016). MR-LDA: An Efficient Topic Model for Classification of Short Text in Big Social Data. *International Journal of Grid and High Performance Computing*, 8(4), 100–113. doi:10.4018/IJGHPC.2016100106

Perera, D. R., Mannathunga, K. S., Dharmasiri, R. A., Meegama, R. G., & Jayananda, K. (2016). Implementation of a Smart Sensor Node for Wireless Sensor Network Applications Using FPGAs. In J. Gazzano, M. Crespo, A. Cicuttin, & F. Calle (Eds.), *Field-Programmable Gate Array (FPGA) Technologies for High Performance Instrumentation* (pp. 213–249). Hershey, PA: IGI Global. doi:10.4018/978-1-5225-0299-9.ch009

Perez, H., Hernandez, B., Rudomin, I., & Ayguade, E. (2016). Task-Based Crowd Simulation for Heterogeneous Architectures. In Q. Hassan (Ed.), *Innovative Research and Applications in Next-Generation High Performance Computing* (pp. 194–219). Hershey, PA: IGI Global. doi:10.4018/978-1-5225-0287-6.ch008

Pourqasem, J., & Edalatpanah, S. (2016). Verification of Super-Peer Model for Query Processing in Peer-to-Peer Networks. In Q. Hassan (Ed.), *Innovative Research and Applications in Next-Generation High Performance Computing* (pp. 306–332). Hershey, PA: IGI Global. doi:10.4018/978-1-5225-0287-6.ch012

Pujari, M., & Kanawati, R. (2016). Link Prediction in Complex Networks. In N. Meghanathan (Ed.), *Advanced Methods for Complex Network Analysis* (pp. 58–97). Hershey, PA: IGI Global. doi:10.4018/978-1-4666-9964-9.ch003

Qian, H., Yong, W., Jia, L., & Mengfei, C. (2016). Publish/Subscribe and JXTA based Cloud Service Management with QoS. *International Journal of Grid and High Performance Computing*, 8(3), 24–37. doi:10.4018/IJGHPC.2016070102

Raigoza, J., & Karande, V. (2017). A Study and Implementation of a Movie Recommendation System in a Cloud-based Environment. *International Journal of Grid and High Performance Computing*, 9(1), 25–36. doi:10.4018/IJGHPC.2017010103

Ramalingam, V. V. S., M., Sugumaran, V., V., V., & Vadhanam, B. R. (2017). Controlling Prosthetic Limb Movements Using EEG Signals. In M. S., & V. V. (Eds.), Multi-Core Computer Vision and Image Processing for Intelligent Applications (pp. 211-233). Hershey, PA: IGI Global. doi:10.4018/978-1-5225-0889-2.ch008

Rawat, D. B., & Bhattacharya, S. (2016). Wireless Body Area Network for Healthcare Applications. In N. Meghanathan (Ed.), *Advanced Methods for Complex Network Analysis* (pp. 343–358). Hershey, PA: IGI Global. doi:10.4018/978-1-4666-9964-9.ch014

Rehman, M. H., Khan, A. U., & Batool, A. (2016). Big Data Analytics in Mobile and Cloud Computing Environments. In Q. Hassan (Ed.), *Innovative Research and Applications in Next-Generation High Performance Computing* (pp. 349–367). Hershey, PA: IGI Global. doi:10.4018/978-1-5225-0287-6.ch014

Rico-Diaz, A. J., Rodriguez, A., Puertas, J., & Bermudez, M. (2017). Fish Monitoring, Sizing, and Detection Using Stereovision, Laser Technology, and Computer Vision. In M. S., & V. V. (Eds.), Multi-Core Computer Vision and Image Processing for Intelligent Applications (pp. 190-210). Hershey, PA: IGI Global. doi:10.4018/978-1-5225-0889-2.ch007

Rodriguez, A., Rico-Diaz, A. J., Rabuñal, J. R., & Gestal, M. (2017). Fish Tracking with Computer Vision Techniques: An Application to Vertical Slot Fishways. In M. S., & V. V. (Eds.), Multi-Core Computer Vision and Image Processing for Intelligent Applications (pp. 74-104). Hershey, PA: IGI Global. doi:10.4018/978-1-5225-0889-2.ch003

S., J. R., & Omman, B. (2017). A Technical Assessment on License Plate Detection System. In M. S., & V. V. (Eds.), *Multi-Core Computer Vision and Image Processing for Intelligent Applications* (pp. 234-258). Hershey, PA: IGI Global. doi:10.4018/978-1-5225-0889-2.ch009

Saadat, N., & Rahmani, A. M. (2016). A Two-Level Fuzzy Value-Based Replica Replacement Algorithm in Data Grids. *International Journal of Grid and High Performance Computing, 8*(4), 78–99. doi:10.4018/IJGHPC.2016100105

Sah, P., & Sarma, K. K. (2015). Bloodless Technique to Detect Diabetes using Soft Computational Tool. In K. Sarma, M. Sarma, & M. Sarma (Eds.), *Intelligent Applications for Heterogeneous System Modeling and Design* (pp. 139–158). Hershey, PA: IGI Global. doi:10.4018/978-1-4666-8493-5.ch006

Sahoo, B., Jena, S. K., & Mahapatra, S. (2014). Heuristic Resource Allocation Algorithms for Dynamic Load Balancing in Heterogeneous Distributed Computing System. In B. Tripathy & D. Acharjya (Eds.), *Advances in Secure Computing, Internet Services, and Applications* (pp. 181–209). Hershey, PA: IGI Global. doi:10.4018/978-1-4666-4940-8.ch010

Sarma, M., & Sarma, K. K. (2015). Acoustic Modeling of Speech Signal using Artificial Neural Network: A Review of Techniques and Current Trends. In K. Sarma, M. Sarma, & M. Sarma (Eds.), *Intelligent Applications for Heterogeneous System Modeling and Design* (pp. 282–299). Hershey, PA: IGI Global. doi:10.4018/978-1-4666-8493-5.ch012

Shahid, A., Arif, S., Qadri, M. Y., & Munawar, S. (2016). Power Optimization Using Clock Gating and Power Gating: A Review. In Q. Hassan (Ed.), *Innovative Research and Applications in Next-Generation High Performance Computing* (pp. 1–20). Hershey, PA: IGI Global. doi:10.4018/978-1-5225-0287-6.ch001

Shahid, A., Khalid, B., Qadri, M. Y., Qadri, N. N., & Ahmed, J. (2016). Design Space Exploration Using Cycle Accurate Simulator. In Q. Hassan (Ed.), *Innovative Research and Applications in Next-Generation High Performance Computing* (pp. 66–79). Hershey, PA: IGI Global. doi:10.4018/978-1-5225-0287-6.ch004

Shahid, A., Murad, M., Qadri, M. Y., Qadri, N. N., & Ahmed, J. (2016). Hardware Transactional Memories: A Survey. In Q. Hassan (Ed.), *Innovative Research and Applications in Next-Generation High Performance Computing* (pp. 47–65). Hershey, PA: IGI Global. doi:10.4018/978-1-5225-0287-6.ch003

Sharma, O., & Saini, H. (2017). SLA and Performance Efficient Heuristics for Virtual Machines Placement in Cloud Data Centers. *International Journal of Grid and High Performance Computing*, 9(3), 17–33. doi:10.4018/IJGHPC.2017070102

Sheikh, A. (2017). Utilizing an Augmented Reality System to Address Phantom Limb Syndrome in a Cloud-Based Environment. *International Journal of Grid and High Performance Computing*, 9(1), 14–24. doi:10.4018/IJGHPC.2017010102

Shojafar, M., Cordeschi, N., & Baccarelli, E. (2016). Resource Scheduling for Energy-Aware Reconfigurable Internet Data Centers. In Q. Hassan (Ed.), *Innovative Research and Applications in Next-Generation High Performance Computing* (pp. 21–46). Hershey, PA: IGI Global. doi:10.4018/978-1-5225-0287-6.ch002

Singh, S., & Gond, S. (2016). Green Computing and Its Impact. In G. Deka, G. Siddesh, K. Srinivasa, & L. Patnaik (Eds.), *Emerging Research Surrounding Power Consumption and Performance Issues in Utility Computing* (pp. 69–83). Hershey, PA: IGI Global. doi:10.4018/978-1-4666-8853-7.ch004

Sirisha, D., & Vijayakumari, G. (2017). Towards Efficient Bounds on Completion Time and Resource Provisioning for Scheduling Workflows on Heterogeneous Processing Systems. *International Journal of Grid and High Performance Computing*, 9(3), 60–82. doi:10.4018/IJGHPC.2017070105

Sk, K., Mukherjee, M., & Maitra, M. (2017). FPGA-Based Re-Configurable Architecture for Window-Based Image Processing. In M. S., & V. V. (Eds.), Multi-Core Computer Vision and Image Processing for Intelligent Applications (pp. 1-46). Hershey, PA: IGI Global. doi:10.4018/978-1-5225-0889-2.ch001

Skanderova, L., & Zelinka, I. (2016). Differential Evolution Dynamic Analysis in the Form of Complex Networks. In N. Meghanathan (Ed.), *Advanced Methods for Complex Network Analysis* (pp. 285–318). Hershey, PA: IGI Global. doi:10.4018/978-1-4666-9964-9.ch012

Sreekumar, & Patel, G. (2014). Assessment of Technical Efficiency of Indian B-Schools: A Comparison between the Cross-Sectional and Time-Series Analysis. In B. Tripathy, & D. Acharjya (Eds.), *Advances in Secure Computing, Internet Services, and Applications* (pp. 128-139). Hershey, PA: IGI Global. doi:10.4018/978-1-4666-4940-8.ch007

Srinivasa, K. G., Hegde, G., Sideesh, G. M., & Hiriyannaiah, S. (2016). A Viability Analysis of an Economical Private Cloud Storage Solution Powered by Raspberry Pi in the NSA Era: A Survey and Analysis of Cost and Security. In G. Deka, G. Siddesh, K. Srinivasa, & L. Patnaik (Eds.), *Emerging Research Surrounding Power Consumption and Performance Issues in Utility Computing* (pp. 220–232). Hershey, PA: IGI Global. doi:10.4018/978-1-4666-8853-7. ch010

Srinivasa, K. G., Siddesh, G. M., Hiriyannaiah, S., Mishra, K., Prajeeth, C. S., & Talha, A. M. (2016). GPU Implementation of Friend Recommendation System using CUDA for Social Networking Services. In G. Deka, G. Siddesh, K. Srinivasa, & L. Patnaik (Eds.), *Emerging Research Surrounding Power Consumption and Performance Issues in Utility Computing* (pp. 304–319). Hershey, PA: IGI Global. doi:10.4018/978-1-4666-8853-7.ch015

Swargiary, D., Paul, J., Amin, R., & Bordoloi, H. (2015). Eye Ball Detection Using Labview and Application for Design of Obstacle Detector. In K. Sarma, M. Sarma, & M. Sarma (Eds.), *Intelligent Applications for Heterogeneous System Modeling and Design* (pp. 186–203). Hershey, PA: IGI Global. doi:10.4018/978-1-4666-8493-5.ch008

Swarnkar, M., & Bhadoria, R. S. (2016). Security Aspects in Utility Computing. In G. Deka, G. Siddesh, K. Srinivasa, & L. Patnaik (Eds.), *Emerging Research Surrounding Power Consumption and Performance Issues in Utility Computing* (pp. 262–275). Hershey, PA: IGI Global. doi:10.4018/978-1-4666-8853-7. ch012

Tchendji, V. K., Myoupo, J. F., & Dequen, G. (2016). High Performance CGM-based Parallel Algorithms for the Optimal Binary Search Tree Problem. *International Journal of Grid and High Performance Computing, 8*(4), 55–77. doi:10.4018/IJGHPC.2016100104

Tian, J., & Zhang, H. (2016). A Credible Cloud Service Model based on Behavior Graphs and Tripartite Decision-Making Mechanism. *International Journal of Grid and High Performance Computing, 8*(3), 38–56. doi:10.4018/ IJGHPC.2016070103

Tiru, B. (2015). Exploiting Power Line for Communication Purpose: Features and Prospects of Power Line Communication. In K. Sarma, M. Sarma, & M. Sarma (Eds.), *Intelligent Applications for Heterogeneous System Modeling and Design* (pp. 320–334). Hershey, PA: IGI Global. doi:10.4018/978-1-4666-8493-5.ch014

Tripathy, B. K. (2014). Multi-Granular Computing through Rough Sets. In B. Tripathy & D. Acharjya (Eds.), *Advances in Secure Computing, Internet Services, and Applications* (pp. 1–34). Hershey, PA: IGI Global. doi:10.4018/978-1-4666-4940-8.ch001

Vadhanam, B. R. S., M., Sugumaran, V., V., V., & Ramalingam, V. V. (2017). Computer Vision Based Classification on Commercial Videos. In M. S., & V. V. (Eds.), Multi-Core Computer Vision and Image Processing for Intelligent Applications (pp. 105-135). Hershey, PA: IGI Global. doi:10.4018/978-1-5225-0889-2.ch004

Valero-Lara, P., Paz-Gallardo, A., Foster, E. L., Prieto-Matías, M., Pinelli, A., & Jansson, J. (2016). Multicore and Manycore: Hybrid Computing Architectures and Applications. In Q. Hassan (Ed.), *Innovative Research and Applications in Next-Generation High Performance Computing* (pp. 107–158). Hershey, PA: IGI Global. doi:10.4018/978-1-5225-0287-6.ch006

Winkler, M. (2016). Triadic Substructures in Complex Networks. In N. Meghanathan (Ed.), *Advanced Methods for Complex Network Analysis* (pp. 125–147). Hershey, PA: IGI Global. doi:10.4018/978-1-4666-9964-9.ch005

Xu, H., Rong, H., Mao, R., Chen, G., & Shan, Z. (2016). Hilbert Index-based Outlier Detection Algorithm in Metric Space. *International Journal of Grid and High Performance Computing, 8*(4), 34–54. doi:10.4018/IJGHPC.2016100103

Xu, R., & Faragó, A. (2016). Connectivity and Structure in Large Networks. In N. Meghanathan (Ed.), *Advanced Methods for Complex Network Analysis* (pp. 180–195). Hershey, PA: IGI Global. doi:10.4018/978-1-4666-9964-9.ch007

Youssef, B., Midkiff, S. F., & Rizk, M. R. (2016). SNAM: A Heterogeneous Complex Networks Generation Model. In N. Meghanathan (Ed.), *Advanced Methods for Complex Network Analysis* (pp. 215–236). Hershey, PA: IGI Global. doi:10.4018/978-1-4666-9964-9.ch009

Zahera, H. M., & El-Sisi, A. B. (2017). Accelerating Training Process in Logistic Regression Model using OpenCL Framework. *International Journal of Grid and High Performance Computing, 9*(3), 34–45. doi:10.4018/IJGHPC.2017070103

Zelinka, I. (2016). On Mutual Relations amongst Evolutionary Algorithm Dynamics and Its Hidden Complex Network Structures: An Overview and Recent Advances. In N. Meghanathan (Ed.), *Advanced Methods for Complex Network Analysis* (pp. 319–342). Hershey, PA: IGI Global. doi:10.4018/978-1-4666-9964-9.ch013

Ziesche, S., & Yampolskiy, R. V. (2017). High Performance Computing of Possible Minds. *International Journal of Grid and High Performance Computing*, *9*(1), 37–47. doi:10.4018/IJGHPC.2017010104

About the Authors

Alberto Garcia-Robledo is Ph.D. in Computer Science from the Center for Research and Advanced Studies, and Erdős Number 3. Alberto Garcia-Robledo has attended courses, participated in projects, or performed presentations in renowned Mexican and international academic institutions, such as the Monterrey Institute of Technology and Higher Education, the National Laboratory of Advanced Informatics, the University of La Laguna and the Università della Svizzera Italiana. From 2013 to 2014, Alberto Garcia-Robledo was appointed technical lead of a financial data analysis research project that involved government, academia and industry at the Geospatial Data Center of the Massachusetts Institute of Technology.

Arturo Diaz-Perez is a Ph.D. in Electrical Engineering from Cinvestav. Since 2006, he is the head of the Cinvestav's IT Lab and his work has focused on promoting information technology developments for the State of Tamaulipas in a joint venture initiative between Cinvestav and Government of Tamaulipas. IT Lab performs projects related to scientific research and technological development in IT field. Prof. Diaz-Perez is member of the Computing and Telecommunications Board at Cinvestav. Arturo Diaz-Perez has published one book in the field of reconfigurable computing for cryptographic algorithms, 16 papers in technical refereed journals, and more than 40 papers in technical conferences.

Guillermo Morales-Luna is a Researcher at Cinvestav-IPN since 1985. He received a Ph.D in Mathematics from the Polish Academy of Sciences, Poland. From 1989 to 1992 he chaired the Cinvestav Computer Science Section. He has refereed texts and books edited by the Sociedad Matemática

Mexicana, the Universidad Autónoma Metropolitana and IPN. He has received several grants for research and technology projects from Mexican CONACyT, UNESCO, PEMEX and the Mexican Institute of Telecommunications. His research interest areas include Logic (model theory, Peano arithmetic, proof theory) and mathematical foundations of Computer Science (recursive functions, computational complexity and algorithms).

Index

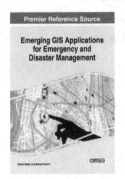
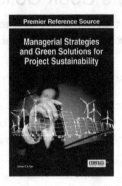

Printed in the United States
by Bookmasters

Printed in the United States
By Bookmasters